A History of the
SAMURAI

A History of the
SAMURAI
Legendary Warriors of Japan

Jonathan López-Vera

Translated by
Russell Calvert

TUTTLE Publishing
Tokyo | Rutland, Vermont | Singapore

"Books to Span the East and West"

Tuttle Publishing was founded in 1832 in the small New England town of Rutland, Vermont [USA]. Our core values remain as strong today as they were then—to publish best-in-class books which bring people together one page at a time. In 1948, we established a publishing outpost in Japan—and Tuttle is now a leader in publishing English-language books about the arts, languages and cultures of Asia. The world has become a much smaller place today and Asia's economic and cultural influence has grown. Yet the need for meaningful dialogue and information about this diverse region has never been greater. Over the past seven decades, Tuttle has published thousands of books on subjects ranging from martial arts and paper crafts to language learning and literature—and our talented authors, illustrators, designers and photographers have won many prestigious awards. We welcome you to explore the wealth of information available on Asia at www.tuttlepublishing.com.

Published by Tuttle Publishing, an imprint of Periplus Editions (HK) Ltd.

www.tuttlepublishing.com

Translated from Historia De Los Samurais
By Jonathan Lopez-Vera
Published by Satori Ediciones
Copyright © Satori Ediciones

English Translation Copyright © 2020
Periplus Editions (HK) Ltd.

LCCN 2022275844

ISBN: 978-4-8053-1535-4

Distributed by:

Japan
Tuttle Publishing
Yaekari Building 3rd Floor
5-4-12 Osaki Shinagawa-ku
Tokyo 141 0032
Tel: (81) 3 5437-0171
Fax: (81) 3 5437-0755
sales@tuttle.co.jp
www.tuttle.co.jp

North America, Latin America & Europe
Tuttle Publishing
364 Innovation Drive
North Clarendon, VT 05759-9436 U.S.A.
Tel: 1 (802) 773-8930
Fax: 1 (802) 773-6993
info@tuttlepublishing.com
www.tuttlepublishing.com

Asia Pacific
Berkeley Books Pte. Ltd.
3 Kallang Sector #04-01, Singapore 349278
Tel: (65) 6741-2178
Fax: (65) 6741-2179
inquiries@periplus.com.sg
www.tuttlepublishing.com

26 25 24 23   6 5 4 3 2   2312VP
Printed in Malaysia

Contents

Contents

For Ginia, who has always been there, and Sören, who has taken shape at the same time as this book.

Note on the Japanese Language

For all Japanese names I have chosen to keep the Japanese rules for word order, with the surname first, followed by the first name. When a name has to be shortened, the usual approach is to only use the surname, but in the case of some particularly important people, it is common to only use the first name, as in the case of Toyotomi Hideyoshi, who we call "Hideyoshi"; in many cases, we shall also do this to avoid the confusion that could occur between members of the same family, for example when talking about the Minamoto. At times, the reader may struggle to follow because a father and son's names look similar since they share one of the two characters used to write them, as in the case of Taira Kiyomori and Taira Munemori.

The names of some emperors begin with the prefix *Go-*. This means there was a previous emperor with the same name, which is why in some texts it is translated as "the second" and why we can find Go-Shirakawa written as "Shirakawa II." Here we have respected the Japanese form.

When talking about early periods, it is common to find the article *no*, which equates to *of*, between the surname and first name, as in "Minamoto-no-Yoshitsune." Here it has been left out and "Minamoto Yoshitsune" used.

I have chosen not to include the many different names the same person may have had over their lifetime—a common occurrence in the Japan of that period and even more so in the case of the samurai—in order to not complicate the telling of the tale.

In the case of the samurai who converted to Christianity and changed their first name to a Western one, most adopted

Portuguese names. So, for example, when talking about Konishi Yukinaga, I refer to his Christian name, "Agostinho."

The Japanese words used in this text have been indicated with italics, but I have chosen to only do so the first time they are mentioned, in order to make the book easier to read. Moreover, with these words, we have kept the Japanese norm of not altering them when used in the plural. Thus, we speak of "the *bushi*" and not "the *bushis*."

The use of the macron has also been maintained. This is a diacritical mark consisting of a horizontal bar over a vowel, as seen in the word *taikō*, which indicates that the vowel should be pronounced with twice its normal length; this has only been omitted with a few Japanese words that have been incorporated into English, as for example with *Kyoto*, rather than its Japanese form, *Kyōto*.

Japanese vowels have the following approximate sounds: the letter *a* is pronounced as in *car*; *e* as in *egg*; *i* like the *ee* in *deep*; *o* as in *bold*; *u* as in *truce*. Consonants are pronounced roughly in the same way as in English, the main difference being that *g* is always pronounced as in *gap*, even if it comes before *e-* or *i-*. I have chosen not to include the Japanese script version of words, names or places, since as I see it, this would not contribute anything to a book of these characteristics.

Preface

This is a book about the samurai, as the title makes clear. The samurai ruled in Japan for no less than seven centuries, which means that to study the history of the samurai over that time span is pretty much to study the history of Japan. Yet, that is not the only way to look at things, because a society or area's history is not only about its ruling class, but the history of all its people. In the case of Japan, between the twelfth and nineteenth centuries, that would also include the peasants—the great majority of the population and foundation of the country's economic system—traders, artisans, clergy, pariahs, etc. It is true that all of them appear in this book, but indirectly, because this is about the history of the samurai, not of Japan, which is dealt with by some excellent books you will find listed in the bibliography. Nor is this a book about the samurai in general; you will find no lists here of Japanese words for all the parts of a suit of armor, images that explain the correct steps for slitting open your stomach or recommendations for films on the subject. There are many other books like that—although I did not consult them and therefore they do not appear in the bibliography—but this, to return to my original point, is a book about the history of the samurai, meant for the general public and not specifically for historians or history students.

The history of the samurai is largely not as unique and exceptional—in the literal sense—as it may appear to be, if we compare it to that of other warrior castes from other times and places. Wherever there have been civilizations, the existence of warriors is something almost inevitable, since different human communities have always needed to defend themselves or attack others who in turn have defended themselves. Those best suited for these tasks have normally ended up forming a defined group of specialists, as has happened with other trades. The difference being that this group, knowing their ability to use brute force conferred on them a certain power, have (almost) always ended up realizing they could use that skill to rule over the rest. In the case of Japan, within the previously mentioned seven centuries of samurai dominance, there were three successive military governments, called Kamakura, Ashikaga and Tokugawa, respectively, each with its own characteristics and idiosyncrasies. There were periods of relative or absolute peace, interrupted by conflicts which were largely local on some occasions and largely nationwide on others. One conflict was total and widespread and lasted more than a century.

There was a single case of aggression by a foreign power—the two attempted invasions by Mongolians, Chinese and Koreans at the end of the thirteenth century—and a single case of foreign aggression carried out by Japan—the attempted invasion of Korea and China at the end of the sixteenth century. This happened to be in harmony with the general dynamics in East Asia, a relatively peaceful region throughout its history, especially if compared with the eternally turbulent and warlike Europe, which put in an appearance off the coast of Japan on two very different occasions, each one the fruit of a very different European or Western context.

First, in the mid-sixteenth century, it was mainly the turn of the Portuguese, but also of the Castilians, followed soon after by their Dutch and English enemies. This was during the era of great discoveries, the new routes to control the spices and silk trade, and the evangelizing zeal of the Catholic Church. Later on, in the mid-nineteenth century, it could be said that the entire West got to Japan, in the guise of the cannons of an American fleet, opening up the country after more than two centuries of almost absolute self-imposed isolationism and almost forcing it to take part in the new global industrial trade. This new world calling at its gates—or threatening to knock them down with its cannons—brought with it, among many other changes, the end of the warrior class. This is the history that we shall review here and conclude with an epilogue of the popular and world-famous samurai myth.

The fascinating samurai myth has led many—myself included—to the discovery of a whole new culture, Japan, which is even more fascinating. So, let me here state my gratitude for the myth, the fiction and the fantasy surrounding the figure of the samurai, because back in the day this is what aroused my interest in many other aspects of an even more fascinating culture, language and, above all history. It could be said that in the end this passion has become my profession. I hope that those who have been attracted to this book by the samurai myth find it to be a good means of approaching the topic from another—more realistic—perspective. Hopefully you will find it as interesting, or more so, than what brought you here.

*　　*　　*

Given that this is a book aimed at the general public, I have avoided using overly academic elements such as footnotes and frequent bibliographical references. For the former, explanations within the text have been used instead to facilitate reading. The latter has been omitted, and the requisite wide-ranging bibliography included at the end. Information has been taken from here and readers can refer to it to widen their knowledge of whatever interests them the most. References appear in Spanish as well as in English and Japanese; a translation of some references listed here in another language may exist, because I have simply included the version I consulted. The same occurs with the year—I have listed the date of the version used rather than the year of publication. Fairly general manuals of Japanese history appear, such as those by Andressen, Hane, Henshall, Gordon or Murdoch; there are books about concrete periods, like those by Beasley, Buruma, Samson or Mutel; works about specific subjects, like those by Boxer, Sola or Goodman; some biographies, like those by Berry or Sadler; academic articles and selected chapters, with a special mention for those pertaining to the indispensable *The Cambridge History of Japan*. Some original archive documents from which I have taken information have not been listed—especially those referring to the subject of contact between Japan and Europe in the sixteenth and seventeenth centuries, currently my main area of research—since I do not consider them relevant for the average reader.

These days we have all the information in the world within arm's reach. It was already available thanks to libraries and now the internet has made accessing it easier than ever before. On the other hand, that can be a big problem, since the more information we have, the more difficult it is to sift the wheat from the chaff. Of all the things my teachers have taught me throughout my academic life, what I value above all is precisely their guidance through the maze of information I had been lost in throughout my years of being self-taught; in that period, I would devour any book I got my hands on that talked about the subjects I was interested in. Reading is like eating insofar as you need it to stay alive (intellectually in this case), but just as there is food that is both healthy and tasty, there is another sort that goes down well but makes you feel ill, and it is not always easy to know which is which.

*　　*　　*

I would like to thank the following people: Ernest Bendriss, who proposed that I write this book, because although the project later ended up taking us down different paths, it would not have been possible without him; Alfonso and Marián, from Satori Ediciones, who published this book in its original Spanish version, for their interest in making this a reality and for making everything so easy; Eric Oey, Robert Goforth, Catie Baumgartner and everyone at Tuttle Publishing, for giving me the amazing chance to take this book to so many new potential readers; Héctor García (Kirai) for the nice long talks in Tokyo and for introducing my book to Tuttle; Russell Calvert, for translating my words into English and being such a good chap; Joan-Pau Rubiés (Universitat Pompeu Fabra,

Barcelona) and Asami Masakazu (Keiō University, Tokyo), the directors of my doctoral thesis, and Josep Maria Delgado (UPF), director of my master's dissertation; Pompeu Fabra University's Humanities Department; all the teachers I have had, both at the Universitat Autònoma de Barcelona and at Universitat Pompeu Fabra University, but also at the Naganuma School of Japanese Language, Tokyo, and Kogakkan University, Ise—including here Mr. Tamada—for giving me the gift of so much knowledge; John Blackthorne and Toranaga-*sama*, for being the spark that lit the touch paper for all this; all the readers and followers of Historia-Japonesa.com; my family and friends for putting up with me and my stories of old Japanese folk.

CHAPTER 1

The Emergence of the Samurai

The First Warriors

Tracing the origins of the samurai is quite difficult, since at the end of the day they are warriors and, in all civilizations—Japan is no exception—warriors have existed almost as long as the civilization itself. When the use of violence or coercion is an easier and more convenient way of obtaining a concrete good than producing it yourself, whoever has that good will want to defend it and whoever desires it will want to take it. In the case of Japan, we know that in the Yayoi period (300 BC-AD 300 approx.)—considered part of prehistory since they had yet to discover writing at that point—rice farming became widespread. This led to populations settling in concrete places and little by little a feeling of belonging to a particular area developed. Also, after this time, surplus harvests could be stored, making them vulnerable to being robbed by other villages and creating a need for their defense. Thus appeared the need for warriors who were able to conquer neighboring villages to steal their surplus harvests in times of need, and who in turn were capable of defending their own surpluses in times of prosperity. At the same time, these sedentary agrarian societies began to stratify, with some individuals devoting themselves to concrete tasks: for example, we know from archeological sites that they started to mass produce ceramic utensils; but each family did not make what they needed, instead the person who was most skilled at the task produced it and exchanged it for other goods. Likewise, only a few of the most capable individuals took charge of the defense of the village—thus giving birth to the first warrior class.

The next significant change—as far as our subject matter is concerned—came about around the year AD 450, within a new period known as the Kofun age (AD 300-552), with the arrival from the continent of a hitherto unknown animal in Japan—the horse. Apart from its many other uses, the horse could be used for combat, affording an army greater mobility and making warriors much more lethal, especially when fighting others who were on foot. The main weapon at that time—and it would continue to be so for a long period—was the bow. An army of archers who could fire from fast-moving horses unquestionably held a great advantage on the battlefield. Regarding armor and helmets, they were not yet recognizable as the typical samurai ones but were very similar to those used at the same time in other parts of East Asia, made up of vertical iron strips, which we can see depicted in some *haniwa*, rudimentary clay figures typical of the Kofun period.

The warrior elites would play a vital role in Japan's process of unification—or at least in part of it—throughout these early periods up until the creation of a kind of state structure in the country's central zone, known as Yamato. Around the year AD 600, the court of Yamato decided to create a great army following the same system used by the Chinese Sui (AD 581-618) and Tang (AD 618-907) dynasties—we find ourselves in one of the moments of greatest Chinese influence over Japan—based on obligatory military service of men aged between twenty and sixty. At certain periods of the year, they had to carry out military tasks wherever they were stationed and also pay the costs of their weapons and other equipment themselves. Despite the previously mentioned advantage the military use of the horse gave, it also represented a considerable expense, both for the cost of the animal—equivalent to a peasant's earnings over five years—and its upkeep as well as for the time needed to learn to ride, and above all, shoot accurately while galloping at full speed. So, the men forced to do military tasks—mainly peasants—made up the infantry, while the cavalry was exclusively made up of those who could afford it—mainly members of the provincial elites.

Fig. 1.1. Haniwa depicting a warrior with suit of armour.
Tokyo National Museum.

These armies were basically stationed at three points around the country: in the vicinity of the capital, to defend the court from a possible attack; on the southern island of Kyūshū, as it was the closest to the continent and therefore most liable to be attacked by the Chinese and Koreans; and in the northern zone of the island of Honshū where, above all in the late eighth and early ninth century, they waged war against the *Emishi*. This is the name given to certain people pertaining to the Jōmon culture, who had inhabited Japan long before the arrival of the Yayoi, from whom it is believed the current Japanese descend, although opinions are divided on this issue. The Emishi were holed up further and further north by the unceasing fights against them. Since this northern zone of the country was the only one where real fighting took place, rather than just patrols and passive defense services, the elite warriors of these regions gained much greater experience than those in the rest of the country. For example, they learned from the battles against the Emishi that it was much more practical to fight in light leather armor than metal suits of armor. Or that, for a sword to be long enough but still be easy to unsheathe on horseback, the blade had to be slightly curved and not straight like those used up until then. These two characteristics would be kept in the samurai age. The court also learned that an army made up mainly of foot soldiers was highly inefficient when facing the Emishi, who used horses and a guerrilla strategy that made use of their great familiarity with the terrain. So, in the year 792 the end of the draft system was decreed, although in some areas of the country it continued to be used for decades.

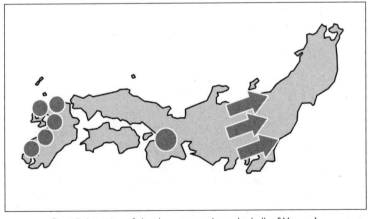

Fig. 1.2. Location of the three areas where the bulk of Yamato's forces were positioned. Author's own drawing.

In the middle of the Heian period (AD 794-1185)—so named because the capital was established in the city of Heian-kyō, today's Kyoto—the use of *shōen* started to be introduced. These were plots of agricultural land declared tax-free by the government for three generations with the aim of encouraging people to farm them. The proliferation of the shōen led to landowners growing rich thanks to the taxes they collected from the peasants who worked their land, thus becoming ever more powerful. Some of these landowners came from the provinces where their land was, but many of them lived in the capital and either could not or did not want to manage their shōen directly, delegating this task to families from the area. These were usually local military clans they had some relation to, who acted as intermediaries and tax collectors, in exchange for which they made a juicy commission.

The central government was already on the wane, which reduced its ability to maintain direct control over its whole territory. This, added to the onset of periods of general scarcity, led to an increase in bandit activity and violence in the provinces that the government could not combat. Because of this, they started to delegate these tasks to local elites, who became ever more militarized, hiring the services of professional soldiers; you could say both the army and the police were privatized, with the government giving up on maintaining its own army and converting the professional warriors into the "claws and teeth" of the State, as the Japanese historians tend to describe the phenomenon. Some of these warrior elites were responsible for dangerous rebellions in the mid-tenth century, which the court smothered using other groups of professional warriors. In exchange, they received posts as governors or low ranks in the aristocracy, which was the first step on their way to achieving a higher standing. As well as this, some noble families—minor branches of important clans—were also posted to the provinces as governors to reduce the burden of an increasingly expensive court. Two of these families were the Taira, mainly based in the southwest, and the Minamoto in the northeast, both related to the imperial family—the two of them would soon play a leading role in Japanese history.

The First Samurai

The provinces and the frontier zones were not the only places where these professional warriors carried out their military tasks; the court itself was under constant threat from some powerful Buddhist monasteries close to the capital, such as Enryaku-ji, Onjō-ji and Kōfuku-ji. These temples had their own armies of warrior monks, who from the early eleventh century often headed for Kyoto (the name adopted for the capital in this century) to pressure the court when it was taking decisions that might be related to their interests, under the threat of creating havoc if their petitions were not listened to. This could either take the form of direct violence or divine curses that they supposedly had the power to invoke. This was one of the reasons why some of the provincial military clans were summoned to the capital and charged with its defense. It could even be said that from that moment on the word samurai was used for these warriors who were under the direct command of the court. Some families pertaining to the Taira and Minamoto clans devoted themselves to the military task of protecting the capital and the former in particular would progressively gain more power at the start of the twelfth century, thanks to the important social and political bonds they were to forge with the court aristocracy.

Origin of the Word Samurai

The most appropriate term for referring to a Japanese warrior is *bushi*, first used at the end of the Heian period, which we are discussing in this section. Before then, we can find different words for this concept, like *tsuwamono* or *musha*, with different origins and nuances that it would be difficult to get into. But you have to bear in mind that in all cases we are referring to professional warriors who were very different from the soldiers recruited from the peasantry to carry out military duties at a certain time of year.

The origin of the word samurai is quite different from what it has come to mean and be used for today. It comes from an ancient verb, *saburau*, which equates to "serving a superior," from which we get the word *saburai*, "he who serves a superior," the pronunciation of which would eventually transform into the term we use today. At first, in the early eighth century, this was the name given to the household servants who looked after the homes of the nobility and carried out all sorts of tasks for them; but when the professional warriors began to work for the Heian-kyō courtiers, the term was also applied to them. Over time the term lost its original meaning and ended up being applied exclusively to the members of these warrior clans, and from the end of the sixteenth century, to an entire social class, access to which was only possible through birth; the son of a samurai automatically became a samurai and that was the only way—with some exceptions, as we shall see later—to be one.

From this point on, we shall use both samurai and bushi interchangeably, or their translation—"warrior."

The rise of the Taira within the court was made easier by the declining power of the Fujiwara family, who had governed *de facto* since the end of the tenth century. Some of its members had held the position of regent on an almost permanent basis when the emperor—as frequently occurred—was a minor. It was even more common for emperors to marry daughters of the Fujiwara family. Naturally this ensured their children—among them the next emperor—would be tied to this clan and even easier to control. If the emperor was an adult, his Fujiwara regent took on the position of chief advisor, and effectively continued to govern; as we shall repeatedly see, in Japan the person who holds power on paper tends not to be the one who actually wields it. But the Fujiwara family had already started to lose power by the early twelfth century and there were constant clashes between members of the clan or with different emperors and former emperors, who also squabbled among themselves.

Retired Emperor

The current emperor of Japan, Naruhito (1960), is the 126th to sit on the Japanese throne, making it the oldest hereditary monarchy in the world today. Despite this, the first sovereigns on this list—from ten to fifteen of them depending on the source—are considered merely part of the mythology and there is only consensus about the existence of those from Emperor Ōjin (third century) onwards. Besides, some historians believe that the dynastic line was interrupted at the start of the sixth century and the monarchs prior to Emperor Keitai—26th on the list—belonged to another dynasty. In any case, where there is complete agreement is on the fact that very few of them wielded any real power.

We could say that there has always been an emperor, but throughout the greater part of history others have governed in his name. These others have varied over time. Sometimes they were regents, because the emperor was a minor and somebody had to take control of the government temporarily. Although, this situation was frequently extended if the regent managed to convince the emperor upon reaching adulthood of the need to abdicate in favor of a cousin or younger brother; at other times the emperor simply died mysteriously. These regents usually belonged to the same family and married into the imperial family, the Fujiwara family being the best example of this. When the hereditary military commanders—the *shōgun*—arrived in the twelfth century, they would wield power, though they supposedly acted on the emperor's orders.

Another matter, which we shall address now, is that of the retired emperors. When an emperor saw that he could not exercise any real power because his life was subject to never-ending rituals and ceremonies that took up most of his time, and because he was immersed in a complicated bureaucratic and administrative machinery with regents and advisors he had not chosen, and who were the ones really taking the decisions, he chose to abdicate and retire. Sometimes the retirement consisted of becoming a monk (in which case we often talk of cloistered emperors), though this did not always happen. In one way or another, from that moment on, he had a lot more time on his hands and could surround himself with a team of hand-picked advisors and confidants. In addition, he was the father of the new and still wet-behind-the-ears emperor, and could have a great influence on him, not just because he was his father, but also because he was the patriarch of the imperial family. This situation placed him in an ideal position to govern indirectly.

This was a recurring phenomenon for nearly a century, from the late eleventh to twelfth centuries, with three consecutive retired emperors, and has occurred on several other occasions, both before and after this time. If the explanation of the system seems complicated, we must add that it also applied to other positions, like that of regent, with the figure of the retired re-gent, or shōgun, also existing, as we shall see throughout our tale. Thus, at times we find a retired shōgun wielding power in the background while in theory the shōgun governs, in the name of the emperor, although the latter is in turn completely under the influence of both his regent and his father, the retired emperor. We could find some even more complicated and con-voluted cases, but this serves as an example. Overall, we could talk of a blurring of authority, which has prevented there being many individuals throughout Japanese history who stand out for having concentrated power in their own hands. This is why we tend to talk more about families or clans.

In 1156, there was a clash within the court in which for the first time, the samurai—both the Taira and Minamoto clans—intervened militarily. This was known as the Hōgen Rebellion. A dispute between Emperor Go-Shirakawa (AD 1127-1192) and the retired Emperor Sutoku (AD 1119-1164) over the succession to the throne led to the creation of two sides supporting one or the other. Each faction was made up of segments drawn from the Fujiwara, Taira and Minamoto clans, which certainly makes for a situation that is rather complicated to analyze. To make things simpler, we could say that the leader of the Taira—called Taira Kiyomori (AD 1118-1181)—supported the emperor, while the leader of the Mi-namoto—Minamoto Tameyoshi (AD 1096-1156)—supported the retired emperor, though this should not be interpreted as it being a conflict between the Taira and Minamoto.

The court showdown—little different from others that had appeared in previous succession crises—was not going to be resolved by politics or diplomacy this time, given that a new factor had entered the equation—military power. So, in mid-July, Emperor Go-Shirakawa's side, led by the head of the Taira, having prevented a large part of the enemy army from reaching the capital, attacked the palace of the retired Emperor Sutoku with a force of six thousand mounted soldiers, taking the defenders by surprise and setting fire to the building. Sutoku managed to escape with his life but was taken prisoner soon after and condemned to exile on the island of Shikoku, from where he never returned. In the following days, those courtiers who had supported Sutoku were also exiled and his side's samurai condemned to death. Since there were members of the Taira and Minamoto clans on both sides, some gestures were made that define the peculiar samurai culture very well, and would be repeated on future occasions: the leader of the Minamoto clan, Tameyoshi, was executed by his own son, Minamoto Yoshitomo

Fig. 1.3. *Tachi*—a type of sword, very similar to the well-known *katana*—belonging to Minamoto Yoshitomo. Kongōshō-ji Temple Museum, Ise. Photograph taken by the author, February 2015.

(AD 1123-1160), who had fought for Go-Shirakawa; the Taira leader, Kiyomori, was given the task of executing his uncle Tadamasa (AD ?-1156). Once the conflict was over, both the Minamoto and the Taira were on the winning side, since Yoshitomo was now the leader of his clan. Both samurai families were rewarded for helping the emperor, although in rather a discreet way, given that, for the court, they were nothing more than simple servants doing what they were ordered to. Perhaps the greatest reward the samurai obtained was the knowledge that now they had the real power to decide who governed the country and it was only a matter of time before the most opportune moment to use it would appear.

A mere three years later, between 1159 and 1160, with Go-Shirakawa already retired as emperor and his fifteen-year-old son on the throne as Emperor Nijō (AD 1143-1165), a new conflict, known as the Heiji Rebellion, occurred. Go-Shirakawa's intention was to control the court from his comfortable position as retired emperor, as Sutoku had done before him. But these intentions appeared to be incompatible with those of his son, who despite his youth was determined not to be anyone's puppet, not even his father's, and began to search for support within the court to strengthen his position. As the Taira were very close to Go-Shirakawa, the Minamoto opted to support Nijō. On this occasion—with minor exceptions—the two clans were clearly positioned on different sides, unlike with the Hōgen Rebellion. As a result, only one of the two families would be victorious this time.

Taking advantage of the fact that Taira Kiyomori was away from the capital on a pilgrimage in Ise, Minamoto Yoshitomo saw a perfect opportunity to act. He stormed Go-Shirakawa's palace and carried him off to his son's palace, who he also had under watch; to a certain extent, his maneuver was aimed less at defending the emperor than at attacking Taira interests. Go-Shirakawa's chief adviser, a Fujiwara who had a great influence over the retired emperor and was one of the main Taira allies, was executed. Another Fujiwara was put in his place—Nobuyori (AD 1133-1160), ally of the Minamoto and one of the instigators of the scheme. Taira Kiyomori was also stripped of his positions and titles. Logically, news of what was happening in Kyoto reached Kiyomori, who returned to the capital immediately. At first, he accepted the new situation, seeing there was little he could do to change it, but a few days later everything changed radically when Emperor Nijō, unhappy with the way Nobuyori and Yoshitomo were behaving, escaped from his palace disguised as a woman and took refuge in Taira Kiyomori's palace. Since they now lacked the emperor's support, the Minamoto were henceforth considered in rebellion against him, while the Taira officially became his defenders. Armed confrontation would not be long in coming, and just one day after Emperor Nijō's flight, the Taira attacked the palace where the Minamoto were gathered, forcing them to leave; once outside, the latter recovered their forces and decided they in turn would attack the Taira base, but were crushed by the defenders and forced to withdraw and flee the capital. Everything had been settled in less than a day.

Fujiwara Nobuyori was condemned to death and executed, while Minamoto Yoshitomo was assassinated when trying to escape from Kyoto; his sons were also sentenced to death—in line with the tradition of the time—although, Kiyomori eventually pardoned three of them: the thirteen-year-old Yoritomo (AD 1147-1199); three-year-old Noriyori (AD 1156-1193); and Yoshitsune (AD 1159-1189), who at the time was just a baby. The first of them was absolved at the request of Kiyomori's own stepmother (who had become a Buddhist monk on becoming a widow), who implored the Taira leader not to execute the young Yoritomo because he reminded her of a son she had lost years earlier and who would be the same age had he lived. Despite the petitions of his advisers, who considered it very important to get rid of any potential Minamoto leadership, Kiyomori decided to grant his stepmother's wishes and exiled the young Yoritomo to an island in the province of Izu, where he would live under the watchful eye of members of the Taira clan. As for his half-brothers Noriyori and Yoshitsune, another woman was behind their pardon, in this case their own mother, Lady Tokiwa (AD 1138-1180), who had been the executed

Minamoto leader's concubine. Kiyomori intended for her to become his concubine, but she flat refused at first and only finally agreed on the condition that her sons Noriyori and Yoshitsune were not executed. This condition was accepted, much to the displeasure of Kiyomori's advisers, and the youngsters were sent to a monastery to be brought up and trained as priests. From that moment on, Taira Kiyomori would take control of the government of Japan, but the day would soon come when he would regret sparing the lives of Yoshitomo's sons.

The Samurai Control the Court

With the Minamoto out of the picture—at least for now—Taira Kiyomori was not satisfied this time with a simple reward in the shape of land or some middle-ranking court position. Knowing he had practically saved the emperor and in a very short space of time too, he had his sights set much higher, and no other samurai clan could stop him now. Kiyomori would make the most of the obvious enmity between Emperor Nijō and his father, Go-Shirakawa, mediating in their constant conflicts and climbing positions within the court. This two-headed system of government, with an active emperor and a retired one competing among one another to have the most possible influence over matters of court, left a crack that somebody smart and hungry for power could use to climb to the top. Thus did Kiyomori—accompanied by other members of the Taira clan—taking on even more important roles within the capital's political structure in the years following the Heiji Rebellion. His meteoric rise culminated in 1167 with him taking over the position of grand minister and from that moment on being the *de facto* governor of the country. He officially abandoned the post just three months later, becoming a kind of retired grand minister, and soon after became a monk, supposedly distancing himself from the political scene due to health issues. Despite this, he carried on holding the court strings. As well as this, just as the Fujiwara had done until then, he astutely linked his own clan to the imperial family by marriage, at the same time as maintaining an ever closer cooperation with the omnipresent Go-Shirakawa, who had also become a monk.

Although Taira Kiyomori and his clan controlled the government of Japan, it would still be too soon to talk about a samurai government since what the Taira did was to continue with the policy that had been developed prior to their arrival; they adapted to the court's way of functioning, rather than the reverse. Things could be summed up by saying there was a samurai in the government but not a samurai government. When Kiyomori was a provincial governor, he defended the idea of a greater political organization among the local landowners rather than the interests of the court, but at that time, as part of the court hierarchy—sitting comfortably, in fact, on the highest step—his policy was typical of the staunchest authoritarian centralism.

The pardoning of the young descendants of the Minamoto clan, their relationship with the retired Emperor Go-Shirakawa and the progressive rift with the provincial warrior clans would be key factors in one of the greatest moments of change in Japanese history, which would occur between the years 1180 and 1185.

Fig. 1.4. Taira Kiyomori, in the last stage of his life, with his head shaven and in monk's attire. Artwork by Kikuchi Yōsai, part of *Zenken Kojitsu*, a collection of biographies of well-known historical Japanese characters.

CHAPTER 2

The Genpei Wars

Young Samurai in Exile

The thirteen-year-old Minamoto Yoritomo had become the leader of his clan upon the death of his father in 1160. But while the Taira had spared his life, he had been condemned to exile, where he would be controlled and carefully watched by his enemies. He was sent to a small village called Nirayama in the province of Izu, the present-day Shizuoka prefecture. It was usual for the Heian court to send those who had been sentenced for political crimes into exile there. He would live at the home of the local lord, Ito Sukechika (AD ?-1182), who was related to the Fujiwara but served Taira Kiyomori. The young Izu lord Hōjō Tokimasa (AD 1138-1215), a Taira family member, was also entrusted with supervising Ito's task of being in charge of the youngster. So, Yoritomo was under the direct strict control of his clan's enemies—a clan he now led despite being completely isolated and cut off from the rest of its members. Thus, twenty long years went by, allowing him time to make a thorough study of what had happened to his clan and prepare himself for when the moment for revenge might come. He also had time for other matters, like courting a young lady called Masako (AD 1156-1225), who happened to be Hōjō Tokimasa's eldest daughter. This was soon after moving to the Hōjō family home because of the incessant problems he had with Itō Sukechika. Clearly, Tokimasa knew that marrying his daughter to the Minamoto's leader would not go down well with Taira Kiyomori, so he hurried to have her engaged to the governor of Izu, a Taira called Kanetaka (AD ?-1180). For the time being we shall take our leave of Yoritomo.

Fig. 2.1. Statue of Minamoto Yoritomo, Kamakura.
Photograph taken by the author, February 2015.

As for his half-brothers, nothing is known about the eldest, Noriyori, in the twenty years following the moment his life was reprieved, but in 1180 he would reappear from out of nowhere. We do have some information about Yoshitsune's early years, although a large part of it falls within the realm of legend and it is not always easy to tell the facts from the made-up parts. It is known that he was sent to Kurama-dera, a temple on Mount Kurama, near Kyoto, where he was supposed to train to be a priest. However, he soon showed little interest in Buddhist scripture and a much greater liking for military texts, such as the Chinese classic *The Art of War* by Sun Tzu (544–496 BC). Temple life turned out to be too peaceful for an action-hungry Yoshitsune who was always dreaming of traveling to the north of Japan, where there was a permanent struggle with the Emishi. This led to him finally escaping to the province of Mutsu—the northernmost island of Honshū—when he was barely a teenager, accompanied by an itinerant merchant who had business with the temple. They say the Kurama monks were happy to see the troublesome boy leave. In Mutsu he ended up living at the residence of Fujiwara Hidehira (AD 1122–1187), governor of the province and member of a branch of the Fujiwara clan, and the person who would quickly become his protector and benefactor.

Minamoto Yoshitsune

The lack of information about Yoshitsune's life in the years from his arrival at the Kurama-dera Temple as a baby to his participation in the Genpei Wars leaves a great number of gaps that were filled with many stories, rumors and legends as time went by. According to the mythology that sprang up around his persona, the young Yoshitsune—known as Ushikawa-maru when living in the temple—had struck up a friendship with Sōjōbō, who lived on Mount Kurama and was the king of all the *tengu*. The tengu are a kind of minor deity that we could class as spirits or demons, normally portrayed wearing a mountain monk's habits and having a part-human, part-crow body, often with red skin, white hair and a long nose; they are expert fighters and normally devote themselves to creating chaos. In the stories about Ushikawa-maru, thanks to his friendship with Sōjōbō, the tengu dedicated themselves to training the boy at night, when he would escape from the temple and go deep into the woods. They were the ones who taught him how to fight, to use a sword and bow, to design military tactics and—according to some stories—even taught him magic so he could get his revenge on the Taira. The legends not only talk of his childhood—one really famous one claims he did not die when we think he did, but managed to escape, left Japan for the continent and ended up there known as none other than Genghis Khan (AD 1162–1227), something which—although it fits chronologically—is very hard to believe.

Something we do know is that from a very young age right up until his death, the most famous warrior monk in Japanese history, Musashibō Benkei (AD 1155–1189) was always at his side. The latter is also known as Benkei, and legends about him abound. It is just one of those legends that explains how he met Yoshitsune and came to be his right-hand man; it is said that one fine day Benkei positioned himself on a busy bridge in Kyoto, ready to challenge any bushi who dared to fight him,

Fig. 2.2. Statue of Yoshitsune in Dan no Ura.

on the condition that if he won the fight, he would keep his opponent's sword. This went on for days as he beat all contenders and piled up 999 swords. But he was unable to reach a round number because his thousandth adversary was the young Yoshitsune, who defeated him. In a sign of respect, he started to serve him unconditionally from that day on. Another of the famous Benkei legends explains how he died—but we will get to that in the next chapter.

Yoshitsune is without question a very well-known character and much loved by all Japanese people. He is considered one of their greatest heroes of all-time and appears in an endless number of paintings, novels, plays, movies, videogames, songs, etc.

Thus, toward 1180, both Yoritomo and Yoshitsune—Noriyori is still a mystery—found themselves under the protection of powerful lords—Hōjō Tokimasa and Fujiwara Hidehira—who at face value supported Taira Kiyomori…, although in times of war, loyalties can sometimes turn out to be rather brittle.

First Phase: Conflict Breaks Out

As was explained in the previous chapter, from 1167, Taira Kiyomori could be considered the supreme governor of Japan and from then on he made himself enemies both within and outside the court. The provincial warrior clans saw how the Taira of Ise—as the branch of Kiyomori, who comes from this province, is known—quickly settled into life at court, changing their old ways and forgetting the interests inherent to the warrior class they had previously defended. As a result, the number of clans unhappy with their government's policy was growing throughout the country. Nor was the Kyoto aristocracy satisfied with the new situation, given that little by little the Taira clan had been rising into positions of responsibility at court, ousting the aristocrats. The latter observed how simple warriors—mere servants from their point of view—were taking over a place they considered belonged to them as of right.

The situation became even more complicated after 1177, when a plot to get rid of the Taira was discovered within the court and some of those implicated turned out to be trusted retainers of Go-Shirakawa; they were executed or exiled, which made relations between Kiyomori and the retired emperor very strained. Two years later, the Taira leader would strike a decisive blow by dismissing nearly forty of Go-Shirakawa's close family from their court positions and seizing their lands, which automatically became property of the clan. He even placed the retired emperor under house arrest. In this way, Kiyomori not only made a permanent enemy of Go-Shirakawa—obviously—but also of a large part of the court and some of the powerful temples on the outskirts of the capital, who were very close to the retired emperor. At this moment, Kiyomori only had to climb one more rung to the top of the ladder and he would climb it in 1180, forcing Emperor Takakura (AD 1161–1181)—fourth son of Go-Shirakawa—to abdicate in favor of his two-year-old son Antoku (AD 1177–1185). The reason is very simple—Antoku was not only Go-Shirakawa's grandson on his father's side but also Kiyomori's grandson on his mother's side, since Kiyomori had married his second daughter to Takakura. So, the new emperor was half Taira and also very young to demand any sort of power, which meant that Kiyomori, having Go-Shirakawa under arrest, could rule Japan with even more authority than before. The Taira clan then took over the highest-ranking posts for good, both at court and in the provinces, filling the post of governor in many of them.

Placing little Antoku on the throne made somebody especially offended—Prince Mochihito (AD 1151-1180), third son of Go-Shirakawa. He had been passed over before for the position and was not prepared to put up with it this time. Kiyomori, having made enemies of practically the entire country, had been building a time bomb under his feet and Mochihito was about to set the timer off,

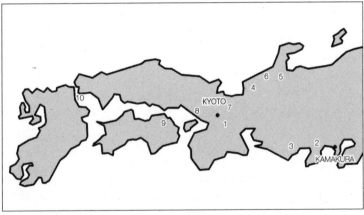

Fig. 2.3. Main battles of the Genpei Wars. 1, Uji (1180); 2, Ishibashiyama (1180); 3, Fujigawa (1180); 4, Hiuchi (1183); 5, Kurikara (1183); 6, Shinohara (1183); 7, Awazu (1184); 8, Ichi no Tani (1184); 9, Yashima (1185); 10, Dan no Ura (1185). Author's own drawing.

triggering the greatest war Japan had seen up until then: the Genpei Wars. This conflict is also known as the Genpei War, depending on whether it is considered a collection of battles from the same war or a series of small wars. As for the name, it comes from the surnames of the two clans—Minamoto and Taira—whose characters may also be read as Genji and Heike. By taking the first part of each surname, *Gen* and *Hei*, and joining them while changing the pronunciation of the latter from *Hei* to *Pei*—something quite common in Japanese with this type of compounds—you get a word which simply means "wars between the Minamoto and the Taira."

The indignant Prince Mochihito decreed an edict in the middle of 1180 asking both the Minamoto, other clans and various temples from all parts of the country to come together to fight Taira Kiyomori. Mochihito had the support of Minamoto Yorimasa (AD 1106-1180), the only one of his clan who had stayed at court after the Heiji Rebellion as he had favored Kiyomori then, although his preferences had changed over the following years. Clearly, after issuing this call to rebellion against the government, Mochihito had put a price on his own head, so he fled Kyoto along with Yorimasa's men and took refuge in the Onjō-ji Temple—also known as Mii-dera—whose monks could protect him. But just days later, a Taira army attacked the temple, forcing Mochihito, Yorimasa, their men and some monks to escape toward Nara.

Warrior Monks

Throughout a good part of Japanese history, the various Buddhist monasteries played a very important role in the country's politic life. With the spread of Buddhism (a religion that had arrived on the islands in the mid-sixth century) in Japan during the Nara period (AD 710-794), some temples began to have more and more power, benefiting from the favor of different emperors and aristocrats, particularly those located in the capital city of the time, Nara. Their influence came to be so great that, among other reasons, it was precisely to escape from their power that the decision was taken to change the capital to Heian-kyō, Kyoto, in AD 794, although from this moment on, the temples of Mount Hiei, near Kyoto, also started to have influence and the Nara temples felt betrayed, which in turn fostered great rivalries. This was because the disputes involving these temples did not begin and end with those they had with the court in the capital city and with the samurai clans. Instead, most disputes occurred between different temples and not for religious reasons, since the main temples belonged to the same Buddhist school; purely economic and political reasons were behind the conflicts.

In many ways we can see these monasteries as just another landowner and in the military sphere they were also like the provincial lords. Just as the provincial lords—as we saw in the first chapter—progressively militarized and formed their own

Fig. 2.4. Late nineteenth-century recreation of a twelfth-century warrior monk. Photograph by Ogawa Kazumasa.

armies, the monasteries did exactly the same thing. This is where the concept of the *sōhei* or warrior monks appears. Although, Buddhism prohibits the use of violence and weapons, these monks were experts in the use of the sword and bow, although their most characteristic weapon was the *naginata*, a kind of spear with a curved blade. In line with their position as monks, they had shaved heads and wore a kind of tunic, although in battle they wore virtually an entire suit of armor underneath. To the typical samurai weapons, they also added some which were exclusive to them, such as a Buddhist rosary which they used to hurl curses. This may seem harmless to us today, but at the time filled people with dread.

By the end of the tenth century and beginning of the eleventh, it was becoming usual for large groups of sōhei to march on Kyoto in threatening kinds of demonstrations to pressure the court and in this way get it to take decisions that were to their benefit. If their demands were not met, they could cause chaos in the city, uttering all kinds of curses and bad omens. Often, they even carried supposedly sacred miniature portable temples with them—like the ones we can see today in street processions throughout Japan in certain festivals—to inspire greater respect.

With the arrival of the bushi at court, the situation changed greatly, since they were not as superstitious as the aristocrats, and were not averse to facing up to the warrior monks, who they saw more as warriors than as monks. One scene, attributed to a young Taira Kiyomori in 1146, when he had yet to become clan leader, illustrates this change of perspective perfectly: in a dispute between a few of his men and some sōhei, Kiyomori gave a clear declaration of intent by shooting an arrow straight at the portable temple the monks were carrying, hitting it squarely in the little gong hanging at the front. The sound of this gong symbolically marked the start of a new era as far as the power of the monasteries was concerned. A sound that many other samurai lords would take it upon themselves to amplify in the following decades and centuries, chief among them Oda Nobunaga in the sixteenth century—but we shall come to this later.

They were intercepted at a village called Uji, where the Battle of Uji was waged, thus beginning the Genpei Wars. The Taira forces were clearly superior so Mochihito, Yorimasa and a few others took refuge in the Byōdō-in Temple, knowing they could not win. The veteran Minamoto preferred to commit suicide rather than be captured by his enemies. This is supposedly the first known case of *seppuku*—what is known in the West as *hara-kiri*. He did not even want the Taira to find his head once he was dead to prevent them showing it off as a trophy, so he ordered one of his men to tie it to a rock and throw it in the river. As for Mochihito, he fled the temple and set off for Nara again, but was captured and executed before making it there. The Taira did not overlook the Onjō-ji temple's collaboration with the rebel prince, so immediately afterwards attacked and set fire to the temple; not content with this, they headed for Nara and did the same with most of the city's temples, including the important Tōdai-ji and Kōfuku-ji.

Gunkimonogatari

The *gunkimonogatari*, or "war chronicles stories," is a Japanese literary genre (dealing, as the name suggests, with armed conflict), which was particularly widespread in the twelfth and thirteenth centuries. The *Shōmonki*, from the late tenth century, is believed to be the oldest of the chronicles and tells the tale of a rebellion led by Taira Masakado (AD ?-940) in 939-940 against the imperial government. Some other gunkimonogatari deal with topics we saw in the previous chapter, like the *Hōgen Monogatari* and the *Heiji Monogatari*, but the most famous of them all is the one dedicated to the subject of this very chapter—the Genpei wars, the *Heike Monogatari*.

This literary work covers the period from the height of Taira Kiyomori's powers within the capital city's court till after the end of the war, so we could say it narrates the rise and fall of the Taira clan—also known as Heike. Of unknown authorship, there are numerous versions, which were written down at different times, but the most popular comes from 1371. These different versions were produced by building upon and tweaking the already existing ones, in a rather chaotic fashion since the stories were usually spread orally, recited by—normally blind—monks. This is known as *biwa-hōshi*, "lute monks." As the saying goes, history is written by the victors, and the *Heike Monogatari* is no exception—despite talking mainly about the Taira, it does so from the Minamoto's point of view. Thus, the former are described as despicable tyrants, warriors who have grown used to life at court and become weaker as a result. But there are two general issues that color the specifics: firstly, beyond the battles, the palace intrigues and the romantic scenes, the whole book talks about the concept of karma, seeing the Taira's terrible fate as a necessary consequence of their bad past actions; and secondly, the inexorable passing of time, the non-permanent character of things and nostalgia for the past, which is made clear in the chronicle's well-known opening paragraph:

> The sound of the Gion Shōja bells echoes the impermanence of all things; the color of the *sāla* flowers reveals the truth that the prosperous must decline. The proud do not endure, they are like a dream on a spring night; the mighty fall at last, they are as dust before the wind (*The Tale of Heike*, 1988).

> Logically, taking into account the way it was passed on and compiled and its one-sided point of view, what the *Heike Monogatari*, or any other gunkimonogatari tells us, cannot be taken as fact, from a historical point of view. There are many debates and studies about the truthfulness of the different episodes that appear in the tome. Some aspects of it have been proved, but it is always advisable for the reader to take into account that we are dealing with a fictional story.

The death of Prince Mochihito did not change the course of events much, because the proclamation he had made a few days earlier had set in motion certain mechanisms in various parts of Japan, which could no longer be stopped, even with its promoter now dead. That very month of June, Yoritomo was visited by his uncle, Minamoto Yukiie (c. AD 1141-1186), who gave him a copy of Mochihito's edict. Yoritomo showed it to his protector, Hōjō Tokimasa, and the two of them agreed to the request made in it, despite—let us not forget—Tokimasa being a relative of the Taira. A few days later, they received more news, first that of the battle of Uji and later that of certain rumors going around Kyoto, claiming Taira Kiyomori might want to carry out a preventive attack on the Minamoto before they decided to obey the edict. The latter rumor merely made Yoritomo and Tokimasa stand by their decision more firmly. So, the Minamoto leader sent messengers to the various clan families telling them to prepare for battle, while he and Tokimasa met in secret with various warlords from the Izu area to get them to join their cause.

Looking at the list of family names of many of the clans who joined Yoritomo, something that may be surprising can be seen: many of those clans—Hōjō, Chiba, Doi, Miura—are in reality descendants of the Taira, among them many who even have the Taira surname, pertaining to different branches of the clan to Kiyomori—the Taira of Ise. In theory, analyzing the name of the conflict—Genpei—we are talking about a war between the Minamoto and the Taira, and this is how it is usually summarized. But reality is usually more complex than it first appears, and it is really a war between two sides: one led by a Minamoto and the other by a Taira. But these two family names can be found, and many others, on both sides, and there were even, as shall be seen later, direct conflicts within the same bloc. Besides, it is more correct to read this war as a struggle between two distinct societies jostling for power: on one side, the waning of the aristocratic refined court government, represented by the Taira bloc, who despite being warriors themselves had adapted to the system; facing them, a new society hungry to make its mark on history, the warriors, soldiers and samurai—those who boasted brute strength, represented by the Minamoto bloc. Having clarified this, from now on, in the interests of making the tale easier to understand, we will continue to simplify it and refer to each bloc as the Taira and Minamoto side.

Reds vs. Whites

During the Genpei Wars, the Taira bloc identified itself with red-colored flags, while the Minamoto carried white ones, and both also had their respective clan emblems, called *mon*. These two colors, red and white, have been very important since then in Japanese culture— as the national flag bears witness—and are used to designate two rival teams in all sort of competitions, like martial arts fights, school sports tournaments, and even the most famous program on Japanese television, on air since 1951, which squares off two teams of singers every New Year's Eve— the red team and the white team.

In September, Yoritomo and Tokimasa set off for the region of Kantō, where most of the Minamoto troops were, along with other forces who had decided to join them, and the first thing they did before leaving Izu was assault the residence of the governor, Taira Kanetaka, and take his head. This was the same Kanetaka who Tokimasa had once promised to marry his daughter to. She had recently been married—to no other than Yoritomo. Having tied up this loose end, they moved deep into the Sagami province (roughly corresponding to the modern-day Kanagawa prefecture) at the head of three hundred men, only to come across a ten-times larger Taira army on reaching Mount Ishibashi. At night, in the

Fig. 2.5. Minamoto (left) and Taira (right) *mon*.

middle of a great storm, the Taira attacked them head on, at the same time as a small reinforcement of three hundred men coming from Izu attacked from the rear; in command of the latter was none other than Itō Sukechika, Yoritomo's tutor and guard when he had begun his exile. Being clearly outnumbered, the Battle of Ishibashiyama ended in a defeat for Yoritomo, that he was only just able to escape from. He finally managed to get to the province of Awa (in today's Chiba prefecture), where he was safe. Yoritomo ended up establishing his base in a village called Kamakura, long since closely connected to the Minamoto, and in the ensuing weeks different clans with thousands of soldiers began to arrive there from various points of the Kantō region, all of them prepared to fight under his banner.

On November 9, 1180, Yoritomo was camped next to the River Fuji commanding 27,000 men when roughly twice that number of Taira soldiers arrived on the other riverbank. Both armies remained in their respective camps for a few days, one on each side of the river, and they agreed battle on the thirteenth. In the meantime, different reports reached both sides, such as the news that in the province of Shinano (the modern-day Nagano prefecture), in the mountainous zone of central Honshū, another big Minamoto rebellion had occurred, led by Minamoto Yoshinaka (AD 1154-1184)—also known as Kiso Yoshinaka—one of Yoritomo's cousins. The Taira also gradually realized the Minamoto had a lot of support throughout the Kantō region and saw that even if they won the battle, they would be venturing into heavily-defended enemy territory and their advance would become impossible. And so, when dawn broke on November 13, the Taira camp had disappeared and what is known as the Battle of Fujigawa failed to take place. At first, Yoritomo thought of pursuing his retreating enemies, but in the end, he heeded the advice of his generals, who recommended returning to Kamakura to first secure his own territory and to wait for the arrival of more clans. By the following month, Yoritomo controlled practically the entire Kantō region—except for a province under the command of his cousin Yoshinaka—as well as three other provinces to the south of the region. He would never again set foot outside Kamakura as long as the war lasted.

Battle Rituals

The essence of a samurai, at least one from the twelfth century— was combat. Let us not forget this is a warrior caste, soclearly it was a fundamental part of their idiosyncrasy and culture. As might be expected then, they had developed a series of war-related rituals, which were carried out both before, after and even during battle. Before going into action, it was usual to pray to certain Shintoist gods, especially Hachiman (one of the most important in Shintoist mythology and the god of war, among many other things), or to Buddha, given that both religions were closely related in that period, and even merged in certain aspects. Also, a ritual meal could be celebrated, eating some food items that were supposedly more propitious for victory. After the fight, if they had been victorious, they would bathe in hot springs, which were good both for curing tiredness and for healing wounds as well as symbolizing purification of the soul. Then came more practical matters, like the drawing up of dispatches in which individual actions carried out during battle were recounted, and the handing over of the heads of the enemies vanquished in combat, a requirement for receiving the corresponding honors.

The battles themselves also tended to take place in certain established phases, typically beginning with a first stage consisting of a hail of arrows between the two armies, at an appropriate distance. The next phase could contain several duels, between soldiers from each side, either horseback archery or sword fighting. These duels generally started with one samurai issuing a challenge to the opposing army, known as a *nanori*, shouting out his name, origin, ancestors and heroic past deeds, thus making his enemies see how much glory and recognition ending his life would bring them. After the duels, the general battle began in which cutting weapons—like spears, swords or daggers—were commonly used, with the bows and arrows staying out of the fight at this stage. At that point, the fighting was much more disordered, with a multitude of individual or group fights, more like the fighting that could be seen in any other part of the world. In addition, in this period, the generals were not positioned on a nearby hill, calmly directing their troops with carefully worked out strategies, as we shall see later; back then, the generals gave their orders before the battle began and once it was underway they fought alongside their men. The military units were usually small—battalions roughly twenty-strong made up of men who were normally related and fought virtually autonomously.

To return to the subject of the phases that preceded the fighting (with their etiquette, organized duels and samurai making elaborate presentation speeches), we must clarify that this is what we have been led to believe by the *Heike Monogatari* and the rest of the gunkimonogatari. So some of it must be true, but clearly so much chivalry forms part of a romantic fictitious vision of reality, which tends to happen with almost everything related to the samurai. As for the battles, in reality many of them were waged through surprise attacks, with troops falling on a fortress or enemy camp in the middle of the night, setting fire to it and massacring those who were fleeing in bewilderment in the midst of the chaos; or else through ambushes or long sieges, something quite different from the aforementioned order and protocol. Furthermore, in the oldest gunkimonogatari references to the Genpei Wars, the nanori are reduced to a simple shouting out of the samurai's name as he launched into his attack, which was almost impossible for the enemy to hear above the roar of battle. The same scene is repeated in successive accounts and each samurai's initial speech—curiously, almost always one from the victorious Minamoto side—gets longer and more detailed with the passing of time. So, the nanori undoubtedly paint a very picturesque and attractive picture, but there are many reasons to believe that, once again, these stories were made up.

In March 1181, Taira Kiyomori died of natural causes, although many saw his death as divine punishment for having ordered the destruction of numerous temples in the capital and in Nara. According to some Japanese chronicles, his last words were: "All that is born has to die, not only I. Since the Heiji era I have served the Imperial House. I have governed the empire. I have attained the highest rank a subject can aspire to. I am the emperor's maternal grandfather. Do I have any regrets? Only one, that I am dying without seeing the head of Minamoto Yoritomo. When I am dead, do not make offerings to Buddha on my behalf, do not read the sacred scriptures, just cut off Minamoto Yoritomo's head and place it on my tomb. Let my sons, my grandsons, men and servants, each and every one of them, follow these commands." The leadership of the clan was passed on to his third son, Taira Munemori (AD 1147-1185).

Three months later, there were two minor battles, at Sunomata and Yahagigawa, in which the Taira defeated a Minamoto army commanded by Yukiie, Yoritomo's uncle—who usually lost all his battles—preventing him from advancing on the capital and forcing him to go back to the Kantō region. After these two battles, the war was forced into a truce which lasted two whole years due to the onset of a period of terrible famines, especially in the western part of the country. Both sides took advantage of the two-year interval to reorganize, enlist more troops and, in the case of Yoritomo, lay down the basis of a kind of embryonic autonomous government in the Kantō area. The Minamoto also had greater success than their rivals in the task of increasing their armies, since unlike the Taira they were not disliked or resented and Yoritomo also allowed any clan to join his ranks, whatever their family name and lineage, as long as they agreed to swear fealty to him; in exchange, they acquired property rights over the lands they lived in, which normally belonged to court nobility.

The fighting would recommence in 1183—this time with larger and better prepared armies—although only one side would be involved in much of it.

Second Phase: Internal Struggle for the Minamoto Leadership

In May 1183, the Taira had prepared a great army of one hundred thousand soldiers entrusted with dealing with Yoritomo's cousin Yoshinaka, rather than Yoritomo himself—for the moment—as Yoshinaka's territory was closer to the capital. But the Taira were not the only stalking Yoshinaka, as Yoritomo himself distrusted him, worried by his independence and increasing power within the Minamoto clan. It appears the Takeda, a powerful clan from the north of the country, had offered Yoshinaka an alliance through the marriage of their leader's daughter to Yoshinaka's son, but the deal had been rejected. As a result, the Takeda had sought an accommodation with Yoritomo and had contributed to heightening his suspicions of his cousin, by telling him Yoshinaka planned to marry one of the Taira leaders' daughters in order to hitch his wagon to them. This was highly unlikely, the way things were going, but it was enough to make Yoritomo distrust Yoshinaka even more. Determined to put an end to this situation, the lord of Kamakura sent an army of ten thousand men to deal with his cousin. Despite the recommendations of his generals, who were in favor of accepting the challenge, Yoshinaka stated that the in-fighting could finish with the Minamoto clan, and that the common main objective at that time should be to take Kyoto and the country, rather than fighting among themselves. So, he formally accepted Yoritomo as his lord and sent his own son to Kamakura as a voluntary hostage and guarantee of his fealty. Thus was this first internal crisis solved without an arrow being fired.

For their part, the Taira sent part of their troops to the mountain passes leading to Yoshinaka's territory. The latter sent two of his generals there with a small force, which resulted in a Taira victory at the Battle—or siege—of Hiuchi. The Taira forces managed to advance in their march on Yoshinaka and entered the Etchū province (roughly in the present-day Toyama prefecture), where they were intercepted at the Kurikara pass by Yoshinaka himself, along with the bulk of his army. The Battle of Kurikara was a turning point in the conflict, after which the Minamoto forces would begin to gain ground and corner the Taira. In Kurikara, Yoshinaka designed a strategy of ruse and distraction which enabled part of his force to surround the enemy and attack them both head on and from behind their lines, quickly finishing off—according to some sources—fifty thousand soldiers, an enormous loss for the Taira army. Yoshinaka then continued to advance toward the sea, winning again at the Battle of Shinohara (where the Taira were commanded by the clan leader, Munemori), a victory that left the way to Kyoto clear for the Minamoto. In his retreat to the capital, the Taira leader tried to get the warrior monks of the Mount Hiei monasteries on his side so they would help out in preventing the Minamoto getting to Kyoto, but he got a blunt refusal for an answer. Not only this, but when Yoshinaka himself camped on Mount Hiei before entering the capital, the monasteries responded by going over to his side. The Taira only had one option left: flight. On August 14, 1183, accompanied by almost the entire imperial family, they abandoned Kyoto, taking the Imperial Treasures with them, and escaped to the west, arriving on the island of Kyūshū on September 5.

With the flight of the Taira, the retired emperor Go-Shirakawa was free again, after nearly four years of house arrest, and the first thing he did was go to Mount Hiei, meet Yoshinaka and accompany him in his triumphal entry into Kyoto. He virtually bestowed upon the Minamoto the status of an imperial army and officially authorized them to pursue the Taira. Go-Shirakawa immediately became the Kyoto court's leading member once more, and summoned Yoritomo—who turned down the invitation—and rewarded him with even more honors than Yoshinaka himself. The latter did not take this well, despite being awarded a high position at court, numerous Taira properties in the capital and the post of governor of one of the provinces. Just three weeks later, Go-Shirakawa placed another of his grandsons on the throne (Go-Toba (AD 1180-1239)), who was only three years old. His brother Antoku is often still considered to be the emperor until 1185 though, since the Imperial Treasures were in his possession until then. This decision was another slap in the face for Yoshinaka, who had proposed one of the deceased Prince Mochihito's sons as the new emperor.

Imperial Treasures

According to Shintoist mythology, the grandson of the goddess Amaterasu—the most important of the gods—came down from the heavens to bring peace to Japan, carrying three sacred objects that appear in a number of famous mythological tales: a sword, a jewel and a mirror. This grandson of Amaterasu is also the grandfather of the alleged first Japanese emperor, Jinmu, and the three objects—the Imperial Treasures—are the representation of the divine legitimization of the imperial dynasty, and proof of a direct link to the gods and to Amaterasu herself. Even today they are still used in the rituals that are followed in each new emperor's enthronement ceremony, although this is celebrated in private and only the new emperor and a few priests get to see the treasures. There is no photo of them and their whereabouts are uncertain, although the sword is assumed to be in the Atsuta Temple in Nagoya, the jewel in the Imperial Palace in Tokyo, and the mirror in the Ise Grand Shrine. Moreover, it is believed the sword is a replica of the original, lost at the Battle of Dan no Ura, as we shall explain in this chapter.

From this point on, it would not be long before an atmosphere of rivalry was created between Go-Shirakawa and Yoshinaka, who was a crude mountain dweller struggling to adapt to court life. His men also had trouble adapting and caused chaos throughout the capital, quickly earning the antipathy of those who lived there. As well as this, Minamoto Yukiie, both Yoshinaka and Yoritomo's uncle, devoted himself to turning the former against the latter, once again straining the relations between the two cousins.

Meanwhile, the Taira had had to abandon the island of Kyūshū—where they also seemed to have few friends—and take refuge on the

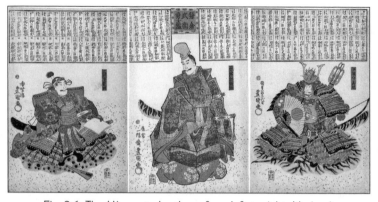

Fig. 2.6. The Minamoto brothers, from left to right: Noriyori,
Yoritomo and Yoshitsune. Artwork by Utagawa Kunisada.

island of Shikoku, whose warrior clans did side with them, where they established their base in the city of Yashima. In December 1183, a Minamoto army led by Yoshinaka was preparing to cross the sea, from the province of Harima (today's Hyōgo prefecture) to Shikoku, to attack the Taira, when they heard rumors Yoritomo had taken advantage of his cousin's absence to send thirty thousand soldiers to take Kyoto. Yoshinaka then quickly returned to the capital. The rumors turned out to be false, but the episode gives us an idea of the climate of mistrust within the Minamoto bloc. Back in Kyoto, the atmosphere between Yoshinaka, Go-Shirakawa, Yukiie and even Yoritomo, despite the fact he was not even there, was becoming ever more strained. The first of them even went so far as to contemplate leaving the city and returning to his northern territories. The tension reached its high point when Yoshinaka learned of a plot concocted between Go-Shirakawa and Yoritomo, who had sent an assassin to the capital to kill him. So, in February 1184, Yoshinaka decided to attack the retired emperor's palace. He managed to carry the emperor off and place him under arrest again and once he had his hands on him he demanded to be granted permission to attack Yoritomo. Go-Shirakawa duly granted this, but at the same time he secretly sent a messenger to Kamakura asking them to send an army to the capital to deal with Yoshinaka.

His request received an immediate response—Yoritomo sent no fewer than sixty thousand soldiers to Kyoto, commanded by two characters who shall be seen again in our story: his half-brothers Noriyori and Yoshitsune.

The two young Minamoto divided the troops to approach the city from two different directions, and while Noriyori was held up for a while by Yoshinaka's soldiers, his brother Yoshitsune was able to steamroll his way forward and quickly free Go-Shirakawa from captivity. A surprised Yoshinaka then had no other option than to try to flee to the north, where his own territories lay, accompanied only by his wife and a few trusted retainers. His escape attempt did not last long: his horse was trapped in a rice field and he was easily slain by his pursuers' arrows, killed at what is known as the Battle of Awazu, his head was taken to be exhibited in Kyoto. Minamoto Yoshinaka's death produced one of the most famous demonstrations of loyalty in Japanese history when Imai Kanehira (AD 1152-1184), saw his lord (who was also his childhood friend and brother-in-law) die and decided to take his own life straight away. So, he unsheathed his sword, placed its tip in his mouth, holding it firmly between his teeth, and leaped to the ground from his horse at full gallop, piercing straight through his head with the sharp blade—or at least that is what the chronicles of the time say.

Tomoe Gozen

Throughout the history of the samurai, female names are few and far between, and when they do appear it is normally as the wife, daughter or sister of some noteworthy samurai. That is not the case of Tomoe Gozen (c. AD 1157-c. 1247), who (although she was Imai Kanehira's sister and—it is believed—Minamoto Yoshinaka's wife) secured a place in the history books in her own right. She earned her place on the battlefield and is without a doubt the best-known woman samurai, the so-called *onna-bugeisha*. It was common for the women of the bushi families to receive some kind of military training, but this was just in

Fig. 2.7. Statue of Tomoe Gozen and Minamoto Yoshinaka, in the Tokuon-ji Temple, in Kiso, Nagano prefecture. Photograph by Koike Takashi.

case they needed to defend their home or family. Tomoe, however, took part in battles just as any another soldier did, as the Heike Monogatari recount: "She was also a remarkably strong archer, and as a swordswoman she was a warrior worth a thousand, ready to confront a demon or good, mounted or on foot [...] and she performed more deeds of valor than any of his other warriors" (*The Tale of Heike*, 1988).

We are not too sure if Tomoe Gozen was Yoshinaka's wife or a concubine. The sources disagree over this, but we do know she was with him fighting at both the Battle of Kurikara and the Battle of Awazu, where Yoshinaka met his death. At this point, different versions emerge once more: according to some sources, Tomoe died in this battle; according to others, she managed to escape and abandoned her life as a samurai to become a monk and thus withdraw from the world. In any case, Tomoe Gozen is one of the best-known characters in Japanese history. She is still popular today with the Japanese and stars in many novels, movies and television series, comics and video games.

Third Phase: Yoshitsune Wins the War

Having dispelled doubts over the leadership of the Minamoto bloc, Yoritomo was finally able to concentrate on fighting the Taira. The latter, oblivious to their enemies' infighting, had had time to reorganize and even to recover the support lost in Kyūshū, guaranteeing them a sizeable number of troops, which they had transferred to their base in Shikoku to protect it and were even planning to reconquer Kyoto. They also had a fortress called Ichi no Tani, on the island of Honshū itself (on the coast of the Suma province, today in the city of Kobe, Hyōgo prefecture), from where they could both protect the entrance to Shikoku and prepare for a march on the capital, if it came to it.

Immediately after Yoshinaka's death, Go-Shirakawa granted a special permit to Yoshitsune and Noriyori to go after the Taira, and the two of them left the capital in March 1184 at the head of an army of 76,000 soldiers that split in two soon after, with Yoshitsune commanding twenty thousand men and Noriyori the rest. The former attacked the Ichi no Tani fortress, in the battle of the same name, playing a leading role in what has become one of the most famous war scenes in the history of Japan: he employed a risky and unexpected strategy, in which the bulk of his troops carried out a frontal attack while a small group, led by Yoshitsune, made up of just a few hundred of his best samurai, attacked from the rear-guard, up a steep cliff, which nobody believed could be used for an attack, much less so on horseback. Coming out of nowhere, they set fire to everything in their path, unleashing chaos and pushing their enemies toward the fortress. In the meantime, his brother Noriyori attacked the fort of Ikuta no Mori, which protected the fortress on its western flank, with forces that were clearly superior to those of his rivals there. Although the majority of the Taira managed to get to their ships and escape to their headquarters in Yashima—among them their leader Munemori—their top generals fell in the battle and the Minamoto easily took the Ichi no Tani fortress, which soon fell victim to the flames. The victory can be put down to the

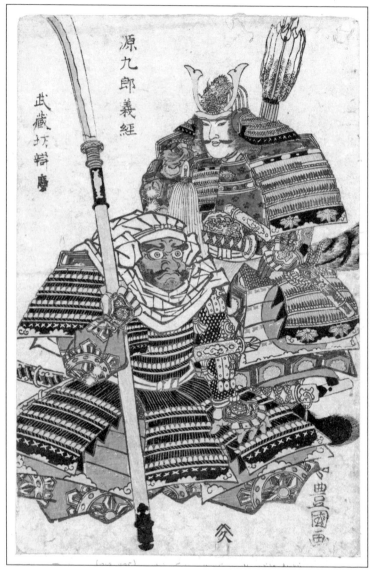

Fig. 2.8. Yoshitsune and Benkei, by Utagawa Toyokuni.

surprise factor of their completely unexpected attack, coming as it had from a theoretically inaccessible place. So, at a stroke they opened up the way to Shikoku and at the same time, protected the capital from a possible Taira attack.

At that point of the war, the Taira controlled the island of Shikoku, the northern and eastern parts of Kyūshū, but only the most westerly tip of Honshū, as well as the Inland Sea, thanks to their naval superiority. There was then a half-year pause, during which Noriyori headed for Kamakura, where a great army awaited him, ready to reinforce the Minamoto forces and put an end to the war once and for all. At the head of this army, Noriyori passed through Kyoto and from there marched toward the west of Honshū, in October 1184, ready to fight his enemies both there and in Kyūshū. His advance was hard going, and it took him four months of tough fighting to get to the Straits of Shimonoseki, which separate Honshū from Kyūshū. The Taira troops were led by Taira Tomomori (AD 1152-1185), Kiyomori's son and, according to many, a general who would have made a much more suitable clan leader than his brother Munemori. In March 1185, Noriyori finally managed to set foot on the island of Kyūshū, where he discovered the local peasants sympathized with the Taira and had fled the villages, taking all the possible food sources with them and transforming the island into a likely death-trap for the Minamoto... unless someone could find a way to avoid that.

After his stunning victory in Ichi no Tani, Yoshitsune had stayed in Kyoto on the orders of his brother Yoritomo, who it seems did not care for the prominence he had gained in his battles and punished him for it by not sending him to the front again. But Yoshitsune became more and more impatient with the news that came of Noriyori's forces slow and arduous advance, and in the end he convinced Go-Shirakawa to send him after the Taira as a general with an imperial mandate. Despite this mandate, when he got to Settsu (in the modern-day Osaka prefecture), where a fleet of over four hundred vessels awaited him ready to cross the sea to Shikoku, a message arrived from the capital, ordering him to return and hand the mission command over to Kajiwara Kagetoki (AD 1162-1200), who in principle had been assigned to him as second-in-command. He was one of Yoritomo's trusted men and a former Taira man who had switched sides at the start of the war. But Yoshitsune ignored the order and decided to go ahead with his plans anyway. At the end of March, he saw a great opportunity to set sail: a strong storm had been unleashed in the area and the fleet could take advantage of the cover it provided to reach Shikoku unseen. But Kajiwara refused as he believed it was too risky and felt the order that in theory gave him the leadership of the mission backed him up here.

Yoshitsune then accused him of cowardice, recruited a hundred and fifty volunteers and set off across a rough sea aboard five ships, heading straight for the Taira. The crossing turned out to be safe and exceptionally quick, and they all made it to the east coast of Shikoku. Despite their small number, Yoshitsune's soldiers began to take the various villages and fortresses between them and Yashima, burning everything in their path. By the time they got to the Taira headquarters, the confusion and chaos was such that Munemori had already ordered the whole clan to retreat to their ships and seek refuge in nearby bays. So just two days after Yoshitsune had set foot on the island, Yashima vanished in the flames. When Kajiwara arrived two days later with his army, he was humiliated to see there was no castle left to attack nor glory to be won. Yoshitsune himself was no longer there either, having set sail again a day earlier to pursue the Taira, who ended up fleeing to a small island in the Straits of Shimonoseki.

Back on Shikoku, Yoshitsune and the rest of the Minamoto began to prepare for the next battle, which looked quite tricky, given that the clan had never been very skilled at naval warfare, unlike the Taira of Ise, who had been expert sailors for generations. Moreover, the Straits of Shimonoseki was a particularly difficult area to navigate due to the strong changeable sea currents. For their part, the Taira found themselves completely trapped between three enemy fronts: to the north, the island of Honshū, controlled by the

Minamoto; to the south, the island of Kyūshū, where Noriyori was at the head of a large—albeit hungry and weakened—army; and to the east, the Inland Sea, where Yoshitsune could appear at any moment. Over the following month, various Shikoku lords would join the Minamoto cause, contributing vessels and sailors that could make up for the clan's lack of naval expertise. One of those lords was Taguchi Iyo (n.d.), who told Yoshitsune that his father, Taguchi Shigeyoshi (n.d.), who was fighting for the Taira, was not very satisfied under Munemori's orders, and that maybe he could persuade him to desert and change sides if he sent him a letter.

On April 24, 1185, the last battle of the Genpei Wars would take place, the most famous in Japanese history—along with the Battle of Sekigahara. On that day, the more than seven hundred Minamoto war junk-class vessels neared the Straits of Shimonoseki, off a village named Dan no Ura, where the Taira fleet's long defensive line awaited them. This was made up of another five hundred similar ships, split into three squadrons and led by Taira Tomomori, a better general than his brother Munemori. When they got within firing range, there was a hail of arrows between the two armies, before they drew closer and started direct combat, with both armies boarding enemy ships to fight with swords and spears. In the first few hours the Taira gained the upper hand, thanks to their better knowledge of the currents and also, perhaps, due to the desperation of knowing that this time there was nowhere for them to run; before the battle had begun, Tomomori had told them their only options were victory or death. But then the battle's development took a new turn when the ships commanded by Taguchi Shigeyoshi lowered the red Taira flag, headed for Yoshitsune's ship and Taguchi himself boarded it.

After this switch of allegiance, the course of the battle was reversed and the Taira quickly began to collapse. The Minamoto also began to concentrate their attacks on a specific part of the enemy fleet in order to get to one particular vessel—the one in which the little emperor Antoku was hiding, along with the Imperial Treasures, and whose exact location Taguchi had revealed to

Yoshitsune. The Minamoto advance was unstoppable and for To-momori, defeat was now inevitable. He then quickly made for the emperor's ship and once there explained that all was lost, that it was better to die than to be taken alive by the enemy and threw himself overboard. His mother, Taira Kiyomori's widow, did the same, and what is more, holding both the Imperial Treasures and her grandson (the six-year-old Emperor Antoku) in her arms. Some ladies who also threw themselves into the sea were rescued alive, like Antoku's mother, and later divers even managed to recover the sacred jewel and mirror, but the sword was lost forever—or so it is believed. The Taira leader, Munemori, preferred to be captured alive rather than commit suicide, which cost him quite a few insults from his mother and brother, and was taken prisoner by the Mi-namoto. Thus, Yoshitsune, who at the time was twenty-four years old, had practically won the war in two battles (at Yashima and Dan no Ura) in the space of just five weeks. Yoshitsune, Yoritomo and Munemori will be discussed in the next chapter.

The Genpei Wars mark the end of the Heian period and the start of the Kamakura period, but the changes brought about by this change of era are unquestionably more profound than the ones produced in other times, given that what is seen here is a complete paradigm shift; the end of a political and social model dominated by a Chinese-style aristocratic court and the establish-ment of a military type government that would last some seven hundred years. And that is how this war should be seen, rather than a simple clash between two clans—something that, as was explained previously, is not so easy to differentiate—it is a matter of a struggle between two political models, one weakened and on the wane, and the other new and dynamic.

This change did not only take shape on the battlefield, as it may appear after reading this chapter and much of the other literature on the subject. Here Yoritomo's role seems to be that of a leader comfortably ensconced in his Kamakura palace while his brothers and generals do all the hard work at the front. Yet, the political and administrative changes carried out by the Minamoto leader were as decisive as his armies' military victories. This part of the process—although it will be dealt with in the next chapter—has not been referred to in detail in these pages as what we are mainly concerned with here is the samurai's role as warriors rather than as politicians or managers. Nonetheless, the importance of this aspect cannot be overlooked.

CHAPTER 3

The First Samurai Government

Tying up Loose Ends

After the Battle of Dan no Ura, Minamoto Yoshitsune had become the great hero of the Genpei Wars, outshining the rest of his side's generals and even the clan leader himself, his brother Yoritomo, who appeared to dislike feeling overshadowed by anybody. Kajiwara Kagetoki, Yoritomo's trusted lieutenant, who Yoshitsune had openly disobeyed, contributed in no small measure to increasing the Minamoto leader's distrust of his younger brother with the reports he regularly sent to Kamakura. Kajiwara, who had been unable to win many honors at the battles of Ichi no Tani, Yashima and Dan no Ura, made Yoshitsune out to be the greatest danger to the Minamoto. The victorious army arrived in the vicinity of Kamakura in mid-June 1185, a little more than two months after the last battle, to be met by Hōjō Tokimasa, Yoritomo's father-in-law, who took charge of the prisoner Taira Munemori and informed Yoshitsune he was forbidden from entering the city. The young general remained camped there for three weeks, asking for permission to enter Kamakura on more than one occasion and even writing to his brother, but his requests were all turned down. At the beginning of July, they handed Munemori back to Yoshitsune, who was told to take him to Kyoto, where he was executed. His head alone was then sent back to Kamakura, to be put on public display.

The Taira from Kiyomori's family had been defeated and exterminated and Yoritomo did not make the mistake of taking pity on any of them, as Kiyomori had done with him and his brothers.

However,—as was mentioned in the previous chapter—the Taira clan had many other branches, almost all of them fighting on the Minamoto side, as well as others fighting for the enemy, who were not persecuted after the war. Some historians are of the opinion that Hōjō Tokimasa, whose clan was also descended from the Taira, made sure of that.

Feudal Period?

With the end of the Genpei Wars, began the Kamakura period (AD 1185-1333) and with it we come to what is commonly known as the "feudal period" or "medieval period" of Japanese history, although strictly speaking these terms are not entirely accurate. Such concepts are inherent to European history and our ethnocentric outlook makes us insist on trying to square them with other societies' history. Having said that, clearly these terms are not used gratuitously or randomly; the said periods are referred to as "feudal" because they share some of feudal Europe's economic and social characteristics, such as the existence of a military-type elite expressed through a lord-subject relationship, for example, although this relationship works in quite a different way in the case of Japan. Regardless of the debate about it among historians, (and above all in the absence of a better alternative), the fact is, these terms are widely used in the vast majority of the literary works available on the subject. For this reason, having clarified this matter, we will also use them here.

Whatever we call it, the Kamakura period surely takes us into that part of Japanese history that we most readily associate with the topic of Japanese history. It is also the favorite period within the collective Japanese imagination—the idealization of a past full of brave loyal bushi fighting out of their loyalty to a lord. This is a more attractive image for most than that of the effete lethargic courtiers of the Heian period, who would, for example, shed a tear over the beauty of a poem about the blossoming of a peony. Leaving aside how idealized and romanticized the vision of this period can be, both for us and for the Japanese, perhaps as happens with the European Middle Ages, undeniably they are very interesting moments in history, which have shaped a good deal of Japanese culture and society, and continue to do so even today.

Yoshitsune, who was prohibited from going to Kamakura, remained in Kyoto. He maintained good relations with the retired emperor Go-Shirakawa, and Yoritomo also perceived a potential danger in that, fearing the court might decide to confront Kamakura, using Yoshitsune as their general. Finally, Yoritomo came to the conclusion that his brother was too big a risk and had to be eliminated, and so sent a small army of nearly a hundred soldiers to the capital. The attack on Yoshitsune's residence took place on the night of November 10, but Yoritomo's men were defeated and a few days later captured and executed. It could be said that the young Minamoto's loyalty toward his older brother and leader disappeared—for good reason—with that night-time attack, which he reported to Go-Shirakawa to request permission from the court to attack Yoritomo. This was duly granted but Yoshitsune couldn't put together an army that could in any way pose a serious threat, so with barely two hundred men he left for Kamakura in late November. To make matters worse, a few days later after having put to sea, a typhoon destroyed the small fleet they were travelling in and put an end to the expedition. Yoshitsune and his closest confidants then sought refuge in the province of Yamato (modern-day Nara prefecture). Meanwhile, Yoritomo had sent his father-in-law to Kyoto, where he took up residence as the Kamakura government's representative in the capital and got the court—who were very given to changing sides depending on which way the wind was blowing—to grant him permission to pursue and punish Yoshitsune for his insurrection.

The situation remained unchanged for months—Yoshitsune remained in hiding, his whereabouts unknown and once again we can find tales of various adventures he supposedly had during this time in different parts of Japan. What is known is that in the spring of 1187 he came to the large northern province of Japan, Mutsu, controlled by Lord Fujiwara Hidehira, who had been his protector years earlier. Hidehira not only controlled this province but also the province of Dewa, another large territory adjacent to Mutsu, accounting for a quarter of the entire country between them. All of this meant another major worry for Yoritomo along with the one caused by his brother. His two greatest potential threats, therefore, were now in the same place.

Hidehira at that time was an old man over ninety years of age, whose end was near, but before dying—at the end of that very year 1187—he made his sons promise to continue protecting Yoshitsune, whatever happened. And what happened was that Yoritomo soon discovered Yoshitsune was in Mutsu, that the lord of that province had died, and his eldest son, Fujiwara Yasuhira (AD 1155-1189), had taken over the position. So, in April 1188, Yoritomo sent emissaries to Mutsu asking Yasuhira to execute Yoshitsune, an order that was endorsed soon after by the court—again at Yoritomo's request. Since the new lord of Mutsu continued to refuse to obey the order, the Minamoto leader petitioned the court again, this time to send his troops to punish Yasuhira, a request that—as one might expect—he was duly granted. When the news reached Mutsu, Yasuhira caved in to the pressure and decided to send a large contingent of soldiers to attack Yoshitsune's residence, in what is known as the Battle of Koromogawa, on June 15, 1189. Greatly outnumbered, the young Minamoto's men could do nothing for their lord this time and Yoshitsune decided to end first his family's life and then his own. As for Benkei, his loyal companion, he stayed on the bridge that led to the residence's entrance defending it until his dying breath and even afterwards—that is, if the legends are to be believed. After killing tens of Yasuhira's men who had the audacity to try to cross the bridge, he was literally cut to pieces by arrows. Nonetheless, he continued to remain standing, and it was not until after the battle was over that his enemies realized he had been dead for quite some time, an event which is known as "the standing death of Benkei."

Yoritomo was thereby able to get what he longed for—Yoshitsune's head, which Yasuhira sent to him along with the head of his own younger brother, who had remained loyal to the promise they had made to their father. In this way, Yasuhira aimed to show his subservience to Kamakura. But as has been seen before, Yoritomo was not keen on leaving loose ends, and he pressed ahead with his plan to send his army to Mutsu. When this army—made up of no fewer than 280,000 men—began its advance to the north, Yasuhira sent emissaries to negotiate his surrender, but Yoritomo refused to negotiate and the lord of Mutsu decided to flee. His flight was short-lived—one of his own men assassinated him and took his head to Kamakura personally. This deed was rewarded by Yoritomo executing the man accused of treason. So at the end of 1189, Yoritomo had eliminated all his possible rivals and could finally devote himself to ruling the country.

Yoritomo's *Bakufu*

After the Genpei Wars, Minamoto Yoritomo established the headquarters of his military government in Kamakura, the same city he had placed his command post in while the war was on—although Kyoto continued to be the capital city. He wanted to escape the court's influence as far as possible and take advantage of the Kantō region's agriculturally abundant plains. He thereby avoided making the same mistakes that had been made in the preceding decades by the Taira, who had integrated into the court, supposedly losing sight of their military nature, and becoming accustomed to the capital's pleasant way of life. Some historians even believe that Yoritomo's main objective was to simply rule autonomously over the eastern part of the country, rather than to take control of the whole of Japan, and that the latter was only a consequence of the former. During the course of the Genpei Wars, Yoritomo had already begun to weave the system of political and military alliances on which he would subsequently base his *shōgunate*. In fact, he did not journey to the capital until 1190, once he was sure of having organized his government and secured his authority in the eastern part of the country. To expand his authority over the rest of the territory, he would have to wait to be named shōgun, which did not happen until the death of Go-Shirakawa, who was firmly opposed to the granting of this position.

Yoritomo was seeking the legitimacy that this appointment provided, because although he had established a military government, the central sacred role of the imperial family was never called into question. Theoretically, Yoritomo acted on behalf of the emperor, although to all intents and purposes he was a completely autonomous figure. He ruled directly in the Kantō zone and indirectly in the rest of the country, holding both political and military power, and was also responsible for policing tasks—duties that did not appear to interest the court much as long as somebody was willing to take on the tedious job of keeping the peace and collecting taxes. He possessed a large number of shōen, although most of them still remained in the hands of members of the court and of large monasteries, and he was even the owner of nine provinces in the Kantō area and seven more in other regions.

Shōgun and Bakufu

The word *shogun* literally means commander of the army, a shortened version of the title *daishōgun* or grand commander of the army and also, in this case, a shortened version of the full title *seiitaishōgun*, which we could translate as something like "the great barbarian pacifying commander." Until then this had been a temporary post given to the general entrusted with the fight against the barbarian peoples of the north, the Emishi, and had only been used by little more than half a dozen generals between the eighth and tenth centuries. Yoritomo lays claim to this title, which should be granted by the emperor, to use it on a permanent and hereditary basis, not to fight against the northern barbarians, but to rule over the entire country, thus inaugurating a completely novel concept. Once again, an easily understandable translation of this term has often been sought, in an attempt to make it fit a more traditional Western concept. Thus, we often find shōgun translated as "military dictator," "*caudillo*," or even "*generalissimo*," although none of these concepts are absolutely right. At the same time, we often call the shōgun's government *shōgunate*, or use the Japanese form, *bakufu*. This word means "government of the *maku*," which was a kind of screen or tent where generals would position themselves during battles to direct the troops from some nearby hill. This term makes it clear we are talking about a government of a military nature. Unlike the other two shōgunate there have been in Japanese history—the Ashikaga and Tokugawa ones—this one does not take the name of its founder's clan, but that of the city it was set up in—Kamakura. It is easy to see why, if we take into account how events developed, but let's not get ahead of ourselves.

The samurai government's systems and structures were not meant to be a substitute for the ones already in place within the imperial system, which had been used since the Taika Reform in the year 645. Instead they were introduced as an addition to them. The bakufu's autonomy, while real and based on its own conditions and regulations, sought to be legitimized by the prevailing power, fitting within the latter's legal framework. In any case, the imperial administration was already quite weakened and, in some cases, held nothing more than a purely nominal role, increasingly so as time went by, shifting the balance of power ever more toward the bakufu's side. This situation did not meet with much opposition from the court, as might have been expected, since the placid day-to-day life of the courtiers and the imperial family was largely unaffected by these changes, and Kyoto continued to be the capital of high culture.

Even before seizing power, Yoritomo could count on the support and loyalty of a group of trusted vassals, known as the *go-kenin*, "men of the house." At first, they were members of his Minamoto clan, although this would slowly change with bushi from other clans joining this select group and ironically it even ended up

Fig. 3.1. Portrait of the shōgun Minamoto
Yoritomo. Jingo-ji Temple, Kyoto.

including numerous members of the Taira clan. Some of these go-
kenin were sent to provinces outside of Yoritomo's direct sphere of
influence, where they acted as his representative. In some places,
they forged alliances with a particular province's clans—in many
cases former enemies—converting them into vassals. To control
and run each province, Yoritomo created two new posts, appointed
by the shōgun himself: the *jitō*, a kind of lieutenant entrusted with
running a shōen, who collected taxes and kept the peace in said
territory; and the *shugo*, a high-ranking position, somewhat like
a governor, who supervised an entire province. Over time, both
positions would become hereditary. By placing loyal vassals in

these positions of responsibility, Yoritomo spun a web of trust in the center of which was the Kamakura bakufu. This fealty was rewarded with land that had been taken from the Taira in the Genpei Wars and from a percentage of the taxes each jitō and shugo raised in the area they ran. The Kamakura government system proved to be more efficient than the previous imperial system, causing the productivity of the shōen to increase and agricultural profits to be greater than they had been until then. This in turn helped to reassure the Kyoto court, given that its courtiers owned a large number of territories that now provided them with greater riches.

The Death of Yoritomo

In 1199, Yoritomo died, which left the bakufu facing a problem since there was no direct successor who could inherit the role of shōgun. As was seen before, one of the first things Yoritomo did after winning the Genpei Wars—suspicious of everything and everyone, especially those closest to him—was to kill off those relatives and members of his clan he felt could usurp him, starting with his brother Yoshitsune. Therefore, with his sons still being too young to govern, there was no Minamoto who had a clear claim to take over the bakufu. His widow, Hōjō Masako, from the powerful clan that had supported Yoritomo during the conflict with the Taira, was the one who took power, backed up by her father and other clan members. In fact, she was then given the nickname of *amashōgun*, "shōgun monk," because upon being widowed she decided to become a Buddhist monk, although everyone knew she was the one ruling in the background.

Three years later, Yoritomo's eldest son, Minamoto Yoriie (AD 1182-1204), came of age, thereby inheriting the clan leadership and the position of shōgun. His mother and grandfather, Hōjō Tokimasa, the Hōjō leader, saw this as a threat to the power they had held since Yoritomo's death. So, they decided to create a new position within the bakufu, that of the *shikken*, a kind of shōgun's regent. In theory this was a person of trust that would advise the shōgun, but in reality, the person who truly controlled the government. In short, it was the bakufu equivalent of the emperor's regent in Kyoto. And logically the first shikken was none other than Hōjō Tokimasa, the grandfather of the shōgun at that time. But Yoriie was much closer to his wife's family and paid much more attention to the advice he was given by his father-in-law, the leader of the Hiki clan, than to what his own grandfather and regent advised him. This once again made Tokimasa fear losing power over the bakufu, so he came up with a plan to end the lives of both, Yoriie's father-in-law and the main Hiki clan members, and even Yoriie's very own son and heir, who was just five years old and Hiki's own great-grandson. After these tragic events, in 1203, Yoriie abdicated, later to be accused of conspiring against the Hōjō and for this condemned to house arrest. A year later he would be assassinated by members of the very Hōjō clan that was headed by his mother and grandfather.

With Yoriie out of the Hōjō's way, the post of shōgun was filled by his younger brother, Minamoto Sanetomo (AD 1192-1219), who was nothing more than a puppet in the hands of his mother's family, and left power completely in the hands of the shikken. During the remainder of this period, this post would always be filled by a member of the Hōjō clan. At first this was the clan leader, but from the mid-thirteenth century on these two positions became independent, with the clan leader being the one really taking all the decisions in the background. So, this quintessential Japanese tradition of power being wielded indirectly was turned up a notch. Let's recap: in Kyoto, supreme power was theoretically in the hands of the emperor, but in practice, real power fell to his regent or *kanpaku*; this influence was offset a little by the figure of the retired emperor, who after abdicating wielded power in the background as the leader of the imperial family; as if that was not complicated enough, in Kamakura we find the shōgun ruling over the whole country, on behalf of the emperor; but we have already seen that was not the case, given that the shikken, the shōgun's regent, who was always from the Hōjō clan, was really the person ruling; and as was just mentioned, from a certain point in time, the leader of

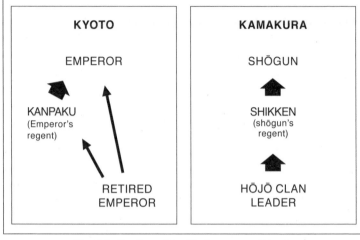

Fig. 3.2. Outline of the "indirect power" in the
Japan of the period. Author's own design.

the Hōjō clan was the one taking decisions in the background in
place of the shikken. Matters could even be complicated a little
more, because after Sanetomo's death, no other Minamoto would
hold the position of shōgun—that is why this shōgunate is named
after the city of Kamakura and not after the Minamoto. From this
point onwards, until the end of the period the norm would be for
the position—stripped of all real power—to fall to members of the
Fujiwara clan or to princes of the imperial family, in an attempt to
legitimize the figure of the shōgun.

The Waning and Fall of the Kamakura Shōgunate

Now let's go back in time a little. In 1198, Emperor Go-Toba was
forced to abdicate on the orders of Yoritomo and his eldest son
ascended the throne. As a result, from then on, he would strongly
oppose the Kamakura government from his new position as retired emperor, a post that had lost a good deal of power since the
shōgunate had come into being, something which obviously also
added to his discontent. A series of disputes about succession

procedures, regarding both the imperial family and the shōgunate, made the retired emperor finally lose his patience. In 1221, Go-Toba began a rebellion against the Kamakura government, the so-called Jōkyū Rebellion, supported by a mixed bag of the bakufu's opponents, such as Taira clan families, other clans from the western regions—at odds with the government for different reasons—and the monasteries close to the capital, pertaining to the traditional sects. These were anxious to put a stop to the growing influence of the new Buddhist sectors, mainly located in the Kamakura area. Just a week after Go-Toba's declaration of war, the Hōjō had readied an army of nearly two hundred thousand warriors (led by the shikken of the time, one of Tokimasa's sons), who immediately began to march on the capital, recruiting even more soldiers on the way. They easily dealt with the opposition they found along the way and took Kyoto from three different flanks, utterly crushing the troops of Go-Toba's allies.

The conflict had been resolved in less than a month and ended with the retired emperor and his two sons (one of whom had also previously been the emperor, and the other was the emperor at that time) being banished to different locations. So, a new emperor ascended the throne, son of the former one and therefore Go-Toba's grandson. Kamakura's overwhelming victory also helped the bakufu cement its authority in the entire country with a series of political and administrative measures. First, a kind of branch of the Kamakura government was established in the city of Kyoto, called Rokuhara Tandai, from which they could control everything that happened in the capital more closely. As well as this, the government reserved the right to actively take part in decisions that until then had been taken exclusively by the court, like matters relating to the succession to the throne or the imperial regency. Finally, a large number of shōen belonging both to the imperial family and to all those who had supported Go-Toba's rebellion were confiscated, and in them a series of jitō who were close to the Kamakura government were placed, many of them members of the same Hōjō clan. After reinforcing the bakufu's power in this way, smothering the rebellion and carefully taking control of the capital, the following half century was characterized by peace and stability. This was also thanks to an efficient governance on the part of the Hōjō. With the country thus pacified, the next threat would come from overseas, with two attempted invasions of Japan by the Mongols, which will be explored in detail in the next chapter.

Despite the bakufu having avoided Japan's being conquered, the Mongol invasion attempts caused an enormous financial and social crisis that in just half a century would end up causing its downfall. On the one hand, the government had incurred major costs defending the country, and victory had not been rewarded by any sort of newly conquered lands or economic booty. Also, the possibility of a third invasion attempt meant the costly security measures were kept in place for decades. Nor, for the same reason, could the bushi who had helped in the defense of the country be rewarded; this time no enemy clan had been defeated whose lands could be seized after victory and shared out among the allied generals. So, for the first time the rule of "rewarding for services rendered," on which a good deal of the system was based, was broken. As a result, the shōgunate's authority began to be questioned.

To make matters worse, some Buddhist monasteries took credit for the double victory over the Mongols, a strange turn of events attributable to the even stranger way events had unfolded during the battles. The famous monk Nichiren (AD 1222-1282) even proclaimed he had forecast the Mongol invasion attempts, as a kind of divine retribution for the country's leaders. Curiously, some monasteries were rewarded for their alleged help in the battle, which contributed in no small part to the samurai discontent. Among the warrior class there was a growing feeling of mistrust toward a puppet shōgunate in the hands of the Hōjō clan—the time when they had sworn loyalty to Yoritomo belonged to the past. The Hōjō even began to lose favor with members of the government itself and of the bushi aristocracy pertaining to other families, because increasingly the positions of responsibility around the whole country were filled almost exclusively by members of their clan.

The Spread of Buddhism

In this same period, new Buddhist sects start to appear (quite different from the traditional ones located in the Nara area) with a much simpler doctrine. This enables them to bring Buddhism—which ever since its arrival in Japan in the mid-sixth century had been a matter for the aristocracy alone—to the common people. These new sects are basically divided into two big movements: Pure Land and Zen: the former is characterized by its worshipping of Amida Buddha and by its rejection of the need for priests and rituals, and sees religious practice as something much more personal and intimate. From an initial sect that gives its name to this Buddhist movement, Jōdo-shū, "Pure Land School," others emerged, like Jōdo Shinshū, "True Pure Land School." Proof of the importance of these two sects is the fact that today they have the greatest number of followers of all of the sects in Japan. The main symbol of the city of Kamakura, the Kōtoku-in Temple's Great Buddha, pertains to this school of Buddhism. The other great religious movement that was widespread in this period was Zen, which in a way acted as a bridge between the traditional sects and the new ones. It had some very important sects such as the Rinzai and Sōtō ones; the former was very powerful and exerted great

Fig. 3.3. The Great Buddha of Kamakura. Photograph taken by the author, February 2015.

influence over the Kamakura bakufu and over the samurai culture in general.

A little later, but still within this period, a new Buddhist sect appeared that did not fit into either of these movements and over time led to the creation of numerous sects: the Hokke-shū sect, or "Lotus School," although it more commonly goes by the name of its founder, the monk Nichiren. It has a noticeably nationalist doctrine and is also very aggressive toward the rest of the sects.

The appearance and spread of all these new sects did not necessarily mean the weakening of the traditional ones, like the Tendai and Shingon sects. On the contrary, the golden era experienced by Buddhism in general, thanks to it being embraced by the common people, also led to these ancient sects enjoying a noticeable resurgence. It is believed one of the reasons for this Buddhist boom was the general climate of pessimism, caused by various natural catastrophes and numerous civil wars and conflicts. As a result, a large part of the population started to think it was all due to the end of the world being near and they turned to religion for spiritual comfort.

At the same time, there was a totally disproportionate increase in the price of rice, and a growth in activities like commerce, manufacturing or monetary transactions. All these factors contributed to the rapid impoverishment of part of the samurai class, who at the end of the day made their living from agriculture, although they didn't farm personally. To cope with this situation, many of the lowest ranking ones and even some jitō had no option but to start to sell their properties, or more often to pawn them and fell into debt. Of course, this crisis did not affect the more powerful and privileged samurai. The bakufu responded to the debt many of the samurai had worryingly fallen into by taking an emergency decision in 1297, declaring an amnesty that cancelled all the debts the warrior class had built up. Obviously, this measure only brought about a short-term solution and made the problem worse in the long term since the samurai, despite being free of their debts, were still just as poor as before and were forced to resort to the services of the moneylenders. The latter, fearing there might be a new government amnesty, made their loan conditions much harsher, with such high interests that the samurai class became even poorer. At the start of the fourteenth century, the disgruntlement of a large part of the samurai—almost all of them in fact, except for the Hōjō and a few others—was becoming almost unmanageable.

We now need to go back a few decades, to 1246, when Emperor Go-Saga (AD 1220-1272) abdicated in favor of his son Go-Fuka-kusa (AD 1243-1304), only to pressure him into abdicating thirteen years later in favor of his younger brother, Kameyama (AD 1249-1305).

After Go-Saga's death, two lines of succession were established based on his two sons, lines that were named after the places where

Fig. 3.4. Statue of Nichiren in the Honnō-ji Temple, in Kyoto. Photograph by Chris Gladis (CC BY 2.0).

each family lived—Daikakuji and Jimyō-in—and new emperors were chosen alternately from the two houses. Understandably, this peculiar succession system caused a lot of tension within the court and within society at large, and even led to the polarizing of cultural or religious matters: one kind of literature was preferred by the Daikakuji and another by the Jimyō-in, and the one that was favored at any given time depended on which branch the reigning emperor was from; there was a religious sect preferred by each branch, a calligraphy style, etc.

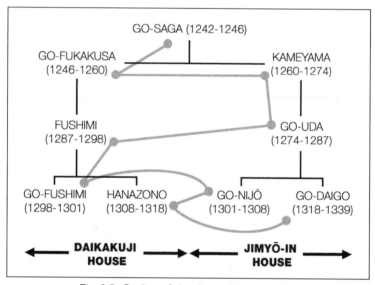

Fig. 3.5. Outline of the alternating succession to the throne. Author's own drawing.

The shōgunate was entrusted with organizing the succession and deciding how to alternate between the two branches, but it got to a point where they decided this system was untenable in the long term. They then introduced a series of regulations whose ultimate aim was to re-establish a single line of succession. One of these rules stated that Emperor Go-Daigo (AD 1288-1339), who had been on the throne since 1318, would not pass his right to the throne on to any of his heirs, thereby initiating the severing of one of the two lines.

Understandably, this was not at all to the liking of Go-Daigo, who was already thirty when he came to the throne and was far from being the kind of emperor without a mind of his own who let others act in his name as they wished. The emperor saw a good opportunity to take advantage of the bakufu's momentary weakness to finish it off and grab real power for himself. After a first attempt in 1324, conflict finally broke out in 1331, in what is known as the Genkō War.

Just as his predecessor, Emperor Go-Toba, had done more than a century before, Go-Daigo sought support among the warrior clans who were unhappy with the shōgunate government, as well as among the monasteries in the Kyoto area. In 1332, the emperor himself was captured by the bakufu army and exiled to the same place Go-Toba had been banished to, although from then on, their fortunes differed. His son, Prince Moriyoshi (AD 1308-1335) and one of his most loyal generals, Kusunoki Masashige (AD 1294-1336), continued fighting the Kamakura army for the year it took Go-Daigo to escape from his exile. The war took an unexpected turn in 1333 when the general sent by the Hōjō to take Kyoto, a descendant of one of the Minamoto clan lines called Ashikaga Takauji (AD 1305-1358), switched sides and decided to support the imperial cause. On reaching Kyoto, he attacked the Rokuhara Tandai, the shōgunate government delegation and took the capital in the name of the emperor. At the same time, in the Kantō area, another samurai leader (Nitta Yoshisada (AD 1301-1338), head of the Nitta clan, and Minamoto kin) also rose up against the Hōjō, quickly conquering Kamakura and so putting an end to the shōgunate.

The Mongol Invasion Attempts

The Great Continental Threat

In the middle of the previous chapter we made a little leap forward, bypassing the two Mongol invasion attempts of the late-thirteenth century. This was done in order to dedicate an entire chapter to them, deservedly so given how important, remarkable and interesting they are. This is an exceptional historical phenomenon because of the nature of those who took part in it. For the first time ever, the samurai would fight, not among themselves, but against foreign enemies, on behalf of the entire country rather than their clan, province or lord. It is also special because of the number of participants, as centuries would go by before there would be battles with such a deployment of soldiers again. And above all, it is unique because of its surprising outcome, which has placed it in the realm of legends, although we are largely dealing with documented historical facts.

After smothering the attempted rebellion that the imperial court was behind in 1221, the Kamakura bakufu, led by the Hōjō clan, not only strengthened its grip on the country and weakened the power of the court, but also led Japan into decades of substantial stability that would only be interrupted by the threat from overseas. By the beginning of the thirteenth century, news was reaching Japan of the stunning expansion of the Mongol Empire across much of Asia—in fact they had even managed to invade areas of Europe and the Middle East, creating the greatest empire of all time—but the time would come when the Mongols would also come calling at the very gates of Japan.

On the continent, a grandson of the near-legendary Genghis Khan had inherited a sizeable part of his empire, ascending the throne with the name of Kublai Khan (AD 1215-1294), and controlling Mongolia and a large part of China. In Europe, quite a lot has been known about Kublai since as early as the fourteenth century, thanks to the famous Venetian traveler Marco Polo (AD 1254-1324) having lived at his court for two decades—al-

Fig. 4.1. Kublai Khan, painting by the Nepalese artist Anige. National Palace Museum, Taipei.

though some current historians not only question many of the assertions contained in the books that recount his travels but even whether or not he ever set foot in China. In their advance through Chinese territory, the Mongols would force the Song dynasty (AD 960-1279) to the south, hence they were known after 1127 as Southern Song. Kublai Khan founded his own dynasty, the first not of Chinese origin, which he baptized Yuan (1279-1368), and which managed to dominate the whole country in 1279 after finishing off the Song once and for all. Japan had maintained friendly diplomatic relations with the Song dynasty since the Heian period, relations that Taira Kiyomori later encouraged and were maintained during the Kamakura government until the Mongol conquered the whole of China. From that moment on, all official contacts and diplomatic missions ceased, but there continued to be some contact both through Japanese monks who visited great Chinese temples and through Chinese traders in Japanese ports, and vice versa. In this way, Japan was kept abreast of what was happening on the continent.

The Mongols were able to implement taxation in their other East Asia territories, on the back of the threat of a possible invasion and conquest that would follow in the event of none payment. This mirrored the system used back in Genghis's day: the Mongols would send a diplomatic mission to another territory and with it request, firstly, fealty and a tax payment, and secondly, that their king visit the Khan's court. On many occasions, after this initial contact, they would provoke this other territory into an unfriendly reaction and use it as a pretext for declaring war, or *casus belli*. They had done this, for example, with Goryeo (called Korea today, encompassing both present-day states), which was easily invaded by the Mongols and made into a vassal kingdom in 1260. Although it was no great change in this case since Korea has always been, to a greater or lesser extent, either under the thumb of or protected by another country, normally China. And they also tried to do the same thing with Japan. The Mongols' first approach was therefore diplomatic and friendly: in 1268 Kublai had a letter sent through the King of Goryeo to the Japanese emperor. Although it was the government, led at the time by Hōjō Tokimune (AD 1251-1284), who was at the same time shikken and clan chief despite being just seventeen years old, that took charge of the matter. The letter went like this:

From the Emperor of Greater Mongolia to the King of Japan. From time immemorial, rulers of small states have sought to maintain friendly relations with one another. We, the Great Mongolian Empire, have received the Mandate of Heaven and have become the master of the universe. Therefore, innumerable states in far-off lands have longed to form ties with us. As soon as I ascended the throne, I ceased fighting with Koryo [Goryeo, Korea] and restored their land and people. In gratitude, both the ruler and the people of Koryo came to us to become our subjects; their joy resembles that of children with their father. Japan is located near Koryo and since its founding has on several occasions sent envoys to the Middle Kingdom [China]. However, this has not happened since the beginning of my reign. This must be because you are not fully informed. Therefore, I hereby send you a special envoy to

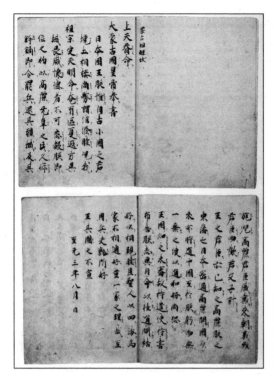

Fig. 4.2. Letter from Kublai Khan to the Emperor of Japan. Tōdai-ji Temple, Nara.

inform you of our desire. From now on, let us enter into friendly relations with each other. Nobody would wish to resort to arms. (Taken from Ishii, 1990).

Except for the last phrase, the letter was not particularly threatening, and what is more it came with a letter the King of Goryeo had added, in which he stated that the Khan was more interested in prestige than in military conquest. But the information the Japanese government had about the Mongols was quite negative, partly because it had reached them via the Song, who at that time were still holding out in the south of China. Also, the letter gave the Korean case as an example, making it clear they had become subjects of the Mongols, not mere friends. As a result—and despite the imperial court manifesting it was in favor of acceding to the Mongols' demands—Tokimune decided not to make any reply to Kublai, and completely ignored his letter. For the bakufu, the Mongol leader's words seemed intolerably arrogant and proud, and the fact he conferred the title of emperor on himself while referring to the Japanese emperor as a "king" was taken as an insult. In the following years, the Mongols sent more letters all of which were ignored, including one that arrived in 1271 stating that if no reply were received, the Mongol army would head for Japan at the end of the year. In spite of this ultimatum, in May 1272 and March 1273 two further letters were sent, which were ignored by the Japanese once again. This finally made Kublai lose patience and abandon diplomatic means.

Despite all these conciliatory attempts to establish relations with Japan, the fact is, sometime before, the Mongols had ordered Goryeo to build a thousand ships and prepare ten thousand soldiers, who along with Mongolian troops, would be assigned to fight against the Southern Song or attack Japan if necessary. For his part, Tokimune had also begun to prepare the defense of Japan following Kublai's first letter, by strengthening the military presence on the southern island of Kyūshū, the logical entry point to Japan from the continent. So, both sides were ready for the clash that was about to take place. The Japanese soldiers had the disadvantage of having lived in peace for nearly a century, since the end of the Genpei Wars, while the Mongols had been fighting right up until that very moment. On the other hand, at that moment, all of the country's samurai worked as one compact bloc that would fight together against the foreign enemy, which made them stronger than they would have been had the Mongol threat appeared at a time of in-fighting.

Unfortunately, we do not have such reliable sources for these events as for the two preceding chapters because one of the most important chronicles of the period, known as *Azuma Kagami*, ends precisely in the year 1266 and the later records which have been conserved are somewhat incomplete and even somewhat muddled in places. But let us get back to wherewere and get down to business.

First Assault, 1274

On October 3, 1274, the Mongol fleet left the Korean coast for Japan carrying fifteen thousand Mongol soldiers and a further eight thousand Korean soldiers, although these figures vary a little depending on the source. Two days later they landed on the island of Tsushima, where in one day they easily defeated the meager hundred-strong Japanese force posted there, which was commanded by the Sō clan, descendants of the Taira. After the victory, they burned down the houses, killed numerous civilians and left a few days later taking the women with them.

Their next stop was on the nearby island of Iki, where they landed on October 14. The island's governor, Taira Kagetaka (?-1274), had already heard news of what had happened on Tsushima, so not only did he prepare his hundred or so samurai, but he also armed the island's civilians with whatever could be used against the Mongols. Despite this preparation, resistance proved useless. Kagetaka took part in the battle himself, but ended up fleeing to his castle, where he committed suicide along with his family. Then, at least according to the Japanese chronicles, the Mongols committed all kinds of atrocities, like piercing the palms of the women's hands to hang them from the sides of their ships before leaving. We also know that some samurai managed to escape and get to Kyūshū to warn of the enemy's arrival. From there, Kamakura was notified, and Tokimune immediately gave the order to inform all the lords in the south of the country and ordered them to send all the soldiers they could muster to the area. This did not happen as there was ultimately no need for it.

We do not know for sure how many samurai were waiting in Kyūshū when the Mongols landed in the Bay of Hakata on October 19, but we do know it was a much smaller number than the Mongol army—figures of around six thousand soldiers are usually given. Despite this numerical inferiority, the Japanese army, although it was forced to withdraw a few kilometers, was able to contain the attack on this first day of battle, causing a large number of

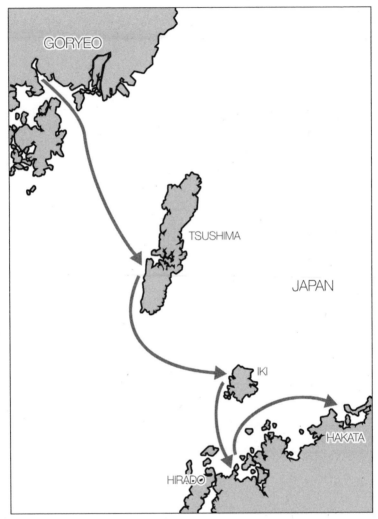

Fig. 4.3. The Mongol fleet's route in the 1274
invasion attempt. Author's own drawing.

casualties among its enemies and regrouping at nightfall to await
reinforcements, which assumed would be enormously superior in
number to the invading army.

After completely burning down the town of Hakata and the

Hakozaki shrine, the Mongol generals, fearing a Japanese night-time attack (which would be devastating as it would be a close-quarters combat, which favored the samurai), ordered their troops to spend the night aboard their ships to rest and rearm before continuing the advance the following morning. The Korean sailors also thought a storm was approaching and that it would be safer to ride it out at sea than on dry land. In a matter of hours, the weather in the area did indeed quickly began to worsen, but much more so than the Koreans had forecast, and before the pilots could take the fleet out of the bay, the ships were trapped there. Although it appears it did not turn into a typhoon, the storm was strong enough to finish off a sizeable part of the Mongol fleet, completely destroying hundreds of ships and drowning thousands of soldiers. The surviving ships made it back to Goryeo more than a month later, on November 27, bringing back with them only a third of the army. The Mongols and

Different Combat Styles

The Mongols had other advantages apart from their numerical superiority and greater combat experience: they were known for their prowess with bows, which they used to produce a hail of arrows with hundreds of archers firing all at once; their great combat skill on horseback was also legendary; they had recourse to such things as poison-tipped arrows and catapults that hurled exploding fireballs, something that had never been seen in Japan. Their combat style was also very different from that of the bushi; the Mongols were in no way as ceremonial as the Japanese and attacked in organized group formations they maneuvered with the sound of drums and gongs, a style the samurai not only considered strange but inferior to their own. It is said the Japanese horses became uncontrollable, frightened by the sound of the drums, gongs and exploding fireballs, which initially disrupted the samurai troops' organization. But despite these advantages, the Bay of Hakata was quite an enclosed terrain where it was hard for the Mongols to maneuver and carry out their great cavalry charges, and it was also well-known to the local samurai.

Koreans who swam to the Hakata shore were captured and taken to Kyoto, where they were interrogated and executed.

Once again, there is the classic version of events, which is what was just explained, and the one given by later historians and even modern-day ones, who question everything related to this storm. On the one hand, late October falls a little outside the Japanese typhoon season, and on the other hand, it is known that a common Mongol strategy was to first send a small expedition to probe the enemy's forces before attacking later with a much larger army. That would make sense here because it hardly seems credible that Kublai expected to invade the whole of Japan with little more than twenty thousand men. There was indeed a storm that night, as several Korean and Japanese chronicles recount, and some of the fleet's ships were trapped in the bay, but the rest might simply have decided to return to the continent.

Anyhow, the rumor quickly began to circulate in the imperial court that a divine wind sent by the gods had put an end to the enemy threat, and that it was all thanks to the prayers given in the country's temples and shrines, especially the Ise Grand Shrine. All these prayers had been made because of the series of strange phenomena in the sky, like comets and eclipses, that had started in 1260 and had been interpreted as ill omens and warnings of great calamities to come; when the possibility of an invasion appeared on the horizon after Kublai's first diplomatic mission, it was quickly associated with those bad omens. Now that—from their point of view—the prayers had done the trick, they redoubled their efforts in praying about the next Mongol attack, an attack which was seen as inevitable in Japan. Hōjō Tokimune's government, much more pragmatically, decided that given the inferiority of the Japanese army, they needed to be much better prepared. Among the proposed defensive measures there was even an invasion of Goryeo, although the plan never got off the drawing board; Japan would take it up again three centuries later, but we will get to that all in good time. What they did do was raise a twenty-kilometer-long wall, three meters high, on both sides of the Bay of Hakata, fifty meters from the shore. This was built by the area's peasants over five years and its remains can still be visited today. A large number of small fast warships were also built, and a much larger army was dispatched posted to the area. This was not the only area to be strengthened, since the Mongols might use a longer sea route and make landfall further north, even on that part of the coast of the Sea of Japan closest to Kyoto, and attack the capital. So, all eventualities had to be planned for.

For his part, Kublai tried another friendly approach, believing that after this first show of force, Japan would be prepared to reconsider his proposal and agree to become a vassal kingdom. So, he sent another diplomatic mission to the islands in April 1275 which even carried the demand that the Japanese emperor—who he kept on demoting to king—visit him at his court in Beijing. But Kublai could not have been more mistaken, and this time the bakufu, instead of ignoring the emissaries as on previous occasions, decided quite simply to behead them and display their heads on the streets of Kamakura as a reply. But despite this clear Japanese act of defiance, the Mongols were too busy at that time fighting the Southern Song to respond and would not think about Japan again until they had taken absolute control of the whole of China in 1279. At that point, Kublai surprisingly persevered with diplomatic channels, sending a new mission and warning that if Japan did not surrender, it would meet the same fate as the Song. Kamakura's response was to again decapitate the Mongol emissaries, this time as soon as they had set foot on Japanese territory. So once again, the time for peace was over.

Second Assault, 1281

This time, in 1281, Kublai Khan planned a far bigger attack, going so far as to create a ministry dedicated exclusively to the conquest of Japan. This ministry ordered Goryeo and the recently conquered regions of the south of China to build nine hundred and six hundred warships respectively, which would join the enormous fleet taken from the Song. The attack, intended for a permanent occupation of the archipelago, would initially be made up of two divisions: the eastern route division, with ten thousand Korean soldiers, ten thousand soldiers from the north of China and thirty thousand Mongol soldiers, who would set off from Goryeo aboard nine hundred boats; and the Chiang-nan division, which would leave from the southeast of China with three thousand five hundred ships housing no less than a hundred thousand Chinese soldiers, who came from areas which had just been seized from the Song. The two divisions made up the largest naval fleet ever deployed at that time, which shows how important the invasion of Japan was for Kublai. Once again, data is lacking on the number of soldiers in the Japanese army, but it was undoubtedly a much smaller figure than the gigantic Mongol-Chinese-Korean deployment.

According to the initial plan, the Korean division was supposed to wait for the Chinese division on the island of Iki and then they would leave together for Kyūshū. But the former, which had left Goryeo on May 3, decided not to follow the plan and headed for Japan without waiting any longer for the southern fleet. This was after first having attacked—not without difficulty—the island of Tsushima and then quite easily invading Iki soon after. Finally, they reached the beach of Hakata on June 21, and we cannot be certain about anything that happened from then until August 15, because once again the relevant sources are rather ambiguous and confusing, and even contradict one another on some points.

But let us try to explain things the way most historians believe they happened. We know that on landing they came across the Japanese wall described earlier, from where the samurai archers caused a lot of casualties among the Mongol soldiers, ultimately forcing them to return to their ships. Upon seeing the enemy withdraw to his ships, the Japanese soldiers set off in pursuit in the small boats they had built precisely for this. These were much more agile in the bay's enclosed waters and they boarded and set fire to numerous Korean ships. Some chronicles tell us of especially strange episodes—whether true or not—such as the one featuring a group of

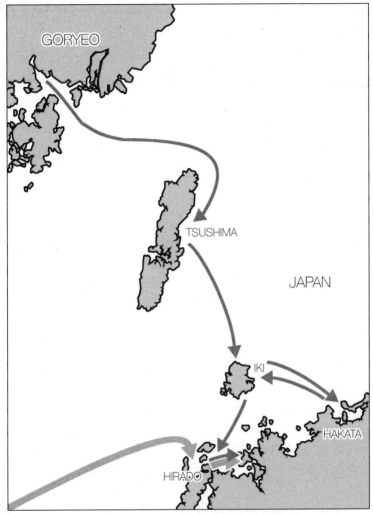

Fig. 4.4. The Mongol fleets' route in the invasion
attempt of 1281. Author's own drawing.

around thirty bushi who swam to an enemy ship, boarded it and
cut off the heads of all of its occupants. Or that of a samurai captain
called Michiari, who is said to have headed straight for the bulk
of the Mongol fleet with his men in two of these little boats. The

Mongols, thinking nobody could be so crazy, assumed it was a Japanese emissary ready to announce their surrender and so neglected to fire upon them, only to be surprised as a handful of bushi then clambered aboard a large enemy ship and killed everyone on it. It is known that the invading army was forced to abandon its plan of taking Hakata alone and returned to the island of Iki to await the arrival of the other division, as the original plan had called for.

Finally, in mid-July, the Chiang-nan division's great fleet got to Japan—to Hirado instead of Iki—and the two divisions came together to head for the nearby Bay of Imari. The plan then consisted of advancing by land from there to the north to take Hakata from behind the wall, but they still found part of the Japanese army waiting for them there, who defended the position during a two-week battle. It is believed one of the reasons the samurai were able to repel their enemies' attacks and stop them from breaking through the Japanese defensive line, despite their clear numerical inferiority, was the lack of determination and motivation of the southern Chinese troops. This was down to the fact the latter found themselves fighting for a side that had been their own enemy until very recently. In any case, the stalemate could not last long as the Mongols' numerical superiority would sooner or later start to tilt the balance in their favor. But, once more, the unexpected happened.

On August 15 and 16, a powerful typhoon completely laid waste to the area, including the Mongol fleet, and this time we do have sufficient high-quality documentation about the event, although there are discrepancies regarding which way the wind was blowing. Unable to disembark because of the attacks by the small Japanese boats and incapable of reaching calmer waters, it is believed the terrible typhoon destroyed around 30% of the ships from the Korean division and 80% of the Chinese ships. Most of their occupants drowned at sea, but it is thought some three thousand managed to reach the shore, only to be captured by the samurai, taken to Hakata and executed. Of the more than four thousand ships that had set sail from the continent, it is believed only about two hundred managed to return.

Fig. 4.5. The defensive wall raised in Hakata. Artwork by Takezaki Suenaga.

Kublai organized a new ministry in 1283 to plan a third invasion attempt, but the operation had to be put off due to more pressing matters such as the conquest of southeast Asia (areas like Vietnam, Burma or Java), which ended up submitting to vassalage; when he was able to turn his attention to Japan once more it was too late for him—the great Khan died in 1294 and his successor, Timur Khan (AD 1265-1307), ordered the project to be abandoned. This entire episode was the greatest—and one of the few—defeats of the all-powerful Mongol Empire, which after having conquered half the known world, in theory should have had no trouble invading Japan.

Obviously, the way the second Mongol invasion attempt ended only increased the belief in a divine deliverance—which had already occurred after the first attempt—with religious leaders like Nichiren taking credit for the Japanese victory, claiming it was down to their prayers to the gods. In fact, both the court and the bakufu accepted this to be true and the various monasteries, temples and shrines were rewarded more than the samurai who had been fighting on the ground. In any case, the samurai could not be rewarded with land given that no new territory had been conquered. What is more, the Japanese government reconsidered the idea of invading Goryeo to prevent a third invasion attempt, but finally went back to their preference for maintaining the defenses in Kyūshū, defenses that were maintained for two more decades, and which ultimately proved unnecessary as the Mongols never came back. For Japan, the attack represented the first foreign threat in its history, since China had never been interested in conquering Japan, nor in general any other country. And Korea had never been strong enough to even think about it. The victory against the legendary Mongols meant the birth of a strong feeling of patriotism and unity in Japan, unknown up until then due to the frequent in-fighting and lack of an outside enemy. But it also meant the start of a crisis that would end the Kamakura shōgunate, as was seen in the previous chapter.

Kamikaze

As far as the Japanese were concerned, the two victories against the Mongols proved beyond a doubt that Japan was the country of the gods, since there was no other way of explaining the arrival of the divine wind that had twice saved them. So, it is no surprise that the next time the country felt itself about to be invaded by a foreign enemy, nearly seven hundred years later, its most desperate military strategy was baptized with that very term—shinpū, "divine wind." At the end of World War II, a special unit was created in the Japanese air force, called Shinpū tokubetsu kōgeki tai, "Shinpū Special Attack Unit," assigned with the task of trying to damage the American fleet through suicide attacks against their ships and aircraft carriers using small dive-bombers fitted with explosives. These planes, and their pilots, are known in the West as kamikaze, a word we have incorporated into our vocabulary and which we use for any type of suicide attack.

The word is usually believed to have come from a reading error by the American army's translators: the term *shinpū* is made up of two characters, which individually are read as "kami" and "kaze," but when joined should be read "shin" and "fū" (and the latter's pronunciation ends up changing to "pū"). So the translators may have chosen an incorrect interpretation, as has happened with other Japanese words popularized in the West. Although, as I say, this is the usual explanation given and one I myself have given on more than one occasion, I have recently discovered it might not be correct. Allow me to explain an anecdote here. I was in the city of Ise in February and March 2015, in a course held in Kogakkan University, when a Japanese professor commented that this city has for many centuries been known as "the city of the divine wind." He said this was because on the one hand it is a very windy place, and on the other, it is the site of the Ise Grand Shrine, the most important site in Shintoism. He said all of this in Japanese and I was surprised he used the word *kamikaze* and not *shinpū*, which I believed to be the correct word in this language. Bitten by curiosity, I carried out a small piece of research and found some very old references to the city of Ise in which its name appeared alongside the word *kamikaze*, or indeed where the city's name was missed out entirely in favor of *kamikaze*. In the same way, we could use "The Big Apple" when talking about New York—a technique known in Japanese as *makurakotoba*. As an example, this anonymous poem which appears in Japan's oldest poetry anthology, *Man'yōshū*, finished in the year 759: Kamikaze ya/Ise no hamaogi/orishikite/tabine ya su ran/araki hamabe ni. The translation—my apologies for its low quality—is something along the lines of: "Snapping the reeds of the beach of Ise, the beach of the divine wind, do they use them to sleep on the shore of a raging sea?" So, even though the term *kamikaze* might have become popular around the world after World War II, due to an error of interpretation, we have proof that the word already existed many centuries earlier.

CHAPTER 5

A Century of Civil War

From the Fall of Kamakura to the Outbreak of War

Let us now go back to where things left off at the end of Chapter
3. When Ashikaga Takauji took Kyoto, he handed the city over to
Emperor Go-Daigo straight away. The emperor wasted no time
in starting to organize everything so that he could take control of
the country himself, without having to submit to any shōgun or
regent. Actually, he handed the position of shōgun to his eldest
son, Prince Moriyoshi—despite it being a military post and not a
court one—and allocated governors posts to members of the capital's aristocracy, thereby ousting the warrior class. He also shared
out the land wrested from the Hōjō among the court nobles, which
understandably caused a great deal of discontent among the samurai, especially those who had actually fought for Go-Daigo. Takauji
himself, had asked the emperor for the position of shōgun, and
although he was generously rewarded, regarded his being turned
down for the post as an injustice. Nor did he agree with plans that
aimed to leave the bushi out of all of the political posts and decision-making roles. Emperor Go-Daigo's government is known
as the Kenmu Restoration and is usually treated as a period in its
own right, separating the Kamakura and Muromachi epochs (AD
1336-1573), although it was only a very short-lived period; at this
stage of our tale, it should be easy to guess why it only lasted a short
time—it tends not to be a good idea to set the entire samurai class
against you, however much of an emperor you may be.

In 1335, Takauji rebelled against Go-Daigo, arrested the shōgun

Fig. 5.1. Portrait of Ashikaga Takauji.

and pointedly took him to Kamakura, where he had set up his base. For this, he was quickly stripped of all of his official positions and declared enemy of the throne. He then ordered Moriyoshi's execution—the post then passing to his young brother Nariyoshi (AD 1326-1344)—and at the beginning of 1336 left at the head of his army for Kyoto, intending to invade it and put an end to Go-Daigo's government; but the imperial forces were too strong and prevented him from reaching the capital, forcing him to take a detour to the south as far as Kyūshū. This detour, rather than a problem for Takauji, turned out to be very beneficial for him, since many other samurai leaders who were unhappy with the emperor joined his cause on the way. They were also encouraged by the promises Takauji himself made them, assuring them of great rewards after victory was achieved. So, in command of a much larger army, in May of that very year 1336 he marched on the capital again and this time had no difficulty taking it, even defeating his old ally Kusunoki Masashige. He entered the city accompanied by Prince Yutahito (AD 1322-1380), son of the former emperor Go-Fushimi—and member of the house of Daikakuji—who with the support of Takauji became Emperor Kōmyō. In order to get to this point they had forced Go-Daigo to give up the Imperial Treasures—which was essential to have a legitimate claim to the throne—although he would later flee to the south of the capital, to Yoshino (modern-day Nara prefecture) and found a parallel imperial court there. He would claim to still have the Imperial Treasures, having only surrendered to Takauji mere replicas which were worthless. Thus begins what could be called the Nanbokuchō subperiod, or "the northern and southern courts" subperiod, which would last until 1392 and during which—anything but peacefully—two imperial courts with their respective emperors would coexist, the northern court in Kyoto and the southern one in Yoshino.

Kusunoki Masashige

As we saw near the end of Chapter 3, Kusunoki was one of Emperor Go-Daigo's most loyal generals and along with Ashikaga Takauji and Nitta Yoshisada, played a part in enabling him to take control of Japan, thus putting an end to the Kamakura bakufu. We don't know much about his origins since he had only been a minor samurai leader up until that point.

In 1336, when Takauji had rebelled against Go-Daigo and was marching toward the capital from Kyūshū, Kusunoki was still one of the emperor's trusted lieutenants. Famed for being an accomplished military strategist, he suggested withdrawing temporarily to Mount Hiei, but Go-Daigo disagreed and ordered

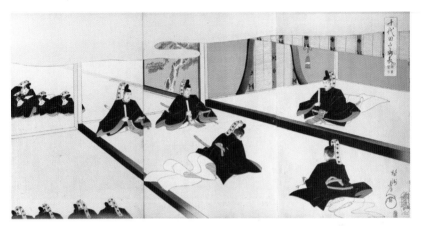

Chiyoda castle (Album of men): Formal Visit to the Shogun (1897)
by Toyohara Chikanobu (1838–1912).

Chiyoda Castle (Album of Men): Visit of the Daimyo (1897)
by Toyohara Chikanobu (1838–1912).

Chiyoda Castle (Album of Men): Yabusame Practice (1897)
by Toyohara Chikanobu (1838–1912).

Chiyoda Castle (Album of Men): Kendo Practice (1897)
by Toyohara Chikanobu (1838–1912).

Chiyoda Castle (Album of Men): Dakyu Practice (1897)
by Toyohara Chikanobu (1838–1912).

Chiyoda Castle (Album of Men): Hunting Practice (1897)
by Toyohara Chikanobu (1838–1912).

Chiyoda Castle (Album of Men): Daimyo Parade (1897)
by Toyohara Chikanobu (1838–1912).

Chiyoda Castle (Album of Men): Kyudo Practice (1897)
by Toyohara Chikanobu (1838–1912).

Ashikaga Takauji and Nitta Yoshisada from *Mirror of Great Warriors of Japan* series (1878) by Tsukioka Yoshitoshi (1839–1892).

Battle of Kawanakajima (1857) by Utagawa Yoshikazu (act. 1850–1870).

A Chronicle of the Subjugation of Kagoshima: Battle around Kumamoto Castle (1877)
by Tsukioka Yoshitoshi (1839-1892).

Famous General Takeda Harunobu Nyudo Shingen by Utagawa Kuniyoshi (1797-1861).

Hatakeyama Shigetada, from *Yoshitoshi's Courageous Warriors* series (1883) by Tsukioka Yoshitoshi (1839-1892).

Heroes of the Shimazu Clan (1877) by Tsukioka Yoshitoshi (1839-1892).

The Battle of Komaki: Kato Kiyomasa and Honda Tadakatsu
by Tsukioka Yoshitoshi (1839–1892).

Katō Kazuenokami Kiyomasa Kneeling by a Banner, from *A Mirror of Wisdom, Benevolence, and Valor in Japan* series (1878) by Tsukioka Yoshitoshi (1839–1892).

Detail from the triptych *The Ghosts of the Taira Clan Attacking Yoshitsune's Ship in Daimotsu Bay in 1185* by Utagawa Kuniyoshi (1797–1861).

The Mongol Invasion of Japan triptych by Utagawa Kuniyuki (act. 1880–1890).

A Most Unlucky Day from *Kuniyoshi's Analogies for the Six Conditions of Nature* series (1860) by Utagawa Kuniyoshi (1797–1861). Mori Ranmaru spears Yasuda Sakubei during the defense of the Honnoji temple after the attack of Akechi Mitsuhide.

Tomoe Gozen from *Mirror of Beauties Past and Present* series (1875–1876) by Tsukioka Yoshitoshi (1839-1892).

Oda Nobunaga in Flames at Honnoji Temple from *Mirror of Famous Generals of Japan* series (1876–1882), by Tsukioka Yoshitoshi (1839–1892).

Tomoe Gozen Defeating Uchida Saburo from *Famous Fights Between Brave Men* series (1865–1866) by Tsukioka Yoshitoshi (1839–1892).

Toyotomi Hideyoshi, unknown author (16th century).

芳年武者无類

彈正彌上杉謙信入道輝虎

Uesugi Kenshin Nyudo Terutora Riding into Battle from Yoshitoshi's
Courageous Warriors series (1883) by Tsukioka Yoshitoshi (1839–1892).

Mount Tobisu Dawn Moon (1887) from *One Hundred Aspects of the Moon* series (1885–1892) by Tsukioka Yoshitoshi (1839–1892). The engraving depicts a general directing his troops at the Battle of Nagashino, 1575.

him to intercept Takauji and attack him head on. Kusunoki was convinced this was an absolutely suicidal strategy which could not possibly work. Nevertheless, he obeyed the order unquestioningly. So, he gathered his troops and took his leave of his eleven-year-old son, reminding him that come what may, he should always be loyal to the emperor—whether this is true or not, it is indisputably a very famous historical moment in Japan. The Battle of Minatogawa took place on 5th July in what today is the city of Kobe. There the tactic duly turned out to be a terrible choice, and Kusunoki's troops were soon over-run by Takauji's greatly superior army. After resisting for five hours, putting off the inevitable, Kusunoki and his men—the few who were still alive—committed suicide rather than be captured by the enemy.

Fig. 5.2. Statue of Kusunoki Masashige, Tokyo Imperial Palace. Photograph taken by the author, February 2015

Logically, Kusunoki Masashige was considered a rebel and a traitor by the Ashikaga government, but a few centuries later, in the Meiji period (AD 1868-1912), with the theoretical reinstatement of the emperor as the country's supreme leader, his reputation was restored, and he was held up as an example of loyalty toward the imperial government. A few decades later, with the rise of Japanese militarism in the 1930s, and above all with the beginning of World War II, this adulation for Kusunoki was taken to a whole new level and he became an inspiration for the young Japanese soldiers, especially for the kamikaze pilots who, like Kusunoki, hurled themselves toward a certain death out of loyalty to the emperor.

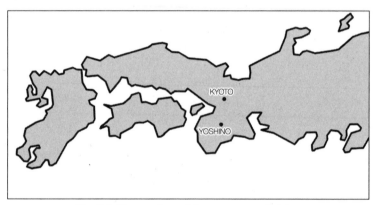

Fig. 5.3. The two imperial courts, around eighty kilometers apart. Author's own drawing.

For his part, Takauji would be rewarded by the emperor with the highest honors and finally, in 1338, with the sought-after title of shōgun, inaugurating the Ashikaga shōgunate, the second shōgunate in history. This meant that in just a decade three different governments had succeeded one another, in a repetition of the struggle between the imperial/courtier and samurai models that had already occurred in the Genpei Wars one and a half centuries earlier.

The Ashikaga Family

The Ashikaga, who were related—albeit distantly—to the Mina-moto, had begun to serve Yoritomo as far back as the year 1180, for which they were rewarded with shugo positions once he seized control of the country. During the Kamakura period, they married off their daughters to form kinship with both the Uesugi—who would be an important family later—and the Hōjō, although as we know, they would end up fighting and defeating them.

The coming to power of the Ashikaga also inaugurates the beginning of the Muromachi period, named after the area of Kyoto in which the bakufu settled. Without question, this is the most conflictive and chaotic period Japan has ever known, characterized by the fragmentation of society and almost endemic nationwide war.

While in 1185 Minamoto Yoritomo had set up his government in Kamakura to escape the pressures of court, Takauji placed his in Kyoto for exactly the opposite reason—to control the court and at the same time acquire the legitimacy his presence there gave him, he certainly needed this if he was to rule over the whole country. Even so, the bakufu failed to enjoy hegemony over the entire Japanese territory: in the provinces furthest from the center they had to resort to using local samurai leaders, transformed into shugo, who recognized the central government's authority, but ruled *de facto* in their territories with a good deal of autonomy. The famous samurai loyalty—which by the way has been greatly called into question up until now—manifested itself between these regional leaders and their men, but not between these men and the shōgunate. The latter's power gradually faded while the provincial lords' power increased, helped in part by the tax system which awarded them a huge share of the tax collected—50% after 1352. These shugo, appointed by the shōgun, shared out 66 provinces between them, where they administered justice, collected tax, took care of policing tasks, smothered any peasants' revolts that appeared—fairly common at that time due to the numerous famines and epidemics—and even had jurisdiction over matters related to land. The areas furthest from the capital, Kyūshū in the south and the territory going from Kantō to the north, were especially difficult to control, and so two regional bakufu offices were located there.

During the governments of both Takauji and his son Yoshiakira (AD 1330-1367), there were frequent wars against the southern court, with the Ashikaga coming as far as briefly losing control of the capital or of Kamakura on several occasions. There was also the treachery of Takauji's own brother, who switched to the enemy side only to switch back a few months later and be forgiven. Ashikaga Yoshimitsu (AD 1358-1408), the third shōgun, who was Takauji's grandson and Yoshiakira's son, was the one who would put an end to the conflict between the two courts in 1392. He did so peacefully by promising to return to the old system of alternating succession between the two royal houses, which convinced the emperor from the southern court—one of Go-Daigo's grandsons—to return to Kyoto, although the bakufu never fulfilled their promise and the second court's line of succession disappeared. But in practical terms, the imperial court of Kyoto never had any real power during this period, which, in any case, was par for the course.

Yoshimitsu accumulated much more power than his two predecessors once the matter of the two courts had been resolved. He not only took the position of shōgun, but also hoarded all the titles he could get his hands on and climbed to the top of both the military and court pecking orders—some historians believe he even tried to usurp the imperial throne. He created the post of *kanrei*, a kind of vice shogun, which bit by bit became something like the Kamakura shōgunate's shikken and although not hereditary was almost always occupied by a member of one of three specific families: the Hosokawa, the Shiba and the Hatakeyama.

Yoshimitsu also established a rule that would last for some time and would have important consequences a couple of centuries later: from then on, in order to obtain the title of shōgun, kinship with the Minamoto would have to be demonstrated. He also became a great patron of art and culture, which enjoyed an age of splendor during his reign, and he was an important protector of and advocate for Zen Buddhism, whose temples and monasteries he particularly favored; for example, with laws that established each province's obligation to have a great monastery which followed this doctrine. He himself gave up the position of shōgun and retired from public life in 1395 to devote himself to being a monk, although in reality he carried on running the country until his death in 1408—as was seen before and will be seen again on numerous occasions. He also sought legitimacy beyond Japan's frontiers, re-establishing contact with Korea and China, now in the hands of the Ming dynasty (AD 1368-1644), before whom he presented himself as the "King of Japan." The main stumbling block to relations with the Ming was still the ancient Chinese practice of treating the rest of the countries as their vassals, although

Fig. 5.4. Ashikaga Yoshimitsu, by then in his monk period, in a painting of the time.

Yoshimitsu appeared to believe it was worth putting up with their vanity for the sake of the commercial benefits to be gained.

After Yoshimitsu, the shōgunate's power started to decline. Just as had happened to the Taira a few centuries earlier, the bakufu samurai began to get used to court life and succumbed to its luxurious carefree lifestyle, spending their money on alcohol, parties and prostitutes. This coincided with a serious financial crisis, the result of the central government's terrible fiscal administration, which they tried to resolve with a generalized increase in taxes—which reached as much as 70% of the harvest—and the creation of new taxes on property, liquor, the use of highways, etc. Logically, this policy was also quickly applied by the shugo in the provinces, who sought to increase their wealth. Such a high tax burden ended up leading to famines, as in 1454 and 1461, when the common people were provoked into important rebellions and there was generalized discontent among the population. There was also an attempt to deal with the extent of many samurai's debts, by decreeing a series of amnesties that cancelled them—once again—which was logically very harmful for commerce and industry.

The elite in the capital, however, were oblivious to this reality and Ashikaga Yoshimasa (AD 1436-1490) himself, Yoshimitsu's grandson, wanted to resign from his position of shōgun in the 1460s to devote himself full-time to living the pleasant life of a Kyoto courtier.

The Kinkaku-ji and the Ginkaku-ji

In the city of Kyoto, you can visit two examples of early Muromachi era art built on the orders of two of the Ashikaga shōgun we have mentioned in this chapter: Yoshimitsu and his grandson Yoshimasa. They are known respectively as Kinkaku-ji and Ginkaku-ji—the Golden Pavilion and the Silver Pavilion.

The first was built on the orders of Ashikaga Yoshimitsu in the year 1397 on the grounds of his property, on the hills to the north of the capital. What we can see today is a replica since

Fig. 5.5. The Ginkaku-ji (left) and the Kinkaku-ji (right), in Kyoto.

the original was destroyed several times during the Ōnin War and even burned down by a monk in 1950. It is in the midst of a well-kept garden encircled by a pretty pond in which you can see its reflection; this is how it is normally photographed and is undoubtedly one of the most famous images in Japan. The second was built at the behest of Ashikaga Yoshimasa in the eastern zone of the city in the year 1474, with the aim of emulating the one constructed by his grandfather. However, they were not able to complete the project as planned, including as its name suggests, covering the building with silver, so what we can actually see is a wooden pavilion. Despite the disastrous economic and social time Japan was going through in the 1470s, with the Ōnin War already underway, the capital almost destroyed and the entire country on the road to utter chaos, Yoshimasa wanted to immortalize his name through this building. Tea ceremonies and poetry readings were often held there—in the finest court tradition—ignoring the cruel reality of the period.

Since he had no sons, he convinced his younger brother, Yoshimi (AD 1439-1491) to give up his life as a monk and adopted him (adoptions between adults were very common in Japan), thereby making him his heir so as to be able to pass on to him what he regarded as the uncomfortable post of shōgun. But before this could materialize, Yoshimasa had a son of his own, Yoshihisa (AD 1465-1489), and although Yoshimasa showed himself to be in favor of leaving things as they were, the child's mother was not of the same mind. The situation became even more complicated thanks to the various succession conflicts in the Shiba and Hatakeyama clans, which—along with all the other problems of the period—ended up leading to the Ōnin War (AD 1467-1477) and with it, to no less than an entire century of civil war.

The Ōnin War: No Winner and Many Losers

At first the two opposing sides were those led by Hosokawa Katsumoto (AD 1430-1473) and Yamana Sōzen (AD 1404-1473), son-in-law and father-in-law respectively. The first, who had held the position of kanrei until shortly before that moment, had always been very close to the shōgun's brother and defended his right to inherit the title. The second, whose family had missed out on the important bakufu posts, quickly positioned himself against Hosokawa by supporting the new-born child as the rightful heir. The shōgunate did not initially take sides and simply tried to avoid armed conflict breaking out, decreeing that whoever started a fight would be officially declared to be a rebel. But Yoshimasa himself paid little attention to the matter and preferred to carry on devoting himself to poetry and the good life. The step taken by the government failed to produce the expected result and war broke out in 1467.

At the beginning of the conflict, the fighting took place in the capital itself, especially in the northern zone, which was quickly reduced to firewood. It soon became clear that, for Yamana, the succession question had just been an excuse to settle old scores with his son-in-law, given that—in a really strange twist—despite supporting little Yoshihisa's candidacy for the shōgunate, when the boy was officially named as heir in 1469, he went over to Yoshimi's side. Not content with that, in 1471 he changed his mind again and then began to defend a completely different cause—giving back the imperial throne to the southern court, reopening a conflict that had lain dormant for nearly eighty years. By this stage of the war, the capital was practically destroyed, and the fighting moved out to the outlying areas and then quickly spread to the provinces, where different samurai leaders began to fight one another. Often times it was rather unclear which side they supported, or indeed what the sides were by that stage.

The real motive was simply the conquest of the loser's territory, although they flew the flag of either cause as and when it suited them. In 1473 two events occurred which together theoretically should have put an end to the war: firstly, both Yamana and Hosokawa died, the first in April and the second in June—thus the theoretical leaders of the theoretical two warring factions disappeared; secondly, Yoshimasa was finally able to give up his boring post and in December his son Yoshihisa was named shōgun, at just eight years of age. But neither event managed to put an end to the conflict, which lasted four whole years longer, up until 1477, when weary of a never-ending stalemate, and worn down to the point of exhaustion, both armies finally abandoned the fight. And not only that: Yoshihisa and Yoshimi—who was both his uncle and adopted brother—made peace.

But that was only the end of the Ōnin War, which had been waged in the capital and its hinterlands and no longer had much, if anything, to do with the innumerable battles that were being fought in the provinces and which nobody could stop now, because out there the war had only just begun.

Beginnings of the Sengoku Period: The Age of Great Names

The Sengoku period—or rather subperiod, since it is included within the Muromachi period—can be described as being the most turbulent and complicated period in Japanese history. It is fascinating to study but at the same time it can be a nightmare because there are many important events, starring an endless number of very diverse figures with many interacting fronts open simultaneously and the whole thing can be analyzed on many different levels. No less than three chapters of this book will be dedicated to dealing with the period, not just because it is so complex, but also because it is so important. The Ōnin War is included as part of the Sengoku period in some chronologies and in others—like this one—it is not, but in practical terms this is of little importance as it just depends on which criteria is used to define each moment. The very name of the period is indicative of its warlike nature: Sengoku could be translated as "country at war," or, even more aptly, "countries at war," since it would be more exact to think of Japan at that time as a territory divided into several countries fighting one another rather than a country at civil war. However, that definition is also correct and perhaps easier to understand. A poem of the time perfectly defines the nature of the period: "A bird with/one body but/two beaks/pecking itself/to death."

As was stated at the start of this chapter, the Ashikaga shōgunate never managed to control the whole country by itself and mostly had to depend on different regional samurai leaders, which placed the central government in a delicate position. At that point in the period, after the 1470s, the Ashikaga were little more than puppets in the hands of the families who between them held the kanrei posts—as had happened with the shikken and shōgun of Kamakura—especially the Hosokawa. As we said earlier, Yoshimasa was finally able to give up his position in favor of his son Yoshihisa, but the latter died aged twenty-five with no offspring. So in a bizarre twist of this tale, Yoshimasa adopted the son of Yoshimi—let's recall, his younger brother and adoptive son—who was also twenty-five and made him shōgun Ashikaga Yoshitane (AD 1466-1523).

Anyhow, it no longer mattered much who was at the head of the bakufu, be it in the post of shōgun or kanrei, because the central government's power extended little further than the capital and the neighboring provinces. If things were bad for the shōgunate, they were even worse for the imperial family, whose capacity to exert any type of authority was non-existent. Maybe because of this, between

1465 and 1585 we see neither abdication nor succession conflicts, with the throne always passing directly from father to son, which would indicate it was hardly a much coveted position. And it is not just a matter of how little real power the emperor had—which in any case was the order of the day—nor did he dispose of the economic resources of bygone days. This is illustrated by the death of Emperor Go-Tsuchimikado (AD 1442-1500), whose corpse had to be kept in the palace for forty-four days since there were insufficient funds for the funeral ceremony that protocol called for. For the same reason, his successor on the throne had to wait no fewer than twenty-one years to be officially enthroned.

Meanwhile, in the provinces, the shugo were gaining more and more power. In some of them, even theoretically minor samurai clans became stronger in this period and began exerting *de facto* control over some territories. Out of this potpourri would emerge the great warlords of the Sengoku period, known as *daimyō*, literally "great name," although many of them had family names that up until then had been fairly insignificant, such as the Asakura, Imagawa, Oda, and others. Logically, where these provincial warlords had the most power was in the areas furthest from the capital, especially in the region of Kantō and the southern island of Kyūshū. These places soon began to stop sending any taxes to Kyoto, which led to greater wealth for the local leaders and a greater decline in living standards for the already impoverished central government.

In this way did these great provincial samurai families effectively become independent from the bakufu—they eliminated the figure of the governor and even went so far as to take over the lands that until then had belonged to the emperor or to members of the court. They only respected those lands that belonged to monasteries, temples or shrines—which also played an important role in the wars, with their armies of warrior monks. These daimyō established bonds of loyalty with their trusted generals, who were rewarded by being put in control of lands and the people who lived in them. This is why from a Western historical perspective this relationship has been qualified as "feudal," as was mentioned earlier. Within their domains, these great lords would build large castles to live in and to defend themselves from possible attacks. Around them commercial hubs would spring up, and bit by bit, new and larger towns, making Japan one of the most urbanized societies of the age.

At the beginning of this period, we could count more than two hundred warring samurai families, although many of them would disappear, either absorbed or defeated by other more powerful ones. The frontiers also varied enormously from one month to another. In the region of Kantō, for example, the most powerful family were the Uesugi, although the Hōjō—a different clan from the one seen in Kamakura—took advantage of a series of fights between different branches of the family to expel them from the Odawara area at the start of the sixteenth century, forcing them to move to the province of Echigo (today's Niigata prefecture). Combat methods were also changing, with much larger armies, whose campaigns required more logistical management and who often depended on the availability of food and therefore on the quality of the harvests in the year in question. The number of casualties, logically, was also a lot higher than in any previous war, and rose from tens of deaths in the battles of the twelfth century to several thousand deaths in the ones of the late sixteenth century. The situation ended up in a kind of stalemate, where no daimyō was powerful enough to take control of a significant territory or of the country's capital, since whenever one of them came close to either of those scenarios, other lords formed alliances to prevent it. Thus, a constant balance of power was established that appeared doomed to last forever and plunge Japan into never-ending wars throughout the length and breadth of its territory.

But in the mid-sixteenth century, something incredible that nobody was expecting would transpire and help to begin to change things. This phenomenon introduced a new element into the equation that would tilt the balance in favor of those who were best able to adapt to the changing times.

The *Ashigaru*

With the start of the nation-wide conflicts, in which each regional leader had to conquer neighboring leaders' territories and at the same time avoid having his own conquered by a third party, the only thing that legitimized these daimyō's authority was their military capability, since none of them had the official support of the bakufu or the emperor. So, having the largest possible army became a matter of life or death, which meant that any peasant was welcome as a soldier. In addition, considering that each soldier was responsible for buying and maintaining their own equipment and weaponry, and that the great majority of them were unable to afford a horse, the number of infantry troops grew enormously.

The Sengoku period is the moment when the use of foot soldiers, the so-called *ashigaru*, was at its peak, to the detriment of the samurai elites' cavalry troops. Clearly, a mounted soldier is more effective than one on foot, but a group of ten ashigaru armed with long spears and united by family bonds or by belonging to the same village, fighting as one unit and

Fig. 5.6. Late nineteenth-century recreation of an ashigaru. Photograph by Ogawa Kazumasa.

having needed far less training than was needed to fight on horseback, could be extremely useful. War was no longer decided by heroic deeds carried out by warriors with illustrious family names charging alone on their horses, but by large infantry battalions moving in a compact organized way, directed by a general located on a nearby hill.

Because of the previously mentioned need for bigger armies and the demographic growth of the time, partly caused by an agricultural revolution that increased the fields' productivity, armies made up of tens of thousands of soldiers appeared. This was something that until then had only been seen very occasionally and for which pretty much the entire country's resources had to be mobilized. Not many decades would go by before, in the year 1600, we would see armies of over a hundred thousand soldiers each on the battlefield—but let's not get ahead of ourselves.

CHAPTER 6

Contact with Europe

Portuguese in Japan

However remote and isolated a society might seem, when its history is studied, it is inevitable that we will discover multiple connections that theoretically we would not expect to find. Consequently, to explain the end of the Japanese Sengoku period and some important changes that took place at that time within the world of the samurai, at this point in the tale we need to hop thousands of kilometers to the west and a good few decades back in time. It is a very superficial summary—let me just say in passing—but a necessary one in order to understand what induced the Europeans to cross the planet and turn up on the coast of Japan.

In the fifteenth century, the unstoppable territorial advance of the Ottoman Empire—the high point of which was the conquest of Constantinople in 1453—cut off Europe's access to the important Silk Road, which had supplied it for centuries with all sorts of goods, some of which were quite essential to daily life there. This very contact with the Muslim world also brought the Old Continent major technological breakthroughs as well as advances in the fields of knowledge and philosophy, introducing or allowing people to rediscover the works of ancient wise men like Eratosthenes (276-194 BC) and Ptolemy (c. AD 100-c. 170), which was key for subjects such as geography or astronomy. All this knowledge also brought a new spirit to Europe, a humanist approach whose ideas quickly spread thanks to the printing press and which would end up leading to the Renaissance. Important figures such as Erasmus of Rotterdam (AD 1466-1536) and Martin Luther (AD 1483-1546) introduced a challenge to the until then unquestioned dogma of the Christian world, a real revolution both in the religious and political fields, splitting Europe in what has been called the Reformation, when numerous countries formally abandoned Catholicism and therefore ceased to be subject to the Vatican's control. Thereby the Catholic countries not only lost—like the rest of Europe—access to the goods brought from Asia, but they also saw the number of adherents to their doctrine decrease drastically in a relatively short time.

Both events were good enough reason to set sail to discover a new way to get to East Asia, so as to trade directly in those lands, and in passing to try to convert its people. Moreover, the new knowledge in the fields of geography and astronomy, instruments like the astrolabe and ships like the caravel offered the chance to try it with a much greater probability of success—albeit still far from guaranteed—than before. Thus, having both the motives and the means, everything was set for departure. The first kingdoms to set off on the search were Portugal and Castile, who both had a papal blessing and used very different routes from one another. The Castilians don't interest us for the moment as they elected to navigate west and thereby ended up finding the American continent by chance. This opened up for them a completely new and unexpected commercial route as well as providing them with millions of new Catholics—even if they had to convert them by the convincing but debatable method of the sword, that is, if they had not first died of the diseases the conquistadors infected them with. Portugal, for its part, founded a modern naval academy, the School of Sagres, from which a route was planned that in theory was safer than the Castilian one, skirting Africa without straying too far from the coast.

Finally, on September 23, 1543, the Portuguese reached Japan (not through any will of their own—rather it is believed they came close to being shipwrecked), on the coast of Tanegashima, a tiny island measuring 57 kilometers from north to south and 12 from

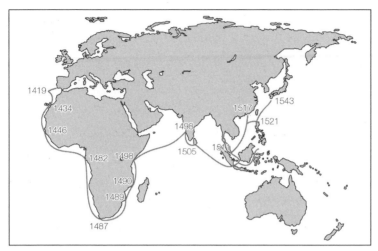

Fig. 6.1. Map of the Portuguese route to Japan. Author's own drawing.

east to west, just to the south of Kyūshū. There were just three Portuguese merchants and the crew of the little Chinese junk they were travelling on; in fact, one of these Chinese sailors, acting as an interpreter, would be the one to introduce the new arrivals as "southern barbarians," as the Portuguese—and later, Westerners in general—were known in China, since they had arrived in their country from that direction. And this is how Westerners would also be known in the Japan of the time, where they were called *nanban*.

The Arrival and Spread of Harquebuses

At the end of the previous chapter, we had left Japan in a stalemate in which none of the main samurai clans could take control of the whole country, or even of the capital and its surroundings. The arrival of the Portuguese would bring about some changes in this scene, although we will never know what would have happened if this contact had not taken place—nor is this something historians should concern themselves with—and the event's importance is still a matter of academic debate. But it is generally agreed that, at the very least, it brought forward the conclusion of the period of warfare. And this is basically due to something the Portuguese merchants (apart from different goods of varying interest to the Japanese) brought with them: firearms. In Chapter 4, the Japanese had already had to face gunpowder during the invasion attempts of Kublai Khan's armies and we also know of a noble from Odawara who had bought a pistol from a Chinese merchant in 1510; the very same year several harquebuses (which had also been made in China) entered Japan which were used in 1548 at the Battle of Uedahara. However, it appears they were very primitive weapons and not very effective in combat—unfortunately, there are no illustrations of these models. On the other hand, the new weapons that had come from Europe were very much so a game changer.

Firearms were a perfect fit for the aforementioned tendency toward a greater user of infantry on the battlefield, since only a few units needed to be armed with harquebuses. With a simple

The Tanegashima

The very place where the first Portuguese to reach the Japanese coast landed—the island of Tanegashima—would henceforth give its name to this type of harquebus in Japan. The local Shimazu clan daimyō soon saw that these new weapons could make all the difference against the bows, swords and spears used up until then, and the first harquebuses sold in Japan fetched astronomical prices. Many daimyō immediately put their armorers to work on the production of harquebuses, trying to copy the Portuguese model by taking one apart and studying it in detail; it took them just two or three years to succeed at their task and a decade later there were already around three hundred thousand across Japan. Not only did they manage to copy the Portuguese models, but the forges of Japan's central region in particular were even able to make harquebuses that were of superior quality to the originals.

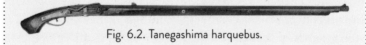

Fig. 6.2. Tanegashima harquebus.

Fig. 6.3. A samurai called Inoue Nagayoshi firing a large-caliber harquebus in the Invasion of Korea, by Utagawa Kuniyoshi.

yet effective design, they were extremely lightweight weapons that could be rested on the user's shoulder unaided—except for some large-caliber models made later in Japan. They measured approximately one meter in length, had a smooth fifteen-millimeter barrel and when fired produced a considerable recoil and a lot of smoke. They could not be used in rainy conditions, but that was no great drawback because both sides' harquebusiers were equally affected. Nor were they to be recommended for a surprise attack because of the loud noise they produced upon firing. The firing rate was only one shot every fifteen or twenty seconds and the range was around five hundred meters—at best—although beyond two hundred meters, shots were wildly inaccurate and rarely proved lethal; quite recently tests have been carried out in Japan with some of these weapons and beyond fifty meters only 20% of shots managed to hit a human target. They only really worked with large targets, like mounted warriors or troops in formation.

Even so, they meant a not insignificant improvement. An experienced archer could shoot a lot more arrows in the same time, and more accurately, but the harquebuses' advantage was that little training was needed to learn how to handle them, unlike the bow. This allowed battalions of harquebusiers to be created, made up of low-ranking ashigaru. The armorers from the town of Sakai, just outside Osaka, had been making copies of some of the rudimentary Chinese harquebuses for several years, but after 1544 they devoted themselves to copying and making the Portuguese model. The smiths of the village of Kunitomo (in the modern-day Shiga prefecture) started to do the same on the shōgun's orders. One of the improvements made by the Japanese manufacturers was to standardize the barrel size of the harquebuses, which they started to make to just two or three fixed measurements. This contrasted with the chaotic mix of sizes used in Europe, which meant almost every unit needed tailor-made munition.

Although the prevailing samurai myth would have us believe this warrior caste rejected the use of firearms as they considered them to be beneath them, the reality, is we know they were quickly incorporated into the samurai troops' standard armament without it causing many moral debates: it was just another tool that could help to achieve victory on the battlefield, and at a time of total and often pitiless war, pragmatism won out over tradition. Despite what is known about the Battle of Uedahara in 1548, it is usually considered that the first time harquebuses (on this occasion, the

Portuguese model) were used in action in Japan was the following year in the province of Ōsumi (modern-day Kagoshima prefecture), which encompassed the island of Tanegashima. Unsurprisingly, the local Shimazu clan made use of them; the powerful daimyō Takeda Shingen (AD 1521-1573) employed three hundred harquebusiers as early as 1555, using them to shore up the defenses of Asahiyama Castle, and in 1569 stated: "From now on, firearms will be the most important thing, so reduce the number of spears and have your most capable men carry harquebuses with them." Both his army and that of Tokugawa Ieyasu (AD 1543-1616) used them when they clashed at the Battle of Mikatagahara, in 1572, and their widespread use from that decade on is taken for granted.

To get back to the moment the Portuguese arrived, China under the Ming had recently ceased trading and cut diplomatic ties with Japan as a protest against the bakufu's inefficiency at preventing Japanese pirates, known as *wakō*, from attacking their coastline. In reality, the vast majority of these pirates were Chinese and the Japanese government, which was incapable of maintaining any kind of control of its own territory beyond the capital's borders, had no way of preventing these attacks. The lack of trade between the two countries presented the Portuguese merchants with a great

Cannons

The use of heavy artillery did not become as widespread as harquebuses. Cannons came to Japan in the year 1551 when the Portuguese, on behalf of the Pope, gave two of them as gifts to the Christian daimyō Ōtomo Sōrin (AD 1530-1587), baptized in 1578 as Francisco. The Japanese armorers also tried to copy them, but never managed to achieve the same quality as the originals. They were normally used from ships or from a largely fixed emplacement in sieges—the clearest example of this being the Siege of Osaka Castle in 1614 and 1615, as we shall see later. But they were hardly ever used as mobile artillery pieces on the battlefield.

opportunity; they became intermediaries, obtaining Chinese goods from their Macao base and selling them in Japan, thereby making considerable profits. With Japan divided into almost autonomous warring provinces, when the Portuguese ships reached their coastline, many of the daimyō wanted their port to be chosen so as to be the first to benefit from trade or—importantly—to get their hands on the firearms the merchants brought from Europe. But rather than the Portuguese merchants deciding freely in which province to berth their ships, it was Catholic priests who decided for them. But which Catholic priests?

Weapons for Souls: The Catholic Mission in Japan

To know what these priests were doing in Japan, we have to return to Europe, where the Vatican responded to the Protestants' demands for reforms with what is known as the Counter-Reformation. This was a strategy that, while allowing for a certain renewal and regulating of the official doctrine and rites, and the foundation or reactivation of religious orders, also strengthened the pope's authority and the Inquisition's institutional role, among other things. One of these new religious orders was called the Society of Jesus—known as the Jesuits—founded in 1534 by Ignatius of Loyola (AD 1491-1556) and six of his classmates from the University of Paris and approved as a religious order in 1540 by Pope Paul III (AD 1468-1549). It was made up of the Church's best-educated men, a kind of intellectual elite, highly disciplined and knowledgeable about all kinds of subjects. They reported exclusively and directly to the pontiff himself, and education—especially that of the upper classes—was one of their main objectives and interests. The Portuguese king, Juan III (AD 1502-1557), a fervent Catholic, quickly took the Jesuits' side and asked the pope to entrust them with bringing the Gospel to the new Portuguese territories. As a result, during those years that Portugal alone had dealings with Japan and China, the Jesuits would be the only Western priests in the area, enjoying a highly-beneficial monopoly.

In 1549, just six years after the arrival of the first Portuguese traders and nine years after the order's endorsement, one of its founders arrived in Japan, the Navarrese priest Francis Xavier (AD 1506-1552), accompanied by two other Jesuits. Xavier had been in other parts of Asia, such as India and Malacca, for eight years, but was unhappy with the results of his evangelizing, which he put down to those areas' inhabitants being uncivilized. Indeed, he decided to journey to Japan because he had heard its inhabitants were—as he put it—"people who are entirely governed by reason," therefore he believed that perforce—from the prevailing Thomist viewpoint of the time—they had to be willing to convert to Christianity. After reaching Japanese shores, what he had been told about the place was confirmed, much to his delight, which made him believe the evangelization of Japan would be a simple task. In his letters, we find continual high praise of the Japanese: "[the Japanese people] are the best to be discovered thus far (…) it seems to me that among the infidels there is not another people to be found that could surpass the Japanese." What is more, he discovered that a single language was spoken in the whole country, which greatly facilitated his mission since only one language needed to be learned; that a large part of the population knew how to read, which made it easier for Christian ideas to be spread; and that different religions and religious schools of thought already existed in Japan, which should make it easier to introduce a new doctrine.

Another factor, which perhaps Xavier was unaware of, would favor his entry: the fact he had come from India, the cradle of Buddhism for the Japanese, conferred great charisma on him. His strategy to convert Japan consisted of two main points: learning everything he could about the Japanese and adapting to their way of life. His first target was the ruling classes—it was a top-down plan, based on the belief that once the elites were converted, the conversion of the lower classes would be almost automatic. Following this logic, Xavier traveled to the capital to try to get in touch with the emperor and ask him for official permission to preach throughout the country, only to discover that in that moment there was nothing in Japan that could be called a central government and the emperor had no authority. So the mission instead tried to curry the favor of the different lords in each region. Xavier was in Japan for barely two and a half years, since having discovered that for the Japanese, China was the cradle of Asian culture, true to his top-down strategy he decided it was more important to convert China, believing the rest of the countries under its cultural influence would then be easily converted. He therefore set off for that country, via India, although he would die in 1552 on the small island of Sanchon, off the continental coast of China.

The strategy designed by Xavier would mark the Jesuit mission's character both in Japan and in the rest of Asia, and a few decades later the Neapolitan Alessandro Valignano (AD 1539-1606), would take it up again even more fervently. Valignano belonged to a younger generation and was Italian, therefore had been in contact with European Humanism and this shows in his way of thinking; he valued experience highly and so believed that in Asia he should deal with things in his own way, because he was the one on the ground and he had personal experience—something the Vatican lacked. On reaching Japan in 1579 (in contrast to what had happened with Francis Xavier thirty years before), he experienced a period of great depression as he did not understand how a society could be so completely different from everything he knew, and even came as far as to fear that it was impossible for Christianity to succeed in those lands. He decided to devote an entire year to simply observing and learning, without taking many decisions until he had enough knowledge of Japanese society. He then came to the conclusion that for Christianity to triumph in Japan, it had to be adapted and things had to be done the Japanese way. To that end, he designed a complete adaptation strategy encompassing absolutely everything. The priests not only had to speak Japanese, but also dress like Buddhist monks, eat what they ate and live like they did. He went so far as to suggest a filter be applied to the Gospels themselves, keeping their spirit and core values, but adapting the rest so that the less important parts did not come into conflict

Fig. 6.4. Francis Xavier and Alessandro Valignano.

with the particular Japanese way of thinking and lead to the whole mission failing. Moreover, all of this should be considered merely the first stage, since Valignano's final objective was for the Catholic Church in Japan to eventually be wholly Japanese, made up of Japanese priests and even bishops.

As was said before, the Jesuits were the ones who decided which fiefdom or province the Portuguese merchants traded with, so the different daimyō soon realized it could be very useful to get on well with them. For that reason, many of these samurai lords authorized the Jesuits to carry out their evangelizing tasks on their land or even personally converted to Christianity—sometimes accompanied by their families or all their subjects. Almost all historians—except for those tied to the Church—believe that as a rule this, rather than any real sense of piety, was the real reason for most of these conversions. So, it is no coincidence the first Christian daimyō were also the first ones to equip their troops with harquebuses.

Fig. 6.5. Typical example of so-called *nanban* art, depicting a European ship arriving at a Japanese port, from which merchants dressed in the Portuguese style are disembarking (along with all manner of goods and animals, and African slaves) and being received by Japanese and Jesuits in long black tunics. Screen work by Kanō Naizen, Kobe City Museum.

In 1580, with the advent of the so-called Iberian Union, the dynastic union of Portugal and Castile, under Philip II (AD 1527-1598), there was a chance of Franciscan, Augustinian and Dominican friars reaching Japan—mendicant orders sponsored by Castile. Understandably, this idea horrified the Jesuits because they were set to lose their monopoly; Valignano himself, in a document dating from 1583, set out the many problems that could stem from the arrival in Japan of the aforementioned orders: he argued it was precisely the Christian uniformity and coherence, compared with the diversity among the different Buddhist sects, that was one of the main reasons why many Japanese converted to Christianity. And this uniformity would be broken if other orders appeared; he added that in order to work in a country that was so utterly different from everything they had known, it was vital to have a lot of experience on the ground and knowledge of its customs—and only the Jesuits had that; finally, the Castilians were feared in Japan because of the way they had conquered half the world and the arrival of their friars could end up convincing the Japanese that evangelization was the first step towards military conquest. Despite these qualms, the mendicant friars eventually arrived in Japan in the 1590s, and their presence and habits caused no end of incidents, both with the Jesuits and with the Japanese themselves. This would be one of the main reasons why both Christianity and the Western presence ended up being persecuted. But all of this takes us away from the matter at hand, so let's leave it here for the moment.

As for the supposed—fleeting—success of Christianity in Japan, Jesuit sources tell us there were around one hundred fifty thousand converts in the country by the early 1580s, although it is clearly an inflated figure as it includes thousands of people considered automatically converted because their daimyō had ordered it. Others speak of one hundred thousand and still others of hardly fifteen thousand at that time. Discrepancies can be found regarding later decades: for 1613, some sources speak of three hundred thousand converts, while others reach figures as high as seven hundred thousand. Take into account that Japan's entire population was below twenty million then. In general, the West has overplayed the impact of the contact with Europe, above all regarding the issue of how Christianity was embraced. An important part of the sixteenth century discourse in Western manuals of Japanese history is devoted to this, but in Japan they highlight the period as the century of the daimyō's ascendancy, with the contact with Europe given far less attention.

When the Sengoku period ended, and the country finally entered a period of unification, the various rulers' personalities, interests, and the prevailing political context would define their varied relationships with the European missionaries, but that is something we shall see later on.

CHAPTER 7

The Unification of Japan

Late Sengoku Period: Fewer More Powerful Rivals

As the Sengoku period developed, the most powerful samurai families—the ones who managed to survive the fighting and take over more territories—started to contemplate a new objective, greater than simple survival or the desire for more land: taking control of the whole of Japan. Before this could be achieved, they had to reach the capital, take it militarily and make a puppet of the shōgun so he would legitimize the daimyō in question as a kind of official unifier, with the right to fight the rest of the clans from that moment on until he had taken control of the entire country. But in order to achieve this new objective, it was not enough just to be stronger than the neighboring territory. It was an enormous undertaking that could not be carried out by any of these daimyō individually. Consequently, numerous alliances between different lords began to appear, alliances that were broken just as easily as they were made, and once again we can see a host of betrayals and side switching—however much the samurai legend likes to swear on their unshakeable loyalty. Some daimyō were hypothetically in a better position to claim victory, such as the aforementioned Uesugi in Echigo, the Takeda in Kai, the Imagawa in Mikawa, Tōtōmi and Suruga, and the Hōjō from Odawara in the entire Kantō region. In the more outlying regions, this process of survival of the fittest had also taken place, leaving the Shimazu in Kyūshū, the Chōsokabe in Shikoku, and the Mōri and the Date in the west and north of Honshū, respectively. The great distance to the capital made them somewhat outsiders as candidates for victory, though. The overall situation had ended up in a kind of stalemate in the mid-sixteenth century, but that would start to change when one of these powerful daimyō made his mind up to try to conquer the capital.

Imagawa Yoshimoto (AD 1519-1560) seemed the most likely to achieve victory, since not only did he possess three important provinces in the center of the country, but he could also count on solid alliances through marriage—his own, a son's and a daughter's—both with the Takeda and the Hōjō. Having all these advantages, he set off on a march to Kyoto in 1560 at the head of a large army—some sources put it at twenty thousand, others at forty thousand soldiers. After several victories that heralded a triumphal campaign, his advance was halted when he was making his way through the province of Owari, his army was massacred and he literally lost his head. All of this was down to a small army of only three thousand samurai, led by a minor daimyō who until a year earlier controlled nothing more than a part of the province, and was surrounded by far more important rivals.

Oda Nobunaga Planted the Rice...

Oda Nobunaga (AD 1534-1582) had been the Oda clan leader since 1549, taking over the leadership at the age of fifteen upon his father's death, despite the opposition of a large part of the clan, who believed the young Nobunaga was crazy, due to his often outlandish behavior. Perhaps that was down to him being a very pragmatic person who judged each situation on its merits and always took the most appropriate action to achieve his goals, even if it meant contravening traditions and protocol or ignoring the others' opinions. So, the same year he took over the clan leadership, he purchased five hundred harquebuses for his troops. He was one of the first daimyō to trust in the firearms' potential and he used them on the battlefield with strategies that were highly innovative, even compared to the ones employed at the time in Europe. And because he quickly showed an interest in these weapons, he also realized that to get his hands on them, it could be very beneficial to have good relations with the Christian missionaries. As a result, he showed a very permissive attitude toward them and met with a number of Jesuit priests on numerous occasions. On the battlefield, his troops moved much faster than any other daimyō's, as he built new roads in his domains and repaired and widened the existing ones. He also raised bridges in many places and had large barges built that could quickly transfer his battalions from one side to the other of Lake Biwa—strategically located in the center of the country. Various factors led to Nobunaga triumphing over the rest: to his just-mentioned pragmatism and innovative spirit, we should add the prime location of his province, Owari, conveniently near to the capital but far enough away not to have been affected by the fighting that had laid waste to it; moreover, luck smiled on him more than once, as shall be seen.

Nobunaga became known throughout the country, suddenly placing himself on the list of the most powerful daimyō, after the Battle of Okehazama, in 1560, where—as we were saying—he crushed Imagawa Yoshimoto's army entirely unexpectedly. After easily taking a couple of fortifications, the Imagawa troops were resting and celebrating their successful advance in a place called Dengakuhazama, a kind of canyon or gorge; Nobunaga, aware his three thousand men could not do anything against such a numerically superior army if they met head on out in the open, decided to take advantage of the enclosed site, which he also knew well, for a surprise attack. So, his little army went around it and positioned itself just above the pass without being seen by the invading troops' lookouts and waited there for the best moment to launch the attack. As luck would have it, the weather changed suddenly and a heavy storm fell upon the area, which had the enemy troops running for cover under the trees. Just as the rain stopped, and making the most of the prevailing confusion as the soldiers were returning to the camp, Nobunaga ordered the charge, literally falling upon the enemy.

The Imagawa soldiers, taken by surprise, were unable to react

Fig. 7.1. Statue of Oda Nobunaga in Kiyosu, Aichi prefecture.

to the attack and there was utter confusion, during which the Oda clan men were the only ones who knew what was going on, allowing them to easily finish off their rivals. Yoshimoto himself was unaware they were being attacked and when he saw a samurai approach him thought it was one of his own men; by the time he realized the truth, he had already been stabbed by a spear and although he reacted quickly unsheathing his sword and defending himself, a second enemy cut his head off with one stroke. With Yoshimoto dead, the few remaining officers from his army went over to Nobunaga's side and the battle ended. After Okehazama, the Matsudaira clan leader also became an important Oda ally—in 1567 he changed his surname to Tokugawa, but that will be discussed in a later chapter. This is one of the most important and famous battles of the Sengoku period, both for its unexpected outcome and, above all, for it being Oda Nobunaga's first step toward the unification of Japan.

After Okehazama, Nobunaga gained a new status among the country's daimyō, and proof of that is that in 1565, in the context of the succession dispute that followed the death of the shōgun Ashikaga Yoshiteru (AD 1536-1565), one of the candidates for the post, Ashikaga Yoshiaki (AD 1537-1597), the dead man's younger brother, asked the Oda clan leader for help—although it is true he had previously asked three other daimyō for help without getting a response. Nobunaga not only agreed to collaborate with Yoshiaki, he saw it as a great opportunity to reach Kyoto (justifying his campaign with the new shōgun's order), if it turned out to be a successful campaign, obviously. But before setting off, he had to prepare everything properly, making pacts with a number of daimyō who controlled strategically important areas and killing others who opposed him. Finally, Nobunaga entered Kyoto in 1568, in command of fifty thousand soldiers, took the city, and installed Yoshiaki as shōgun, thus achieving what so many samurai clans craved. Yoshiaki gave him the title of kanrei, but Nobunaga turned it down, since this position—let's recall, a kind of vice shogun—meant being at the shōgun's command, and he had not taken the capital for that; on the contrary, he intended to use Yoshiaki as a puppet who would do what he decided. Thus, as lord of the provinces of Owari, Ise and Mino, and legitimized by his control over the shōgun, he threw himself into the conquest of the rest of Japan.

From that moment on until his death, Nobunaga was permanently at war, sometimes in different parts of the country at the same time, fighting here and sealing alliances there to reach his objective. One of the main stumbling blocks to achieving it was the great power in the hands of some of the Buddhist monasteries in the area near the capital, which had lands and armies in the same way the samurai clans did. For the pragmatic Nobunaga, if the monasteries behaved like the daimyō, they should be treated as such, so he fought them with the same ferocity he did with anyone else, setting aside traditions, religious considerations and superstitions. True to this belief, in 1570 he laid siege to Ishiyama Hongan-ji, a real fortress and headquarters of the powerful Buddhist group Ikkō-ikki, who for decades had been rebelling against any samurai-type government. He did not manage to defeat them on that occasion, but he did in a second siege that lasted four whole years, from 1576 to 1580. More famous would be his attack on the Enryaku-ji monastic complex on Mount Hiei in 1571 (a place already seen in previous chapters). This was a real massacre in which Nobunaga deployed thirty thousand soldiers who first surrounded the mountain and then climbed it in unison, burning every building they came across and killing anyone who crossed their path, be they a warrior monk, a simple monk, a woman, or even a child—nobody was spared. In a single day, the whole of Mount Hiei was completely devastated; not one of its three thousand buildings was left standing and it is believed around twenty thousand people died.

In parallel to the campaigns against these religious institutions, Nobunaga completed the conquest of the country's central region, defeating clans such as the Asakura and the Azai there. Once he had all this zone under his control, he was able to start to plan his advance to the west, since for the moment the north, his rearguard, was quite secure thanks to his alliance with the leader of the Tokugawa. They had finished off the Imagawa—or what was left of them after the Battle of Okehazama—and now possessed the provinces of Mikawa and Tōtōmi, and had the Hōjō under control. The north was also secure thanks to the stubborn unending rivalry between the Takeda and the Uesugi, which kept them too busy to attack Nobunaga and made them fear that if they tried to, their rival would take advantage of the occasion to attack their own lands.

The relationship between Nobunaga and Yoshiaki had been

deteriorating almost from the start, from the moment the latter saw the Oda leader had his own plans. By 1572 it was so bad the shōgun began to concoct a plot to get rid of this bothersome samurai, contacting in secret with the leaders of several of the most powerful bushi clans, none other than the Mōri, the Uesugi and the Takeda. The latter were the only ones to respond to his proposal and Takeda Shingen himself set off on a march to the capital at the head of his army. The Tokugawa intercepted them when they were passing through their territory, near their fortress in Hamamatsu, in what is known as the Battle of Mikatagahara. The Tokugawa forces were clearly inferior to the Takeda forces, some eleven thousand soldiers against thirty thousand and the latter had an almost legendary cavalry regiment, so the Tokugawa were soon forced to retreat. When the Tokugawa leader managed to get to Hamamatsu, he ordered the fortress doors to be left wide open, partly to allow any soldier who managed to flee there from the enemy to enter, but also partly to project an image of confidence.

And his strategy worked because when the generals Takeda sent to Hamamatsu to inspect the site prior to an attack on the castle saw the doors open, they believed it had to be some kind of trick, and recommended not attacking, thus allowing the Tokugawa to escape a near certain defeat. After this battle, Takeda Shingen, fearful of an attack in his rearguard by Uesugi Kenshin (AD 1530-1578), decided not to continue advancing on the capital for the time being, preferring to return to his lands, and reprise his plan a few months later, by which time the snow would have blocked the roads between his territory and the Uesugi's. So, in January 1573, the thirty thousand Takeda samurai were on the march again, only to stop once more when Shingen was hit by a harquebus shot during a battle. In April when he had recovered from his wound, they set off again, but then he died suddenly—according to some sources of an illness, and according to others because the bullet wound had reopened. One way or another, it seemed fortune had smiled on Nobunaga once more.

Takeda Shingen and Uesugi Kenshin

As we were saying, Nobunaga was not, *a priori*, one of the main candidates to take control of the country. It seemed logical that many other daimyō, like the late Imagawa Yoshimoto, who were more powerful than him, could achieve this with greater ease. A little to the north of Imagawa's territories, two other daimyō were becoming increasingly powerful: Takeda Shingen, of Kai, and Uesugi Kenshin of Echigo, also known as "the Tiger of Kai" and "the Dragon of Echigo." It is often said neither of them managed to take over the whole country precisely because they focused their efforts on finishing each other off instead of first trying to take the capital.

The Takeda were a very ancient clan, related to the Minamoto—which would have opened the way to the shōgun post for them—and Shingen became their leader on coming of age. Although to do so, he had to wrest the position from his father, who felt open contempt for him and intended to make another of his sons his heir, for which he was banished. Despite what

Fig. 7.2. Statue of Takeda Shingen and Uesugi Kenshin depicting the famous fan defense scene, in Nagano, in the identically named prefecture.

his father thought of him, Shingen showed himself to be a great clan leader, highly respected by all his men, and a great daimyō, famous for his ability as a military strategist and, above all, for being a brilliant administrator of his lands, a task many other lords disregarded. He was also known as a great Buddhist devotee, a cruel judge with criminals—who he used to boil in a large cooking pot, and a great womanizer; he had two wives, several dozen concubines and even a fairly stable relationship with one of his leading generals. Upon taking over the Takeda clan and securing his province after defending it from some attacks by neighboring daimyō, he decided to expand his domains by conquering the adjacent province of Shinano. His advance would be halted from then on by the person who would become his arch enemy. Uesugi Kenshin did not really belong to the Uesugi family. His name at birth was Nagao, an Uesugi vassal. He became the leader of his family by fighting one of his brothers and soon after conquered the entire province of Echigo. Kenshin lived for battle and was far more interested in conquering new territories than in running the ones he already had. He was always at war with other daimyō, for example fighting the Hōjō from Odawara in the name of the Uesugi, a clan that had been very powerful but now was much weakened. With time he came to control this clan and so began to use its name, which was of much more ancient lineage than his own since the Uesugi were related to the Fujiwara. Kenshin, like Shingen, was also very religious, but unlike the latter he never married nor had offspring and it is even believed he remained celibate; his piety did not, however, stop him from regularly drinking copious amounts of alcohol, an addiction that is thought to have caused the illness that killed him. He is also credited with having a deep sense of honor, even with his enemies—something that was very unusual at the time, despite what the chronicles say. Faced with the Takeda advance in the province of Shinano, other daimyō asked him for help to halt the Tiger of Kai's samurai.

Shingen and Kenshin clashed five times over eleven years: in 1553, 1555, 1557, 1561 and 1564, in what are known as the Battles of Kawanakajima, but all but one of these clashes were nothing more than small skirmishes or face-offs, which for one reason or another finished as soon as they started. What has gone down in history is the fourth battle of Kawanakajima, where the two armies—both of them around twenty-thousand strong—did indeed confront one another. There was a high casualty rate—almost two-thirds of the Kai soldiers and three-quarters of those from Echigo. Kenshin was finally forced to retreat, but we cannot really say the battle was a great victory for the Takeda. The most famous moment of the battle—whether or not it really happened—occurred when Kenshin himself personally managed to get to the enemy camp on horseback and charge right at a surprised Shingen. The latter had to defend himself from several sword strokes with only a metal fan he normally used to direct his troops on the battlefield before his men forced the Echigo lord back. But the tiger and the dragon, as the Chinese tradition goes, are equally matched and in the end neither of these two powerful daimyō was able to beat the other, nor did they manage to unify the country. When Kenshin found out about his rival's death, he claimed to be saddened by it, banned music from being played in his castle for three days as a sign of mourning and refused to take advantage of the Takeda's momentary weakness to attack them.

Having dealt with the shōgun's unsuccessful plot, in 1573 Nobunaga decided to put an end to the problem once and for all, and in passing to show he was so powerful by then that he didn't need the legitimization that he had been making use of since 1568; he expelled Yoshiaki from the capital and relieved him of his post. As a result, the fifteenth Ashikaga shōgun would be the last, thus ending both the Sengoku period and the longer epoch it forms part of—the Muromachi period. The following period is given the name Azuchi-Momoyama (AD 1573-1603), formed by the names of the places where first Oda Nobunaga and later his successor would locate their castles. The country's new ruler, now alone and without the help of any shōgun, did not concern himself with obtaining this nor any other equally pompous official title. His pragmatism was put into practice here as he believed his military power was enough to legitimize his authority. Nobunaga was much more fixated on continuing to conquer territories until he had taken over the whole country.

The Daimyō Castles

The few remaining authentic castles in Japan—the great majority are fairly recent reconstructions—date back to the end of the Sengoku period. In previous eras, the fortifications tended to be simpler, and cannot really be classed as castles; they were often temporary rather than permanent structures and were meant for a specific campaign. In the northern area of Honshū, where the fighting against the Emishi took place, it was common practice to build simple stake fences, which made the most of hillsides. The very same structures even appear at much later times, as in the wars between the northern and southern courts, in the Nanbokuchō period. In fact, there are no significant changes before the beginning of the sixteenth century, at which time the different daimyō, normally potentially at war with all of their neighbors, started to build fortresses on the borders of their lands, usually taking advantage of hilltops. An even larger

Fig. 7.3. Himeji Castle, photograph by Bernard Gagnon (CC BY-SA 3.0).

fortress—a castle—was normally built in the center of their territory, where their headquarters was located. Today none of these constructions are still standing, although there are several modern replicas, and what we know about them we have gleaned from chronicles, paintings and engravings from the era. The lower portion of these castles normally had wooden walls while the upper half consisted of clay walls over a wooden structure, crowned by a pitched roof to avoid the clay part getting wet and weakening. This type of walls would continue to be used, but at the end of the sixteenth century, a new element would be added, which is very characteristic of this type of building: an enormous base made up of great stone blocks. These stones were firmly embedded in a mound of earth and on their exposed side were well sanded down and assembled in such a precise way that they formed a slope. This made the base very difficult to climb, and when doing so there was the risk of being riddled with arrows or stoned from the openings included in the upper part for just that purpose. In addition, this stone structure acted as a solid foundation which allowed for the construction of large tall buildings on top of it. If we add that it was usual to surround the castle with moats and that in front of the main gate a long wooden bridge was normally built, we can now conjure up the typical image that comes to mind when we think of the samurai castles.

Oda Nobunaga built his great castle, Azuchi, in 1576, and it would become the greatest example of its age of this type of fortification: a massively proportioned castle designed to impress his enemies both with its defenses and with its well-appointed chambers. It was destroyed by Akechi Mitsuhide in 1582 and today only its stone base remains; it has not been reconstructed, at least not in its original location, although it has reappeared in a kind of theme park called Azuchi-Momoyama Bunka Mura, in Ise. Toyotomi Hideyoshi wanted to match Nobunaga and built the giant Osaka Castle, which can be visited today, although it is a very modern reconstruction that has little in common with how it was in its time, especially inside. Another great example is Odawara Castle, where the Hōjō managed to repel both Uesugi Kenshin and Takeda Shingen's attacks, although they would fall in 1590. The castle is currently the city of Odawara's greatest tourist attraction, despite being a contemporary reconstruction and much smaller than the original. The most famous of the original castles remaining in the country is undoubtedly Himeji Castle (in the Hyōgo prefecture), which was declared a World Heritage Site by UNESCO and is considered one of Japan's National Treasures. Various wars, fires and earthquakes, along with political decisions taken during the Edo period, and above all, during the Meiji period, are the reasons behind the scarcity of authentic castles today.

Takeda Shingen was succeeded as clan leader by his son Takeda Katsuyori (AD 1546-1582), although the son had not inherited his father's skills either as a military strategist or as a territorial administrator. Just two years later, in 1575, he tried to invade Mikawa, the Tokugawa's province, laying siege there to Nagashino Castle. On seeing he would not be able to defend it for too long in the face of the fifteen thousand Takeda clan soldiers, the general in command of the fortress asked his Tokugawa clan leader for help, and he in turn asked Nobunaga for help. Between them, the reinforcements sent to the rescue added up to almost forty thousand soldiers, thus beginning the Battle of Nagashino, one of the most important in Japan's history.

Nobunaga, who was aware the main threat came from the Takeda's powerful cavalry, came up with a very novel strategy, based mainly on the strength of his harquebus battalion, made up of no fewer than three thousand men. We have already seen that by 1575 the use of harquebuses was far from unheard of, but Nobunaga added a few innovations at Nagashino: he built palisades from behind which the harquebuses would be fired, surrounded by infantry carrying spears that were much longer than normal—nearly six meters—thus protecting the harquebusiers from the impact of any cavalry that escaped their shots; but most importantly of all, he stationed not one but three rows of harquebusiers so that after the first row had fired, the second one was already ready to fire and by the time the third row had fired, the first row had had time to reload—in a nutshell, continuous relay firing. And this was some two decades before the first time this revolutionary system would be used in Europe.

He also positioned his men so that there was a small yet muddy river between them and their enemies, in which the cavalry charge would be mired, and left with barely two hundred meters to pick up speed again. Despite having everything against him, not least bring overwhelmingly outnumbered, Katsuyori made a great show of his famous bravery—or rather recklessness—and decided to charge the enemy in any case. He believed the heavy rain of the night before would have rendered most of the Oda's harquebuses unusable and so his cavalry would be able to penetrate the enemy lines and leave a gap for his infantry to exploit. So, on the morning of June 28, 1575, the Takeda cavalrymen set off, crossed the river and launched into a gallop against the Oda-Tokugawa coalition's defensive emplacement. In spite of the understandable nervousness caused by seeing the mythical Takeda cavalry advance toward them at full speed, Nobunaga's harquebusiers waited for the order to open fire, which was only given when the enemy was fifty meters away, an effective range for a harquebus shot.

The weapons worked, as did the relay system, and the attacking samurai, both the mounted knights and the foot soldiers, quickly began to fall under the incessant defensive fire; those who managed to reach their objective were then halted by the enormous spears that appeared from behind the palisades, and those that remained were repelled by the swords or (normal sized) spears of the samurai who were waiting for them. After several hours of combat, the Takeda began to retreat and were then chased, and in many cases eliminated, by their enemies. There were around ten thousand casualties on the attacking side and approximately half as many among the defenders. The importance of the battle is that it was a turning point as far as the way of understanding and approaching military strategy was concerned; it was the moment firearms not only participated in a battle but were decisive in its outcome.

After his great enemy Takeda Shingen's death, Uesugi Kenshin also began to think about taking over the capital by defeating Nobunaga. As early as 1574 he had initiated his advance, conquering a number of areas and coming dangerously close to Kyoto after defeating Nobunaga and his allies' armies in several battles, the most notable being Tedorigawa in 1577. But the next year as he was preparing for the final attack, Kenshin died, struck down by some sort of disease in the course of just four days—a death that has led to all kinds of theories and stories. Once more, lady luck had smiled on Nobunaga and with the Uesugi clan greatly weakened after the loss of its leader, he had little difficulty finishing them off. He also decided to finish with what was left of the Takeda clan once and for all, and so in 1582 he mobilized a massive—and most likely unnecessary—army of one hundred fifty thousand soldiers. This was vastly superior to the twenty thousand Katsuyori had and the result was a crushing victory. Although the Takeda leader was able to escape with a few dozen of his samurai, he was captured and killed soon after. Thus, the only remaining potential threat in the country's central region came from the Hōjō, although for the moment they were closely controlled by the Tokugawa. So, Nobunaga then decided to concentrate on the western part of the country—which was mainly under the control of the Mōri and their allies—and chose his best general, of whom more later, to lead the campaign.

But in this very year 1582, Nobunaga's good luck suddenly ran out, in what is known as the Honnō-ji Incident. On his way from his base in Ōmi, where his impressive Azuchi Castle was located, to supervise the campaign against the Mōri, he decided to send one of his generals ahead—Akechi Mitsuhide (AD 1528-1582)—while he stayed behind in Kyoto for a couple of days to await the arrival of the Tokugawa leader. He decided to lodge in the Honnō-ji Temple, as was his custom when he visited the capital, although this time he was only accompanied by a hundred or so samurai, and not the two thousand soldiers that he usually took with him. At the halfway point on his way to the western campaign, Mitsuhide suddenly gave his troops the order to turn around and head for

Fig. 7.4. Part of a screen depicting scenes from the Battle of Nagashino, showing the high palisades, the three rows of harquebusiers and behind them the ashigaru armed with long spears. Tokyo National Museum.

Kyoto. On reaching the city, at dawn on June 20, they attacked Honnō-ji. Nobunaga and his men, who were greatly outnumbered and completely unprepared for the attack, preferred to set fire to the temple and be burned alive rather than fall into the traitors' hands. Nobunaga committed seppuku, although as his body was never found, all kinds of stories emerged about this. Immediately after the attack, Mitsuhide ordered his men to do the same with Nijō Castle, also in Kyoto, where Nobunaga's son and heir Nobutada (AD 1557-1582) was staying. He ended up committing seppuku just like his father. The reasons behind Akechi Mitsuhide's betrayal have been discussed at length by the historians who have studied the matter and several hypotheses put forward. The usual explanation is that it was personal revenge as Mitsuhide blamed Nobunaga for the death of his mother three years earlier; but some scholars argue that the general quite simply wanted to take control of the country.

Yasuke, the Black Samurai

Although it is something we rarely talk about, as well as taking an active part in the goods trade between Europe, China and Japan, The Society of Jesus also participated in another kind of trade that was common in that era but is of course much more questionable from a modern-day perspective—the slave trade. When Alessandro Valignano reached Japan in 1579, one of the people who accompanied him was an African slave, from Mozambique according to the Jesuits' chronicles, who was nearly one meter ninety tall and worked in the service of the priests as a slave. When Valignano traveled to Kyoto in 1581 he took him along and his presence caused such a stir and was so astonishing that the news came to Oda Nobunaga's attention. So, the powerful daimyō sent a message to the Jesuits asking them to come and see him and to bring with them the black-colored person everyone was talking about. The visit took place that very same year on 23rd March according to the Japanese chronicles, which describe the slave as a very strong youth, who was roughly twenty-five years old and of healthy appearance, whose entire body was black "like an ox" and who also spoke some Japanese. His appearance made quite an impression on Nobunaga, who made him strip off to the waist and ordered servant girls to scrub his skin with all kinds of soaps, oils and ointments to check if his color was natural and not some kind of dye or paint. Once he was sure the prodigy was real, he asked the Jesuits to let the youth stay with him, to which the priests—who were greatly interested in getting on well with the man who was by then the ruler of most of the country—agreed, giving him the youth "as a gift."

The name given to this black slave was Yasuke (until recently the reason for this was unknown—investigations carried out in Japan not long ago claim his real name was Yasufe) and from then on he always accompanied Nobunaga as a kind of body-guard. It is worth pointing out that henceforth he was no longer a slave, since he received a salary for being in the daimyō's service and enjoyed the same comforts as other vassals. He was granted the rank of samurai and occasionally even shared a table with Nobunaga himself, a privilege few of his trusted vassals were afforded. We know he was at his master's side in the Hon-nō-ji Incident, fighting Akechi Mitsuhide's men, and managed to escape with his life and get to the place where Nobunaga's son was staying. When the latter was also attacked, he fought like the rest once more, with the difference that when they saw they were going to be defeated, he did not commit seppuku like many of his companions did, but instead surrendered to the enemy. Akechi decided to spare his life, although it seems more out of contempt than mercy; he stated Yasuke was more of an animal than a man, so could not be considered a samurai, and therefore could not be held to account with his life as was expected of a defeated samurai. So, he was given back to the Jesuits and from that moment on history loses track of him, although it is believed he ended up returning home. A certain English sailor—of whom more later—is often credited with being the first Western samu-rai, but Yasuke got there a few years before him.

At the time of his death, Nobunaga had managed to unify the country's entire central region, placing 32 of Japan's 68 provinces—approximately a third of the country in terms of area—under his control. Of note was his policy of creating cities around castles in these territories, where a new spirit of entrepreneurship and commerce sprung up. This was due to Nobunaga's government facilitating commercial activity; free market operations were favored with measures such as the abolition of tariffs and tolls. As far as his relationship with the Europeans was concerned, Nobunaga showed an interest in favoring the Jesuit mission, with whose priests he held friendly meetings on numerous occasions. Clearly it is easy to see a direct relation between this friendship with the missionaries and his massive use of harquebuses: being such a pragmatic person, Nobunaga understood it could be very much in his interests to get on well with the Catholic priests, in the same way as he fought against some Buddhist monasteries, putting aside religious questions.

For his part, Akechi Mitsuhide, proclaimed himself shōgun after he had finished off the Oda clan leadership, something he was lawfully allowed to do given the Akechi family was related to the Minamoto. In any case, his name does not usually appear on the list of shōgun in Japanese history because he did not last long in the post. A mere two weeks later, Oda Nobunaga's best general managed to avenge his death.

...Toyotomi Hideyoshi Cooked It...

Toyotomi Hideyoshi (AD 1537-1598) was born in the province of Owari, on Oda clan land. He was the son of a simple peasant called Yaemon, who (as peasants used to when called upon) had served for a time as a foot soldier in the clan's army and died a little later when Hideyoshi was seven years old. As we can see, this is the story of someone who got to the top from the humblest of beginnings, which is unusual in Japanese history, more given to great families, proven pedigrees and ostentatious family names. Since he was of working-class background, little is known about his childhood— and of course that gap has been filled with all kinds of stories and legends—but it is believed that from a very young age he devoted himself to traveling around different provinces in the service of various lords, always carrying out minor tasks as a stable boy or servant. Apparently he returned to Owari in 1558 and started to work for the Oda, undertaking all kind of jobs, the best-known and most famous of which was as Nobunaga's personal sandals carrier.

His legendary self-belief and his apparent natural talent for standing out from the rest helped him to make a meteoric rise from this humble position. Once more though, little is known about him until in 1570 he was entrusted with the command of three thousand of the Nobunaga army's soldiers in a campaign against the neighboring Asakura clan. In 1574, after defeating the Azai clan, he was rewarded by Nobunaga with the defeated side's territory—the Ōmi province—and a stipend of one hundred eighty thousand *koku*, as a result of which the son of the peasant Yaemon

Fig. 7.5. Statue of Toyotomi Hideyoshi
in Toyokuni Shrine, in Osaka.

officially became a daimyō. Shortly afterwards, in 1577, his official
biography, written by his secretary, begins.

Koku: Rice as a Currency

The koku was a unit of measurement of rice, in theory equivalent to the amount of rice eaten by one person in a year. Although the amount varied, we could put it at around 150 kilos. The wealth of a fiefdom or the stipend granted to a samurai was calculated in koku.

Over the following years, as well as ruling his province, Hideyoshi took part in numerous campaigns as one of Nobunaga's leading generals, winning all of his battles. For example, he was at the aforementioned Battle of Nagashino fighting the Takeda in 1575, and subsequently was entrusted with the campaign against the powerful Mōri clan and their allies. In this campaign, Hideyoshi showed himself to be a great strategist and, above all, a brilliant negotiator, since many of his victories came about before he had even set foot on the battlefield, by convincing the enemy to switch sides. In one way or another, Hideyoshi went on advancing toward the west, gaining territory after territory. As a result, Nobunaga rewarded him again in 1580, this time with two of the provinces he had acquired in his advance—Tajima and Harima. Here he established his operational base, ready to continue fighting the Mōri. In 1582 it was the turn of the Bitchū province, where one of the most famous battles in Hideyoshi's career took place—the Siege of Takamatsu Castle. Taking advantage of the lie of the land where the castle was located and the close proximity of a river, Hideyoshi ordered a long dike to be built—nearly three kilometers long, over seven meters high, twenty-two meters wide at the base and eleven at the top. The result was that all the territory surrounding the castle was flooded. Hideyoshi, who expected the Mōri to come to the aid of the castle's defenders, then asked Nobunaga to send him reinforcements. The latter decided to send him an army led by Akechi Mitsuhide before going in person to supervise the operation. It was then that the aforementioned Honnō-ji Incident occurred.

Mitsuhide's strategy took into account that Nobunaga's principal generals were scattered over different parts of the country at the time, fighting on various fronts. The most dangerous adversary of all of them was undoubtedly Hideyoshi, but Mitsuhide knew his attention was fixed at the time on the siege of the flooded Takamatsu Castle, which he could not leave; if he did so and headed for the capital on hearing of Nobunaga's death, he could be attacked by the Mōri from his rear-guard. So, he sent the Mōri a messenger, informing them of Nobunaga's death. Luckily for Hideyoshi, they managed to intercept this messenger and just two days later agree on a negotiated end to the siege with the Mōri—with highly advantageous terms for the latter, who remained unaware of what had happened in Kyoto. So, having settled this business, Hideyoshi and his troops headed for the capital as fast as they could, covering an average of forty kilometers a day. Meanwhile, Mitsuhide proclaimed himself shōgun, presenting himself in Kyoto as the country's savior, the one who had finished with the dictator who had hijacked the central government. When he learned Hideyoshi's troops were approaching, he decided to head out to meet him, taking advantage of his being able to look for an optimum spot at which to face him. The clash of the two armies took place in a village called Yamazaki, after which the battle is named. In just one day, Hideyoshi's troops massacred all the enemy troops, other than those who managed to flee. Akechi Mitsuhide himself also started to flee, only to be slain by bandits in a nearby village called Ogurusu. Only thirteen days had gone by since Nobunaga's suicide and Toyotomi Hideyoshi was the man who had avenged him.

After the death of the Oda leader, a conflict broke out within the clan between the three possible successors—two of Nobunaga's sons and a grandson—although in reality it was a conflict between three clan factions, each of which supported one of these possible heirs. Hideyoshi led one of these factions and, after fighting some and making pacts with others, and bolstered by the legitimacy bestowed on him by the fact he was the one who had avenged Nobunaga, managed to claim the leadership. Nobunaga's grandson, who he supposedly supported as successor, nominally took control of the Oda clan, but since he was only two years old, power was, *de facto*, in Hideyoshi's hands. In 1585 he had a Kyoto noble from the Konoe family adopt him, as they were descendants of the Fujiwara, and thereby reclaimed the title of kanpaku, or imperial regent. Just one year later, in 1586, Emperor Ōgimachi (AD 1517-1593) abdicated and Hideyoshi placed the previous emperor's grandson on the throne, Emperor Go-Yōzei (AD 1571-1617), who was only fourteen years old and a mere puppet in his hands. Hideyoshi thereby managed to take control of both the military and the court, concluding his rise from the bottom to the top of Japanese society.

During the 1580s and in an astonishingly short time, he would manage to impose his control over all the provinces of Japan—thus unifying the country for the first time in over a century—using negotiation more than battle and managing to get those who until then had been fearsome enemies to side with him. Throughout these years Hideyoshi favored the idea of pacifying the country, rather than conquering it, and even brought many of the daimyō he had defeated on the battlefield over to his side, which helped to reduce the opposition of those who were still independent. In this way, it only took him around eight years to control the whole country—in comparison, Nobunaga needed ten just to subdue the Takeda. Those in the furthest-flung regions, like the Shimazu of Kyūshū, were not so aware of his power. Moreover, they refused to obey the orders of a peasant's son, but were soon defeated by the increasingly gigantic armies mobilized by Hideyoshi: two hundred thousand samurai to conquer Shikoku and no fewer than two hundred eighty thousand for Kyūshū. In 1590 the Hōjō finally fell, after the famous Siege of Odawara Castle, and then the only territory remaining outside Hideyoshi's reach was that belonging to the Date, comprising a large part of the north of Honshū, but their leader, Date Masamune (AD 1567-1636), went to the kanpaku's camp and swore loyalty to him.

Thus ended the long process of Japan's unification, which had been underway ever since the outbreak of the Ōnin War had sent the country's already weak stability up in smoke. Hideyoshi governed Japan with a firm hand, but not as a dictator; he was really at the head of a federation of three hundred or so samurai lords from all around the country, two hundred of whom could be considered his longtime allies and the remaining hundred former enemies. He personally owned rather a modest amount of land—if he is compared with previous rulers—amounting to a couple of million koku. Among many other measures, he allowed the reconstruction of the temples and shrines Nobunaga had destroyed but made sure they did not meddle in political affairs again. From the start, he ordered a complete census of land and productive resources to be compiled and implemented profound changes in the political sphere. He decreed that peasants would henceforth be the owners of their land (which they were duty bound to till and would pay taxes on) and that the land would no longer belong to the samurai. The latter mainly moved to the new towns that had sprung up around the castles, where they got a koku stipend taken from the taxes the peasants paid on the lands they controlled. In addition, from that moment on, the samurai would be the only ones authorized to carry weapons; they were requisitioned from all the non-samurai who possessed one, be it a sword, spear, bow or any other weapon. The peasants would no longer take part in battles and would devote themselves to peacefully ploughing their land, as would their sons, given that from then on social class would be hereditary—a strange policy coming from the son of a peasant who had managed to become the most powerful samurai in the country. Many of the institutions and laws created by Hideyoshi would establish important foundations on which the Japan of the following three centuries would be based.

Peasant Weapons

When Toyotomi Hideyoshi prohibited everyone who was not a samurai from using weapons, the peasants were left defenseless in the face of potential bandit attacks, so had to find a way to, if not exactly disobey, get around this new legislation. It is believed this is when various implements that until then had been used as farm tools started to be used—either as they were or in some modified form—as weapons. This is how weapons such as the *nunchaku*, the *tonfa*, and the *kusarigama* among others appeared. The Ryūkyū islands' archipelago was conquered by Japan in 1609 and added to the domains of the Shimazu clan, who imposed the prevailing Japanese legislation, which included the abovementioned ban on possessing weapons. It is believed that the use of these tools as weapons originated there, especially on the island of Okinawa, along with the development of an empty-handed fighting style, that was later known as karate, literally "empty hands" in Japanese.

Hideyoshi resigned from his position as kanpaku in 1591, passing it on to his nephew Hidetsugu (AD 1568-1595), who he had named as his successor some time earlier when his only male child had died at the age of two, and became *taikō*—retired regent. Hideyoshi is normally referred to by this term and despite the role's theoretical remit, he ruled the country from this position until his death. From the moment he took control of the whole country, Hideyoshi's biography includes some points that have been greatly criticized and which contradict with the attitude he had shown up until that moment, such as his gradual adoption of the ways and customs of the court—perhaps to make up for his humble beginnings. Particularly noteworthy was his great enthusiasm for the tea ceremony, which he occasionally held for an enormous number of guests, and even had a luxurious portable tea house built so he could hold the ceremony anyplace. His decision to invade China and Korea has also been much criticized—but this will be discussed in the next chapter—as has the fact that shortly after managing to produce a son in 1593, he ordered his nephew Hidetsugu (who until then had been his heir) to commit seppuku, accused of conspiring against him. Although this was nothing more than an excuse to get rid of him now that he had a son of his own to succeed him. The same order was given to Hidetsugu's entire family and his vassals, and those who refused to commit suicide were executed, children included, though that was nothing unusual at the time.

When he took control of the Oda clan, Hideyoshi was just as tolerant and even friendly with the Christian missionaries as Nobunaga had been, and for the same reasons. But once he had taken over the south of the country, in 1587, things began to change: with Japan almost conquered it was no longer so urgent for him to have good relations with the Europeans and he also began to realize that, especially in Kyūshū, they had a strong influence over some daimyō, who, for example, had gone so far as to destroy temples and shrines on becoming Christians. Upon reaching this island, he saw with his own eyes the power the Jesuits had there. They had even controlled the city of Nagasaki ever since Ōmura Sumitada (AD 1533-1587)—the first daimyō converted to Christianity, called Bartolomeu after being baptized—had given it to them as a gift. As a result, the idea of a potential invasion of Japan by the Castilians and Portuguese—now under the same crown—helped by the armies of the Christian daimyō, began to gather strength in Hideyoshi's mind. This was not a possibility he was prepared to tolerate. In July 1587, he proclaimed what is known as the "Anti-Christian Edict," in reality called Bateren Tsuihōrei, "Priest Expulsion Edict," which would mark a turning point for Christianity in Japan, decreeing—as its name makes clear—the expulsion of all of the country's Catholic priests, although not the rest of the foreigners, meaning the traders. Nagasaki and the rest of the Jesuits' property was also confiscated and from then on the port city answered to Hideyoshi personally. Understandably the priests were very surprised by this sudden change in the then kanpaku's attitude toward them and played for time arguing they could not leave Japan until six months later because there were no galleons to Macao until then, to which Hideyoshi agreed. When the day came, the Jesuits decided to disobey the edict, simulating a departure in which the only priests to leave the country were those who had other matters to attend to in China, and continued to carry out their missionary work, albeit from then on in a very discreet and almost clandestine way. Hideyoshi was obviously aware of this, but opted not to do anything about it and the edict was never implemented.

Only a few churches were destroyed and some daimyō forced to renounce their faith. The kanpaku knew if he expelled the priests completely, Philip II would not allow Portuguese trade in Japan, so for the time being he hoped the Jesuits would have got the message and would avoid meddling in political affairs and be sure to carry out their mission without making too much noise; what is more, he already had a law to turn to if necessary should the priests become overly confident and start to act freely again. They had to learn that the period of civil war was over and it was no longer of any use to curry the favor of any of the daimyō since these lords were no longer absolute rulers of their lands but the kanpaku's men, subject to his orders. Years later, at the end of 1596 (by which time other orders, like the Franciscans, had priests in Japan), after what is known as the San Felipe Galleon Incident, Hideyoshi resurrected the persecution of the Catholic mission in Japan when the idea of an invasion attempt using the priests as a vanguard reappeared more forcefully. This galleon, which covered the Manila-Acapulco route was shipwrecked on the Japanese coast carrying a large quantity of goods, money and weapons, and when the crew was interrogated by an envoy of Hideyoshi's, the pilot— with the aim of impressing the Japanese—showed the enormous number of territories under the control of Philip II on a world map. On being questioned about how a single monarch had managed to get so much land, the pilot explained that first the priests and friars were sent to a new land, with the task of converting part

Fig. 7.6. European engraving from 1628 depicting the crucifixion of the Martyrs of Nagasaki, by Wolfgang Kilian.

of the population and the elites so that in this way conquest was easier when the Castilian armies arrived soon after—and this is what had been done in Peru and New Spain. There are many versions of this event as well as debates and controversies, but what is certain is that Hideyoshi ordered 26 men to be executed in early 1597, who were crucified and pierced with spears—the so-called "Martyrs of Nagasaki." It is not known how his relationship with the Catholic mission would have continued since Hideyoshi died only one year later.

Toyotomi Hideyoshi died of natural causes in September 1598, but before that he formed a council of five regents, his five trusted generals, who he made responsible for governing the country until his heir Hideyori (AD 1593-1615), just five years old at the time, reached adulthood. But despite his planning, it did not take long for divisions to appear in this council and for war to break out among his generals, a conflict from which the last of the three great unifiers of Japan would emerge victorious.

...and Tokugawa Ieyasu Ate It All Up

Tokugawa Ieyasu (AD 1543-1616) was born with the Matsudaira surname, the son of the leader of that clan, a rather less important family from the province of Mikawa that lived surrounded by two more powerful clans, the Oda and, above all, the Imagawa. In order to survive, the Matsudaira were forced to become vassals of one of those two opposing clans. Ieyasu's father chose the latter, and his servitude was accepted on the condition he sent his son and heir as a hostage to guarantee his submission. This was quite a common custom of the period. So, at the age of five, Ieyasu was separated from his family to be sent to live with the Imagawa, although the cortege he was travelling in was then intercepted by the Oda and the young heir kidnapped. A year later, Ieyasu's father died of natural causes, and the little six-year-old became the Matsudaira clan leader. A pact between the Oda and the Imagawa finally resulted in Ieyasu going to live with the latter, and he would

Fig. 7.7. Statue of Tokugawa Ieyasu in his
hometown, Okazaki, in the Aichi prefecture.

spend his childhood and adolescence with them. Demands kept
on coming from the Matsudaira in Mikawa for the Imagawa to
free the man who was now their leader, but Yoshimoto balked at
releasing him from his status as a hostage and after a few years
made the young Ieyasu begin to take part in his battles, at the
head of the Matsudaira army but always under the orders of the
Imagawa. In Japan, Tokugawa Ieyasu is credited with having one
virtue above all others: patience. He was capable of seeing the best
thing is often to calmly wait for the appropriate time to act, and
this episode of his biography is a good example—the moment to
cease to be a hostage would come all in good time.

When Imagawa Yoshimoto began to advance on Kyoto in 1560—to return to the beginning of this chapter—a small part of his large army was made up of men from Mikawa led by Ieyasu. One of the victories the Imagawa soldiers were celebrating when Nobunaga's troops fell on them in Okehazama was precisely the conquest of a fortress by Ieyasu's Matsudaira men, who thanks to this were not at the fateful site of the battle. With Yoshimoto's death, the young Ieyasu was set free from his agreement with the Imagawa—if not formally, at least *de facto*—and so returned to his Mikawa province to finally rule his clan and his domains. And as a matter of fact one of his first decisions as Matsudaira leader was to become allies with Oda Nobunaga, who in a way could be considered his liberator. Straight after this, he initiated a campaign to free his wife, son and other relatives, who were still hostages of the Imagawa clan, who he would finish off for good a few years later. From then on—as was previously seen—he made a very important contribution to Nobunaga's unification of Japan: if Hideyoshi was his best general, entrusted with going about the conquest of new territories, Ieyasu was the loyal ally who enabled stability to be assured in the rearguard, where the Hōjō, Uesugi and Takeda were an ever-present threat. And he managed this both by fighting them and signing pacts and alliances with them at concrete times—so many and so volatile that it is not worth describing them here. In 1567 he changed his surname for Tokugawa and the following year his troops formed part of the army with which Nobunaga took the capital and control of the country's vitally important central region. The most important test—at least from our perspective—of Ieyasu's loyalty toward Nobunaga would come in 1579, when the Tokugawa leader's wife and eldest son were accused of conspiring along with Takeda Katsuyori to kill Nobunaga; an accusation that Ieyasu resolved by ordering his own wife to be executed and his heir to commit seppuku.

When Nobunaga died in 1582, Ieyasu remained almost on the fringes of the struggles for the Oda clan leadership, only getting involved near the end, supporting one of the bands opposing

Hideyoshi, but quickly agreeing an alliance with him. He did not mind staying in his shadow, as he had done before with Nobunaga. From then on, he collaborated with Hideyoshi in the conquest of the rest of the country, and played a particularly key role in the fall of the Hōjō of Odawara in 1590. After this, Hideyoshi swapped Ieyasu's five provinces for the ones they had conquered from the defeated clan. He did this to distance him from the national political center and to break the bond the Tokugawa had with their territory, two measures aimed in principle at limiting the increasingly powerful Ieyasu. Many members of his clan then regarded this transfer as virtually an exile or even a banishment. But this change would turn out to be highly beneficial for the Tokugawa.

They came to control the entire prosperous Kantō region, and decided to establish their base in a place called Edo, which at the time was nothing more than a handful of houses scattered around a castle, but which he would change into a prosperous city that would come to have the largest population of its age and which is known today as Tokyo. They assimilated the area's rural samurai and even accepted many former Hōjō vassals without stripping them of their rank. Starting from scratch in a new territory, Ieyasu was able to devote himself to organizing and administering his new domains over most of the following decade, largely applying the same systems he had learned after snatching the Kai province from the Takeda, since one of Takeda Shingen's greatest virtues had been that he was a great administrator. Ieyasu was able to devote a lot of time to these matters because having already pacified Japan under Hideyoshi's government, he did not participate in the wars with Korea and China, unlike many other lords. This is one of the reasons why the lord of Kantō became the most powerful daimyō in the whole of Japan, only surpassed by the Taikō himself.

Consequently, once Hideyoshi died in 1598, Ieyasu was undoubtedly the strongest candidate to succeed him. Logically he formed part of the council of five regents the Taikō had constituted to govern until his son Hideyori's coming of age, and when—as was said earlier—there was a split among the members of this council,

Fig. 7.8. Part of a screen depicting the Battle of Sekigahara: in the image we can identify Ishida Mitsunari on a white horse, in the lower right-hand side. Gifu City Museum of History.

Ieyasu was the leader of one of the two opposing blocs. One of the other four regents had died of natural causes and the remaining three had united, supporting the one who had taken on the role of leader of the bloc opposed to Ieyasu, a daimyō called Ishida Mitsunari (AD 1560-1600), who supposedly defended Hideyori's interests. Each side resorted to alliances and pacts with different samurai leaders around the country and two large daimyō federations were formed, which, broadly speaking, could be summed up as east against west, the first led by Ieyasu and the second by Ishida. The two sides would clash at the famous Battle of Sekigahara in the year 1600, the other great battle in samurai history along with Dan no Ura, which would conclude a series of prior small battles and sieges from that same year.

There is no official data about the number of soldiers that took part in the Battle of Sekigahara, but historians calculate around one hundred eighty or two hundred thousand (so we may be talking about the largest battle ever to take place on Japanese soil), who at first were almost equally divided between the two sides. Ishida Mitsunari's troops arrived in Sekigahara (in the modern-day Gifu prefecture) before dawn on October 21, 1600, a few hours before the enemy side, meaning they had time to plan their strategy. This consisted of first holding back the charge of Ieyasu's forces in the battle's center, later to deploy an encircling maneuver in which the army of the young Kobayakawa Hideaki (AD 1582-1602)— Hideyoshi's nephew—would attack by coming down a hill on the left flank, followed by Ishida himself on the right and the Mōri in the rear guard. Although the eastern confederation's armies had arrived a little before eight o'clock in the morning, the battle did not begin until then because they had to wait for the dispersal of a thick fog that made combat impossible. When fighting broke out, the main action developed in the central zone, where the two sides' forces were evenly matched.

For the first three hours, they traded attacks without either army gaining a significant advantage over the other. Both armies used harquebuses as part of their arsenal, although they were not decisive as they had been at Nagashino. Ishida's forces even went so far as to use five cannons, something highly unusual on the battlefield. At this stage, at around eleven in the morning, Ishida decided to initiate the encircling maneuver, sending Kobayakawa a signal for him to come down from the hill where he was stationed with his fifteen thousand samurai. But Hideyoshi's nephew stayed exactly where he was for some time and when he finally reacted, he did so by ordering his men to attack Ishida's army, thus betraying the western confederation. His first objective was then Ōtani Yoshitsugu's men, a daimyō (AD 1559-1600) who had fought in Korea alongside Ishida Mitsunari, which had given rise to a strong friendship between them, and who was taking part in the battle despite being seriously ill with leprosy; he was by then practically blind and unable to stand and had to be carried around on a palanquin. When Kobayakawa ignored Ishida's orders, Ōtani had been suspicious of his intentions and had taken the precaution of deploying his men to defend against a possible attack of his. As a result, when this did indeed take place, they were able to resist longer than if they had been taken by surprise. But this resistance did not last too long and seeing his army's defeat was near, Ōtani had them put him down from his palanquin and ordered one of his men to cut off his head and hide it to stop it from ending up falling into enemy hands. Kobayakawa's betrayal meant the forces were now uneven and it ruined Ishida's strategy, leading to two things happening: many of the clans that made up his bloc, such as the Mōri and the Chōsokabe, opted not to enter into combat, and those who had begun to fight fled. Seeing that victory was now highly unlikely, Ishida Mitsunari himself also decided to leave the site, and the battle then came to an end at around two o'clock in the afternoon.

A few days after Sekigahara, Ishida was captured and executed, as were many of his allies. Ieyasu also decided to send the little Hideyori to live in Osaka Castle. So with the way clear after having wisely bided his time for decades, he took control of Japan and in 1603 obtained the longed-for position of shōgun from the emperor. Thus ends the Azuchi-Momoyama period and begins both the Edo period (AD 1603-1868) and the Tokugawa shōgunate, the third and final one in history.

CHAPTER 8

The Invasion of Korea

Possible Motives and Preparations

The previous chapter ended with Tokugawa Ieyasu recently made shōgun, but now we have to go back a decade to explain something that was skipped when talking about Toyotomi Hideyoshi because it undoubtedly deserves a chapter all of its own. Once Japan was unified, the Taikō decided it was a good moment to embark on one of the greatest ambitions a Japanese ruler could ever contemplate: the conquest of China. Once this had been achieved, he intended to transfer the Emperor of Japan to its capital, making him Emperor of China, while one of his sons would occupy the Japanese throne; not satisfied with this, the next step would be to conquer India and the whole of south-east Asia. There has been much debate about the motives that might have been behind these plans, and those who are most critical of Hideyoshi's persona tend to argue he more or less went crazy in his final years, falling victim to sick delusions of grandeur that made him want to be a kind of world monarch. To support this idea, people normally put forward the death sentence handed to his nephew Hidetsugu, his sudden taste for luxury and court ceremonies, and above all the fact he himself declared on more than one occasion that the conquest of China was a task the heavens had entrusted him with at birth.

Admittedly these are sufficient reasons to support this theory. But against this supposed sudden madness Hideyoshi had been weighing the idea of invading China for quite a long time, as there is written proof of a conversation as early as 1586 with the Jesuit

Gaspar Coelho (AD 1530-1590) in which he spoke to him of the matter; in fact, this idea had appeared in some Jesuit documents attributed to none other than Oda Nobunaga in 1582. In addition, we already said in the previous chapter that the Hidetsugu episode—however cruel it may seem to us—was nothing unusual for its time. It seems much more logical to think, as more and more historians assert, that invading the continent was seen as a way of keeping Japan unified and at peace—as well as being down to Hideyoshi being quite ignorant of its sheer size and characteristics. Also, as has been seen, Hideyoshi had conquered many Japanese provinces without having to resort to fighting by convincing the daimyō to join him. And many of those he had defeated on the battlefield were even later pardoned and incorporated into his bloc. Although this way of doing things saves many lives and resources in general, it also has its disadvantages, such as not being able to reward one's own generals with the territory wrested from the defeated enemy. This situation in which there were a good number of daimyō who had gone unrewarded after years of warfare was a time-bomb that might go off whenever one of them tried to extend their land at the expense of their neighbor's, given that national unity was still something quite recent and fragile. So tying them all up in a new war may have been regarded as a good solution to this.

Despite this chapter's name, the Taikō never intended to invade Korea. His original idea was for that country to become a Japanese vassal state and to actively collaborate in the attack on China (which once again shows a great ignorance of the region's political reality) and this is what he communicated to the Korean government through a diplomatic mission. The Japanese emissaries, who understood the relationship between Korea and China much better than Hideyoshi did, softened the message before delivering it, changing it into a mere request for passage through the Korean peninsula. But Korea, a country that was historically a vassal of and protected by its Chinese neighbors, did not accede to the Japanese leader's petitions, so—after several more fairly unsuccessful missions—Hideyoshi took the decision to invade first Korea and

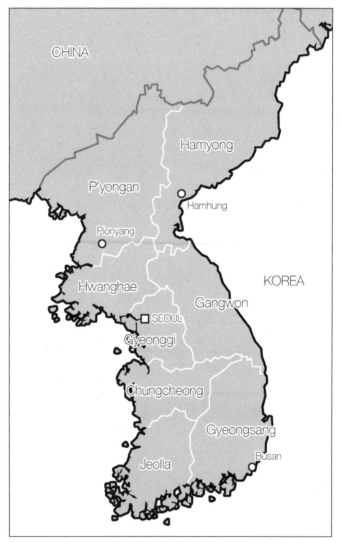

Fig. 8.1. Map of the provinces of Korea of the period. Author's own drawing.

then China. At the end of the day, for an army supposedly capable of conquering the entire Chinese territory, adding the small sliver of land that was the Korean peninsula was no big deal.

Fig. 8.2. Toyotomi Hideyoshi in conference with his generals, planning the invasion of Korea and China.

In September 1591, Toyotomi Hideyoshi ordered all of Japan's daimyō to start to collect more taxes and prepare troops for the invasion of China. Although in theory they all had to contribute toward this undertaking, the share-out turned out to be very unfair and we can see how the lords of Kyūshū contributed many more resources than those in the east of the country. The former also had to pay the enormous construction costs that the great castle Hideyoshi ordered to be built from scratch in Nagoya entailed. This was not the Nagoya that today is the country's fourth biggest city, in the center of Honshū, but another one in Hizen, the closest province to the continent, in Kyūshū. The castle was a gigantic operational base and headquarters that was built from start to finish in just six months, had all the luxuries and comforts demanded by the Taikō and could accommodate tens of thousands of soldiers. A large number of workers charged with building and transport tasks were forced to participate in both this great construction project and the expedition to the continent. Among the daimyō there were also many who obeyed the order despite being in complete disagreement, but there was only one case of insurrection; this was immediately and cruelly crushed (including the wife of the rebel in question being burned alive) as an example of what would happen to any other general who didn't toe the line… and it worked.

So by the start of 1592, the largest army Japan had ever seen was ready in Nagoya, made up of no fewer than 158,000 men. They were divided into nine divisions, each one under the command of a general, plus another 27,000 who remained stationed in Nagoya under Hideyoshi's personal command, and a further 75,000 who would make up the reserve and who would not journey to Korea—for the moment.

First Invasion and Truce

On May 23, 1592, the first division arrived in the Korean port city of Busan—curiously the same place the continental fleets had set sail from in the Mongols' two invasion attempts in the thirteenth century. This first division, led by the Christian daimyō Konishi Yukinaga (AD 1558-1600), reached the coast of Korea unopposed and once in Busan requested permission from the city authorities to pass through on their way to China. Again the Korean response was a categorical refusal so the Japanese then attacked the city and conquered Busan in the course of a single day. The Japanese superiority was overwhelming, mainly due to their modern harquebuses, which contrasted with the few firearms the Koreans had—outdated Chinese pistols. It also would have to be taken into account that Korea had been enjoying almost uninterrupted peace for around two centuries, while war had been almost continuous in Japan for half a millennium, especially over the preceding hundred years, and the samurai were battle-hardened. In Busan something that would be a persistent feature of the war became apparent: the Japanese soldiers would fight with great ferocity, more so than at any time in their history, sparing the life of no-one and inflicting a large number of casualties.

According to the initial plan, the first division was supposed to wait in Busan for the arrival of the second, led by the daimyō Katō Kiyomasa (AD 1562-1611), and they were then to head north together, but Konishi decided to advance alone, maybe because of the strong enmity he had with Katō. Konishi's advance was easy,

Castilians Against Samurai?

When the Christians in Kyūshū passed on news of the enormous mobilization of Japanese troops to the Castilians in Manila, they went into panic mode believing Hideyoshi had resolved to conquer the Philippines. They hurried to improve the city's defenses as well as they could and asked Philip II's court to send money and more soldiers urgently. But for their peace of mind, when the first of the nine divisions left Japan in April, it did so in a westerly and not southerly direction, heading for Korea.

Regarding this matter, we have to clarify that combat between Castilian troops and a samurai army (which as we were saying, was an idea that terrified the Castilians in Manila) is something that never came to pass. Every so often the Spanish press publishes some reference to an alleged battle in 1582 in which Castilian soldiers defeated samurai troops, but this is a distortion of the facts, since what has been dubbed the Cagayán fighting was in reality a number of skirmishes between Castilian ships commanded by Captain Juan Pablo de Carrión (AD 1513-?) and wakō, simple Chinese and Japanese pirates. A quick search through the documents of the General Archive of the Indies, in Seville, makes this self-evident with the chronicle of the events written by Carrión himself. Yet, the Spanish writing of history, especially that of the mid-twentieth century—little given to historical rigor when it harmed national pride—made sure this misrepresentation took root in the collective imagination and is still often revived today to the delight of some.

meeting with little resistance on his way to the vicinity of Seoul, where, days later, the two divisions finally met up—the second also having found no resistance en route—to decide on the best way to take the capital. It was not an easy decision since both Konishi and Katō wanted to be in charge of the city's conquest and take the personal glory that entailed—the chronicles of the time say they almost came to blows in their discussion. Finally, they agreed both divisions would march on Seoul by different routes and the first to arrive would have the right to attack, or to put it another way, they challenged one another to a race. Konishi arrived first, on

June 10, but there was no glorious battle as what they found was a deserted city, abandoned by the army and without a king, since the Korean monarch had fled for Pyongyang just one day earlier. With or without a battle, the Japanese had taken the capital of Korea in less than three weeks of campaigning in the country, a lightning advance, which would never again be so rapid.

Katō Kiyomasa and Konishi Yukinaga

To lead the first two divisions of the Korea campaign, Hideyoshi chose two daimyo that had already shown themselves to be not exactly the best of friends. This could equally have hindered their mission or been an extra motivation that would make them compete to outdo one another on the battlefield, and maybe this is what the Taikō was thinking when he chose them. What is clear is that Katō and Konishi were already rivals before going to Korea, they showed themselves to be so while there and continued their rivalry after returning to Japan.

Katō Kiyomasa had been born in the province of Owari, just like Hideyoshi, and began to serve him when he was still very

Fig. 8.3. Statues of Katō Kiyomasa and Konishi Yukinaga, both in the prefecture of Kumamoto.

young, shortly after the Taikō had become a daimyō. From then on, he took part in several campaigns which formed part of the country's process of unification and his climb up the ranks was as swift as the rise in his stipend. During the conquest of Kyūshū, Hideyoshi decided to reward him with approximately half of the province of Higo, taken from a rival lord, thus making him a daimyō. As for Konishi Yukinaga, he was from Sakai, in modern-day Osaka, and worked for the daimyō of the province of Bizen, but joined Hideyoshi's service just before he conquered the area. He took part, as did Katō, in the conquest of Kyūshū, receiving the other half of the Higo province as a reward. From that moment on, as neighboring daimyō, there were problems between the two, mainly because Konishi was a Christian—baptized as Agostinho—while Katō was a staunch supporter of the Nichiren school Buddhist doctrine and cruelly persecuted Christianity in his lands, which bordered Konishi's.

Once in Korea, as well as competing to claim the greatest number of conquests, their differences of opinion during the truce negotiations with China were crystal clear, since Konishi backed an understanding with the Ming as a pacific way out of the conflict, while Katō was a firm believer in total war, whatever the cost. The latter, known to the Koreans by the nickname Kishokan, "demon general," was famous for being a great warrior and lived purely to fight; the engravings in which he is seen hunting tigers with his spear in Korea during the—for him—boring truce are very famous.

With the war over after Hideyoshi's death, Katō ended up forming part of Tokugawa Ieyasu's bloc, which is probably one of the main reasons Konishi chose the opposing side. The two then fought in the armies that clashed at the Battle of Sekigahara, after which Konishi was executed; he refused—as a Christian—to commit suicide after the defeat, unlike many of his companions. For his part, Katō received his old enemy's lands as a reward, and henceforth possessed the entire province of Higo.

With Seoul conquered, Konishi and Katō parted ways: the first stayed in the capital for a while, while the second marched north pursuing the Korean king, who had fled. But as we were saying, from then on the advance slowed down considerably, and one of the reasons for this was the existence of a number of wide fast-flowing rivers in the northern region of the country, from which the Koreans had removed the boats they used to cross them and whose shallow zones the Japanese had absolutely no knowledge of. So, the second division was held up for weeks on the southern bank of the River Imjin and only managed to cross it on July 6 thanks to the Korean army's recklessness: safely stationed on the northern bank, the Koreans decided to cross the river in their boats to attack the Japanese, and were crushed by them, thereby handing the Japanese a means of transport to get to the other side. At that moment, it was decided that Konishi would be the one to advance toward Pyonyang in pursuit of the Korean king—accompanied by the third division—while Katō was entrusted with clearing a path to the north-east coast of the peninsula. As the remaining divisions arrived in Korea, they would be entrusted with securing the provinces in the southern half of the country. Moreover, the same policies that were being established in Japan in each new territory that was added to Hideyoshi's bloc were also applied here; so, taxes were collected from the population, weapons requisitioned, censuses drawn up and anyone who disagreed was eliminated.

Toward the end of July, Konishi Yukinaga reached the outskirts of Pyongyang with thirty thousand samurai and at that very instant the Korean king—who cannot have particularly trusted the ten thousand soldiers defending the city—decided to flee for the north once more, taking refuge almost on the border with China. The samurai found themselves with the same problem there they had faced on reaching the Imjin, since the city of Pyonyang was on the north bank of another fast-flowing river, the Taedong. The solution to the Japanese problem would once again be provided by the recklessness and overconfidence of the Koreans, who instead of remaining safely inside their fortress, decided to attack the Japanese camp with three thousand soldiers during the night of July 22. Although at first the Korean offensive was successful, taking the Japanese by surprise, the situation soon turned around and the Japanese left just a few Korean soldiers alive in order to see how they returned to the city,

Fig. 8.4. Siege of Dongnae, one of the first battles of the
war. Korea Military Academy Museum, Seoul.

thereby discovering the shallow areas of the river where it could
be crossed. So, two days later, Konishi's army got to the north bank

ready to fight the seven thousand Korean soldiers that presumably must have been left in the city, but once again they found the place deserted—the defending troops had fled during the night.

As for Katō Kiyomasa, he arrived in the north-east region of Korea without any great difficulty, left half of his soldiers—ten thousand of them—in the city of Hamhung and started to advance along the coast, taking various cities and fortresses, many of which were abandoned after news of the Japanese victory at the Battle of Songjin on August 23 reached them. At one point in the campaign, Katō changed his heading and began to advance northwards, away from the coast, after being told that two Korean princes had fled in that direction. What he found on reaching the city of Hoery-ong, almost on the border with China, was that the two princes had been taken prisoner by the very inhabitants of the city, who despite being Korean had no liking for the far-off government of Seoul. They therefore handed the princes over to Katō along with another gift—the governor of the province. Since he was so close to the frontier, the Japanese general decided to make a small raid into the Chinese territory of Manchuria, at which point no fewer than three thousand Hoeryong men offered to accompany the Japanese forces, both as guides and soldiers. Once in Manchuria they clashed with the local clan, the Yurchen (later known as Manchurians), who were forced to retreat after suffering nearly ten thousand ca-sualties at the hands of the Japanese and Koreans. After this victory, the Japanese troops returned to Korea, to the northernmost tip of the coast, and from there went down to the point where they had turned off to penetrate the hinterland, thereby having taken the whole Hamgyong region, and by October 12 had met up with the ten thousand men they had left behind in Hamhung.

Up until then, the Japanese advance—lightning fast at first and a little slower afterwards—had been unstoppable and although the samurai generals were much more aware of the great difficulty of the objectives than Hideyoshi was back in Nagoya, for the moment everything was looking good for the Japanese. Things began to change at the start of 1593, when China decided to intervene in the conflict. But even before this, two other factors had already started to weaken the Japanese conquest from within Korea itself. Firstly, various groups of Korean civilians had started to fight the samurai throughout the conquered territory in a kind of guerrilla warfare, which also involved warrior monks, thus significantly harming the communications and transport network the Japanese had put in place. Secondly, and even more importantly, the Korean fleet defeated its Japanese counterpart in some decisive naval battles, preventing them from achieving one of their plan's fundamental objectives: to control the west coast sea routes so as to quickly transport both soldiers and supplies to the northern region of the country, which was essential when it came to the subsequent attack on China. These naval victories are still a source of patriotic pride within Korean history, which is not exactly teeming with triumphs, and the famous "turtle ships"—vessels covered with a kind of wooden armor—are always credited with a starring role. Despite this fame, the reality is that this type of ship's contribution was little more than anecdotal, and the difference came down to the Korean ships' use of heavy artillery, and above all the skill of Admiral Yi Sun Sin (AD 1545-1598), a real national hero in Korea, and deservedly so. As a result of the defeats suffered by the Japanese in the battles of Sacheon on July 8 and Hansando on August 13—along with other minor defeats—the samurai generals came to regard the conquest of China as something increasingly unfeasible.

As was mentioned earlier, the situation would become even more complicated with the appearance on the scene of the Chinese army, who finally decided to intervene to defend their Korean vassals, who were incapable of expelling the invaders by themselves. A small group of just three thousand soldiers had already made a raid in late August, attacking Pyonyang by surprise, but had easily been eliminated by the almost twenty thousand samurai who were in the city. China would enter the war—this time for real—in February 1593, sending an army of more than forty thousand soldiers. They would be joined by around ten thousand Koreans, made up of soldiers and volunteers, and around five thousand warrior monks. For their part, the samurai forces were already greatly depleted after several months of privation due to the lack of supplies reaching the city, which was almost cut off by the Korean guerrilla activity along the Japanese supply lines. From then on, the nature of the war changed and the Japanese had to go on the defensive, feeling themselves incapable of taking the next step in their plan, despite hardly having lost a battle.

In Pyonyang, the Chinese generals ordered a direct attack from all flanks, which was initially repelled by the Japanese harquebus fire, causing so many casualties the attacking soldiers were able to use the piles of dead bodies to scale the walls. The Japanese were greatly outnumbered and it was only a question of time before they would be defeated, so Konishi Yukinaga decided the only option was to withdraw and—as the Koreans had done before—the Japanese abandoned the city in secret during the night and headed for the safety of Seoul. Some fifty thousand samurai came together there since the situation in other northern parts of the country was similar to Pyongyang, with a lack of supplies and the Chinese army approaching. Japan was therefore forced to give up the entire northern half of Korea, the part that provided them with access to what was in theory the main objective of the entire campaign: China. In Seoul, things were not much easier either as the soldiers were becoming weaker and weaker. Although they won some important battles, like the Battle of Pyokje on February 26, they also suffered a heavy defeat trying to assault the fortress of Haengju on March 14. Finally, the Japanese generals reached an agreement with the Koreans and took the tough decision to leave the capital and regroup in the south-east coast of the peninsula, in a series of fortresses in Gyeongsang, the closest province to Japan. The Chinese troops then entered Seoul in mid-May to discover the city had been practically razed to the ground by the Japanese, who had set fire to a large number of buildings to cover their retreat.

With the Japanese concentrated on the south-east coast there were a few more battles, the most noteworthy being the Siege of Jinju Castle. This fortress had already resisted an attack in 1592 and

Hideyoshi took its conquest personally, sending reinforcements from Japan with the express purpose of achieving this. The siege lasted about five weeks and ended in the greatest defeat suffered by Korea in the entire war—a massacre in which no fewer than sixty thousand Koreans died. It was also the last battle of this first phase of the invasion; a stalemate had been established in which the Japanese were incapable of gaining more territory but seemed able to resist indefinitely in their strongholds. So both parties decided to call a truce and begin a negotiating process to find a peaceful solution to the conflict. This process would last around four years during which time more than forty thousand Japanese would live in Korea—in samurai castle-style fortresses, whose stone bases can still be visited today—doing the same thing they had done in Japan in peacetime. Thus, the action moved into the field of diplomacy, which can sometimes prove to be just as dangerous as the battlefield, or even more so.

Tallying up and Inspecting Heads

Traditionally, the samurai were in the habit of collecting the heads of the enemies they had defeated in battle so that later they could prove how many adversaries they had killed. This was essential so they could be duly accounted for and the samurai subsequently rewarded. In the case of the heads of generals or important figures, a whole ceremony was normally performed, beginning with the head being washed and its hair combed, followed by the blackening of the teeth with a special dye. They were then placed on a board or pedestal; at this stage, they were presented to the victorious army's leader for inspection, and sometimes later put on public display.

The fact these negotiations were only held between Japan and China is highly significant—at no time did either of them take into account what Korea might have to say on the subject. The Koreans were not even informed of what was being discussed, thus making it clear that China was not helping its vassal state out of the goodness of its heart, but was simply trying to get the Japanese to move away from its sphere of influence—the Chinese were protecting what was theirs. Since ancient times the Chinese Empire had played the role of regional center in East Asia, around which the rest of the countries revolved. They recognized China's superiority through diplomatic missions and tributes and in exchange for this submission the Chinese—among other things—conferred legitimacy on the kings of each country in question, giving them a gold seal declaring them to be monarchs recognized by China. And this Sino-centric system was what Japan was daring to attack—thereby altering the regional order—as was shown by the fact the King of Siam had offered the Ming military aid to fight the Japanese. It could be said that the negotiations between China and Japan to end the invasion of Korea were still-born, since the former insisted on the condition that the Japanese recognize their vassalage to China. Hideyoshi was in no way willing to do anything of the sort, stating more than once that Japan was "the country of the gods."

So, throughout the four years of negotiations there was nothing but misunderstandings; to start with, because the Taikō believed he was negotiating nothing less than China's surrender, as a result of which he drew up a document that established seven conditions. These included the four provinces of the southern half of Korea passing into Japan's hands, the resumption of Sino-Japanese commercial relations and one of the Ming emperor's daughters marrying the Japanese emperor—conditions that clearly contrasted with the reality of the situation. For its part, China was convinced it was negotiating Japan's submission. This was, above all, down to the people charged with the mediation between the two governments (Konishi Yukinaga on the Japanese side). Seeing the conditions their respective leaders demanded were overly ambitious and unacceptable for the other party, they often toned down the original words they were supposed to convey. In fact, they even went so far as to falsify the document containing Hideyoshi's demands with one in which Japan recognized Chinese superiority in exchange for much more modest conditions than the original ones, one of them being the recognition of the Taikō as the King of Japan, something Konishi thought would calm Hideyoshi down. The Ming showed themselves to be pleased with this new Japanese attitude and prepared everything necessary to accept the agreement, including a gold seal.

October 23, 1596, when the Chinese emissaries visited Osaka Castle, was supposed to be the day the end of the war would be agreed upon, but clearly, with both parties at the meeting, it would not take long for the truth to come out. At first, the Taikō appeared delighted with the gold seal which recognized him as the King of Japan, and at the ceremony celebrated the following day appeared wearing the Chinese-style monarchical robes that had been brought by the emissaries as a complement to the seal. In the exact moment the document drawn up by the Ming government was read out, peace was shattered. It did not include a single one of Hideyoshi's seven conditions and only referred to Japan's vassalage to China. The Taikō flew into a rage, proclaimed the negotiations over and declared the imminent start of a new invasion of Korea.

Second Invasion and Outcome

Although Korea had played no part in the misunderstandings or ruses of the negotiations, Hideyoshi blamed the Koreans for everything that had happened. And for him their guilt could be traced back to before the start of the campaign, for having refused to collaborate with Japan in the conquest of China. And since they were guilty, they deserved to be punished. As a result, during the second invasion—or second part of the invasion, in reality—the objective was no longer China, but to teach the Koreans a lesson and conquer their country. The Japanese troops therefore fought even more fiercely and committed all kinds of atrocities with the Korean soldiers and people as they advanced toward the north of the country. An enormous number of men were sent from Japan, who joined those already waiting in the fortresses of the northeast coast, forming an army of over one hundred forty thousand troops. This time the advance would be led by two divisions, called the "Army of the Right" and the "Army of the Left," respectively, made up of thirty and fifty thousand soldiers.

The first battle happened on August 28, 1597, at Chilcheolly-ang. This was the only naval battle where the Japanese were victorious—maybe because it was the only one Admiral Yi Sun Sin did not take part in—and practically finished with the Korean fleet. As for the two Japanese armies, they would advance from the south-east coast conquering cities and fortresses; some were taken by force, as in the Siege of Namwon on September 26, and others

Account of the Atrocities

We have numerous Japanese accounts of the Korean campaign, but almost all limit themselves to praising the great deeds of the samurai who took part in the fighting. They are epic, bombastic tales which are very similar to the gunkimonogatari we talked about in Chapter 2. Undoubtedly they are a very useful source of information, but we must remember these are self-serving accounts, often written on the orders of a particular general for his personal glorification. So, we should be rather wary of what they say and always double check information in other sources.

But we said that *almost* all of them are like this because there is one exception: among all these documents the *Chōsen Nichinichiki*, stands out. It was written by Keinen (n.d.), a Buddhist monk who had journeyed to Korea as a doctor, accompanying the Bungo province's daimyō. The diary Keinen wrote is far from an epic tale of the grandeur and honor of combat. On the contrary, it details the atrocities committed by the Japanese army during the second invasion, which is when the monk joined the campaign. It describes in detail the scenes he himself witnessed in person, and on numerous occasions he compares what he has seen with hell itself. This idea is perfectly summed up in his phrase: "hell cannot be in any other place." This diary would turn out to be so embarrassing for Japanese governments it was completely ignored and remained unpublished for the better part of four hundred years, until 1965.

were found abandoned when the Japanese soldiers arrived, or were surrendered with little resistance, like the fortress of Hwangseoksan. The samurai armies thereby closed in on Seoul and set up their base nearby, awaiting the reinforcements and supplies that were supposed to arrive by sea, skirting the west coast of Korea.

These were essential for the assault on the capital since the Chinese had stationed a large army there to defend the city. But the Japanese reinforcements and supplies would never arrive, dashing the samurai's plans, and once again this was thanks to Admiral Yi. On October 26, 1597, an important naval battle took place at Myeongyang, roughly at the vertex of the peninsula's southern and western coasts. In what has gone down in the history of Korea as "the miracle of Myeongyang," Admiral Yi, with the only thirteen ships the Korean navy had at its disposal (which had survived Chilcheollyang by having withdrawn in time), confronted around one hundred thirty Japanese ships. They finished off more than thirty of them, thereby eliminating the transport that was needed to attack Seoul. When the news reached the Japanese generals posted near the capital, they saw that the attack would be impossible and that the best option was to—once more—pull back and fortify their positions in the south-east coast fortresses, and go on the defensive—yet again.

From that moment on, the Japanese army abandoned all plans of attack and the war became a succession of Chinese and Korean attempts to expel the samurai from their fortresses and from Korea. Perhaps the most important of these offensives was the Siege of Ulsan, on January 29, 1598, when they took advantage of the fact the walls surrounding the castle were still only half-built, which meant many Japanese soldiers still lived camped outside it, unprotected. At Ulsan, the Chinese and Koreans completely encircled the castle when they attacked, but despite their numerical superiority were helpless against the constant fire coming from the Japanese harquebuses; once again the accounts paint a picture of soldiers scaling walls thanks to the number of dead bodies piled on top of one other. Katō Kiyomasa's forces were able to hold out inside the

Fig. 8.5. Fragment of a painting depicting the
siege of Ulsan. Fukuoka City Museum.

fortress until February 8, when reinforcements reached the area
and the Chinese generals, fearing an attack in their rearguard,
ordered the retreat.

Ulsan was a heavy blow for China, and since the Ming were not
prepared to see it happen again, they mobilized an even larger army
to fight the Japanese. They came to have more than one hundred
thousand soldiers on Korean soil, which meant Hideyoshi's army
was outnumbered for the first time, especially after around seventy

thousand Japanese soldiers left Korea because the south-east fortresses could not accommodate more than sixty thousand men. The war thus seemed doomed to last quite a bit longer and cost tens of thousands of more lives; neither of the two sides seemed willing to give up, and on the horizon all that could be seen were long sieges of the Japanese bases—which could be reinforced with more troops brought from Japan—by a Chinese army that could always be supported by more troops.

But in September 1598 everything changed with the death of Toyotomi Hideyoshi, which was discussed in the preceding chapter. The five generals in the council that succeeded him in the government were very clear that they should leave Korea as soon as possible, and try to bring as many Japanese soldiers back alive as possible. In order to achieve this, they felt it wise to keep the Taikō's death a secret while the evacuation of the Korean fortresses was carried out. Over the three months it took to complete the process, the Chinese and Koreans—unaware of the news—continued their ceaseless attacks on several fortresses, such as Ulsan—once again—Sacheon and Suncheon: in the second Siege of Ulsan the Chinese found themselves forced to retreat, just like the previous time; in Sacheon they suffered the biggest defeat of the entire war, as a large burial mound in the area still bears witness today. In it no fewer than thirty thousand Chinese soldiers' corpses are buried—without their noses; and in Suncheon, the battle ended with another retreat by the attackers. As in most of the conflict, the Japanese were winning the battles, but losing the war.

They signed off, though, with a defeat, as the final battle of the whole campaign would take place at sea. At the Battle of Noryang, on December 17, 1598, the last of the Japanese were already leaving the Korean peninsula when they were attacked by the invincible and indefatigable Admiral Yi Sun Sin. The Korean fleet finished off half the Japanese ships that set sail from the continent that day, but not satisfied with this, Yi then ordered the pursuit of the ships that had managed to escape the attack. This was perhaps an excess of greed, which he would pay for dearly, as a Japanese harquebusier aboard one of the ships being chased managed to shoot the admiral and end his life. So, one of the last people to die in the entire war was one of the main architects of the Japanese defeat. At the end of that December, the last Japanese ships reached the Bay of Hakata.

The Great Nose Mountain

During the invasion of Korea, the Japanese soldiers caused so many casualties that the samurai practice of collecting their fallen enemies' heads soon became impractical, since they had to be sent to Japan to be checked and tallied and took up a lot of space on ships, which had to be virtually set aside for that purpose. So they opted to only collect noses (which were much smaller and lighter) and send them to Japan in barrels, preserved in salt. These days, in Kyoto, there is still a knoll called Mimizuka—although it is given little publicity as a tourist attraction—under which all these thousands of Korean noses are buried. The mound was erected on the grounds of a temple by order of Hideyoshi himself to watch over the souls of the buried noses' former owners, and at first was named Hanazuka, which literally means "nose mound," but sometime later was

Fig. 8.6. Mimizuka.

inexplicably changed to the present-day "ear mound." Most Japanese are unaware of its existence or downplay its importance, and the visitors who go to Mimizuka are almost always Korean tourists who want to pay their respects and pray for the souls of the dead who are partially buried there. Strangely, the Koreans are more interested than anyone in preventing the place from being destroyed and preserving it there as a reminder of the atrocities committed by the samurai. The Shintoist shrine right beside the mound is Toyokuni-jinja, built in 1599 to be consecrated to—of all people—Toyotomi Hideyoshi.

We talk of a Japanese defeat because Japan failed to achieve any of its objectives, but this does not mean there was a Korean or Chinese victory: once more the outcome of the war was defeat for all of the contenders. Japan had lost thousands of lives and an enormous quantity of resources such as ships, weapons, supplies, etc. China had also lost thousands of lives and in turn an enormous quantity of resources. This loss had added to an economic crisis the Ming government had already been dealing with, considerably worsening it and was one of the reasons behind the fall of the dynasty half a century later. And Korea had lost more than anyone, both in terms of human lives and resources, since the fighting had occurred in its territory and its population had been massacred, robbed and raped at the hands of the Japanese army—and of the Chinese army, however strange that may seem and however much it tends to be kept quiet. The Koreans had also suffered the great humiliation of seeing China and Japan deciding their future without ever asking their opinion. The country would take several generations to recover. Moreover, it would be invaded twice in the seventeenth century by the Manchurians, who by the time of the second invasion would be ruled by the Qing dynasty. So here we bring to a close this little digression, which should be situated chronologically within the preceding chapter.

CHAPTER 9

The Tokugawa Shōgunate

Ieyasu, Laying Down the Foundations of the Dynasty

At the end of Chapter 7, Tokugawa Ieyasu took control of the whole of Japan after the famous Battle of Sekigahara, in1600. After this he inaugurated the shōgunate that bears his name (and the period that bears the name of his government's capital, Edo) on being named shōgun in 1603 by Emperor Go-Yōzei. For that to happen, he had to prove he was a descendant of the Minamoto, a condition that, let us recall, Ashikaga Yoshimitsu had introduced as a requirement for obtaining the title. The kinship claimed by Ieyasu was somewhat distant and the proof presented rather scant and not particularly convincing, but when it came to the crunch what really counted was the power one had, and Ieyasu had little trouble proving he had plenty of that at that point in time. Nor had anyone believed for one second, a few decades earlier, that Toyotomi Hideyoshi, the son of humble peasants, was a descendant of the Fujiwara when he took the title of kanpaku. But that hardly mattered in the case of someone who could muster more than one hundred thousand soldiers on the battlefield without batting an eyelid. In fact, it was very common in that period for those who had become samurai recently—before Hideyoshi himself banned mobility between classes—to invent supposed lineages that related them to distinguished bushi family lines of the past to further legitimize their membership of this elite.

In any case, just two years later, Ieyasu decided to abdicate as shōgun in favor of his son Tokugawa Hidetada (AD 1579-1632), to then take up the role of *ōgosho*, or retired shōgun, despite which—and this should by now come as no surprise to us—he continued to wield real power for the rest of his life, from his new castle in Sunpu, in present-day Shizuoka. However powerful Ieyasu may have been, nothing could guarantee him that after his death his successor would be capable of keeping control of the country; the two previous rulers of Japan had been just as powerful as him, but when they died, power had not lasted long in the hands of their families and this is something Ieyasu himself had witnessed—and even contributed to in the case of Hideyoshi.

The Tokugawa hegemony, despite the victory at Sekigahara, was still very fragile and to a large extent based on a whole series of pacts and alliances Ieyasu had managed to forge thanks to the marriage of his no fewer than eleven sons and five daughters with members of other important bushi families. But nothing guaranteed these alliances would outlive Ieyasu himself, so he had to strengthen his family's grip on power before dying. One of the mechanisms he found to avoid the question of the succession to the shōgun's position becoming a moment of dangerous weakness was for it to be carried out when he was still alive and in possession of all of his faculties. Although, as was seen earlier, he was not the first one to think of this. In addition, the fact he had so many children allowed Ieyasu to establish several secondary lines of succession to guarantee the existence of an heir in the event of their not being one in the main line. These three family branches were known as *sanke*, "the three houses," and originated from Ieyasu's ninth, tenth and eleventh sons. They were allowed to keep the Tokugawa surname while almost all the others returned to the previously used Matsudaira. Maintaining these reserve lines of succession, if they may be called that, might seem overly cautious to us, but sometime later it would prove necessary to resort to this mechanism to choose the eighth Tokugawa shōgun. Logically, these measures related to the succession were not enough to ensure the dynasty's success, and the first three Tokugawa shōgun had to apply a whole series of policies aimed simply at maintaining stability. They were so successful their government managed to last right up until 1867, always headed by a Tokugawa, fifteen of them in all.

The main focus of instability the Tokugawa had to deal with urgently stemmed from the two blocs the country's daimyō had divided into for Sekigahara; defeat on the battlefield alone was not enough to solve the problem and an opposition that was too strong would not make things any easier for the new bakufu. So, no fewer than 88 rival daimyō were eliminated after the battle and their fiefdoms confiscated. At the same time, many others saw their territories reduced or were transferred to other regions, thereby severing their traditional ties to a particular area. This should not be seen as repression or cruelty that was anything out of the ordinary for the Japan of the age, since these punishments were commonplace. Likewise, the lands obtained after all this were assimilated by the shōgunate or shared out among his allies as a reward for their loyalty. Numerous new daimyō were also named, around seventy in the first two years, and their domains were considerably smaller than those of the ones who, shall we say, they substituted. The transfers both of old allies and of rivals were intended to shape a map in which the encirclement of isolated potential adversaries by trusted men would reduce the chances of any rebellion.

Moreover, the bakufu's own lands were surrounded by the territories of allies, who could protect them in case of any attack, and the same applied to Kyoto to prevent a rival daimyō from seizing the emperor. Furthermore, in spite of the fact all the daimyō were the shōgun's vassals, a classification was established which distinguished between two categories, depending on whether they had fought for or against Ieyasu at Sekigahara: the latter were called *tozama* daimyō. There were about eighty-five of them and the bakufu considered them a potential danger, despite the fact they were the ones who had been spared the executioner's block and had not been eliminated out of hand. The members of this group were forbidden from accessing all government posts and were always under suspicion. The fact some were Christian only added to the motives for this since they were liable to ally with the Europeans;

the first ones were called *fudai* daimyō, and numbered around a hundred seventy-five. They were considered the Tokugawa's true vassals, allowed to accede to official posts and their fiefdoms were located at strategic points such as great cities, important roads and, above all, close to tozama domains, with the aim of keeping watch over them. The shōgunate's wariness toward the tozama would be shown to be justified centuries later.

Before he died, Ieyasu was able to remove the greatest potential threat to his dynasty—which was none other than the existence of Hideyoshi's heir, his son Toyotomi Hideyori. The latter had been confined to Osaka Castle since the defeat of his supporters at Sekigahara, but as long as he was alive, there was the risk that some of his former followers—all of them tozama who were not particularly satisfied with their current situation—would rise up and call for his return. Until 1614, Ieyasu had treated Hideyori cordially and he had even become related to the Tokugawa marrying one of Hidetada's daughters in 1603, when he was still a boy. But that year a strange incident related to a bronze bell—or perhaps he used this as a pretext—caused Ieyasu to adopt a suspicious attitude toward Hideyori, going so far as to ask him to send his mother to live in Edo as a guarantee and sign of good faith—a request that was intolerably refused. Moreover, Osaka had for some time by

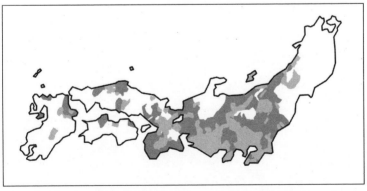

Fig. 9.1. Territorial distribution: tozama (white), fudai (dark gray) and Tokugawa bakufu (light gray). Author's own drawing.

then been witnessing the arrival of numerous samurai who had found themselves bereft of a lord after the elimination of tens of daimyō for opposing the Tokugawa at Sekigahara, and even some tozama—especially the Christians from the south—were also moving to the area with a large number of soldiers. Conflict was thus becoming inevitable.

At the end of that very year 1614, Ieyasu decided to launch an attack on Hideyori, beginning what is known as the Siege of Osaka, which would be divided into two campaigns (winter and summer) and would be the samurai's last armed conflict for more than two centuries.

The Hōkō-ji Bell Incident

Ieyasu knew Hideyori had a great fortune, which he had inherited from his father, and this was a reason for him to worry about and distrust the Taikō's son, so he pressured him into spending large sums of money on the reconstruction of various temples and shrines. One of these temples was the Hōkō-ji, in Kyoto, and as part of the renovation works, a large bronze bell had been forged, which included a series of inscriptions carrying good wishes, as is the custom with these objects. But within these inscriptions there were some words that Ieyasu was none too happy with. He felt they went against him, and took them to be either curses or simply public criticism. To begin with, there was a phrase that at first glance said nothing more than "may the country be peaceful and prosperous," but two of the four characters it was made up of are the same ones that are used to write the name *Ieyasu*, and he interpreted this as an offense and bad omen, based on an ancient Chinese taboo about the writing of first name characters. In addition, part of the inscription, in the phrase "may both the ruler and the servants be wealthy and contented," which was also made up of four characters, the two characters from Toyotomi's surname appeared and the meaning could be interpreted as wishing for this family to rule again.

So, the inauguration ceremony was suddenly interrupted by emissaries of the shōgunate and the complete cancellation of the bell's consecration was ordered. This incident caused a radical change in Ieyasu's attitude toward Hideyori, although it seems a rather insufficient motivation on its own and the most widely accepted opinion is that the Tokugawa leader simply used this event as a pretext to eliminate the Toyotomi.

Fig. 9.2. Part of the Hōkō-ji bronze bell, with the "controversial" characters highlighted in white.

The figures are around two hundred thousand attackers against about one hundred fifteen thousand defenders in the winter campaign, and around one hundred fifty thousand attackers against ninety thousand defenders in the summer campaign. Officially, the attack was led by Hidetada, who held the position of shōgun, but once again it was his father who was the one really in charge. This was not only because he was also the one who ruled the country *de facto*, but because he had extensive military experience too, while his son had only taken part in the Battle of Sekigahara. And he had not even formed part of the main front there, having arrived late because he had been held up laying siege to a castle on the way—something that his father apparently never forgave him for. The situation differed little in the other bloc: Hideyori was nominally the leader, but in reality left the strategic decisions to his generals, the most important of whom was Sanada Yukimura (AD 1570-1615), who had already fought against Ieyasu at Sekigahara and from then on had been forced to live as a monk.

Throughout the month of December, the Tokugawa side's troops took up positions near the castle, having won a few minor battles on the way relatively unopposed, due to the other side's decision to take a defensive stance and barricade themselves inside the castle, which was reputed to be the most impregnable in Japan. Its defenses had also been greatly improved by Sanada over the preceding weeks. When the fortress was finally attacked in the first days of January 1615, its reputation proved to be well deserved and one of the fortifications Sanada had built (dubbed Sanadamaru in his honor) turned out to be a stone in the attacking army's shoe. Ieyasu then ordered the castle to be bombarded, which was highly unusual in Japanese battles, using large cannons he had obtained from the trade with the Dutch and English thanks to his adviser William Adams (AD 1564-1620). The artillery attack began on 8th January, and greatly intensified a week later. Although it did not cause major structural damage, since the great stone bases of Japanese castles made them almost impervious to cannon-fire, the intention was to psychologically sap the defenders; in this respect, Ieyasu's tactic was indeed successful, and Hideyori found himself forced to propose a truce to negotiate a surrender.

William Adams

In Chapter 6, when we were talking about the contact between Japan and Europe, we focused on the first stage of this contact, initially monopolized by the Portuguese and later widened to include the Castilians when the two nations united under the same king in 1580; but they were not the only two European nations to set foot on Japanese soil. In April 1600, a Dutch ship named Liefde, with its crew fading fast, reached the coast of the Bungo province (currently in the Ōita prefecture), piloted by an English sailor called William Adams.

We have little information about Adams's past prior to his arrival in Japan, and what we do know comes from the letters and diaries written by the man himself. It seems he was born in Gillingham and as a young man fought against Philip II's famous Spanish Armada. His story, though, starts to be of interest to us ten years later, in June 1598, when he signed on in Rotterdam as the pilot of a ship whose mission was to reach the Indies via the dangerous Cape Horn to obtain the spices and Asian products which at the time were monopolized by Castile and Portugal, enemies of both England and Holland (at the time called Republic of the Seven United Netherlands). The fleet was made up of five ships, but only three of them managed to make it to Pacific Ocean waters, and only one, Adams's Liefde, reached Japan, with barely two dozen crew members aboard, most of them sick. Logically, the Jesuits were none too happy when Adams and his men turned up, as this was even worse than the arrival of the friar orders seven years earlier, since these Dutchmen were also enemies of their Crown and not even Catholics—this at a time of great rivalry between Catholics and Protestants. What Japan knew about the rest of the world had until then been filtered by the Portuguese and Castilian priests, who were also the only source of information in Europe of what was happening in that part of Asia, but this state of affairs was now in danger.

So, they wasted no time in accusing the new arrivals of being pirates and thieves, and asked the Japanese authorities to expel or even execute them—they would do the same thing with the English, who arrived a few years later. Ieyasu ordered a representative of these new Europeans to meet with him in Osaka—at that time he was one of Hideyori's five regents, this just before Sekigahara, and there he got to talking with Adams, who gave him a rather different vision of European political and religious affairs from the one he had had until then. Incidentally, this interview obviously had to take place through an interpreter, and only the Jesuits were qualified for that. From then on, Adams became Ieyasu's adviser on all matters related to foreign trade and politics, sharing these tasks with others, including the Portuguese Jesuit João Rodrigues (AD 1560-1634). He was known as Tçuzu, "the Interpreter," both for his remarkable knowledge of Japanese (he was the author of the first Japanese-Portuguese dictionary and of the first Japanese grammar) and for being Ieyasu's official interpreter. This adviser's post carried with it privileges and duties, and the former included being officially named *hatamoto*, which is normally translated as "standard bearer." In the Edo period, this meant being in the direct service of the shōgunate, thus occupying a very high position within the samurai ranks, which is exactly what Adams would henceforth be—a samurai. As hatamoto, he was given a property valued at between 150 and 250 koku in the Miura peninsula (modern-day Kanagawa prefecture), close to Edo. From then on, in Japan he was named Miura Anjin after his fiefdom (the second word means "pilot" in Japanese). His main duty was subsequently to remain in Japan, he was not permitted to return to Europe and had to abandon the wife and two children he had in England. Sometime later he got married

Fig. 9.3. Painting which has been used to portray William Adams since 1934, although there is no contemporary image of him.

to a Japanese woman, who he had two children with, and we know he also had a consort in Hirado with whom he had another child, born after Adams's death. But it seems he always took financial care of his English family, periodically sending them money once the sea traffic with the Dutch and English had been normalized.

The merchants from these two countries arrived in 1609 and 1613 respectively, and Adams took part in the negotiations between them and the bakufu, although his importance both in this and in other events has been greatly exaggerated—the Japanese sources downplay his role to that of a mere interpreter. As for the hostile posture the bakufu would end up adopting toward Christianity, the documentation also greatly plays down the English sailor's influence, but the Catholic missionaries laid most of the blame on him, perhaps because it is always easier to blame an outside enemy than to carry out self-criticism. Adams died in Hirado in 1620 and was quickly forgotten. His persona was not revived until the end of the nineteenth century, in England, and became quite popular after 1934, when a serial saga was published narrating his life, albeit adding large doses of fiction and exaggerating his influence in the Japanese context. Despite its lack of truthfulness, this text laid the foundations for many later ones and created a mythologized image of Adams, which has been adopted in literature, television and even a musical.

The negotiations lasted a few days and finally an agreement was reached by which Hideyori solemnly promised never again to oppose the Tokugawa and to consult them about all his decisions and movements; in exchange, Ieyasu spared the lives of all his generals and soldiers and allowed both Hideyori and his mother to stay in Osaka or move to whichever province they wished, where they would be given a fiefdom equivalent to the one they had at the time. But this treaty was doomed to failure before it was even signed, since neither side really intended to abide by it. Ieyasu had not started this war to leave things as they were before it began— before he died he had to finish what he had started at Sekigahara

Fig. 9.4. The present-day reconstruction of Osaka Castle.

so his dynasty would have some chance of remaining in power. So, he took advantage of the recently signed truce to order his men to demolish the castle's outer defenses, arguing they were no longer necessary since they had made peace. As for Hideyori, he and his generals were planning to attack Kyoto to take the emperor and pressure him into officially declaring the Tokugawa traitors to the empire. At the end of May, this climate of mistrust led to Ieyasu attacking the already weakened castle, on the pretext that a large number of troops were gathering again in Osaka. Yet, at the same time in Osaka they were saying that these troops were returning precisely because of the rumors of a new attack by the Tokugawa. Whatever the truth of the matter may have been, Ieyasu sent armies from Kyoto to attack the castle, but they were surprised half-way there by a Hideyori army, resulting in a battle which signified the commencement of the summer campaign of the Siege of Osaka.

This second campaign did not develop like a classic siege, as had been the case with the first campaign, since Hideyori's side knew the castle would not hold out for long without the outer defenses Ieyasu had demolished during the short ceasefire. As a result, they opted to leave the fortress to fight out in the open and halt the attackers' advance there. Over the course of just a few days there were several battles—Dōmyō-ji, Yao, Wakae—in which the Osaka forces were either defeated or made to retreat, until on 4th June the final battle was fought, the Battle of Tennō-ji. Here, the Tokugawa armies, which were larger and better organized, gained one position after another and advanced on the castle (taking several prized heads on the way, such as Sanada Yukimura's). They reached the castle gates on the afternoon of that same day and it was soon enveloped by flames. Seeing they were defeated, many of the Osaka bloc's generals committed suicide, while Hideyori took refuge in a storehouse with his mother and sent his wife—let us recall, Hidetada's daughter—to negotiate with the attackers. The following morning, having received no news, Hideyori committed suicide, followed by his mother. Just a few days later, Ieyasu ordered the beheading of Hideyori's son, who was barely seven years old, thus ending the short-lived Toyotomi dynasty.

Tokugawa Ieyasu himself did not live much longer, dying just one year later, it is believed of stomach cancer. He was ill for quite a few days, which gave him time to meet with his son Hidetada several times, and with his main generals and advisers. Right up until the end he was giving instructions about how things should be done when he was no longer around. Unlike Hideyoshi, Ieyasu died with the satisfaction of having left no loose ends, with a successor who had already been shōgun for years, a grandson who seemed more than fit to succeed him one day, the main threat recently eliminated and the least trusted daimyō under control.

Hidetada and Iemitsu: Stabilizing the System

Although Ieyasu had laid down the groundwork for the dynasty's success, both Hidetada and his son Iemitsu (AD 1604-1651) had to finish the task of securing a system that would provide the stability needed for it to endure. In the absence of military victories like the ones that had legitimized Ieyasu's hegemony, his two successors developed and implemented a series of strategies and policies already set in motion by the ōgosho before he died—some had been established even earlier by Hideyoshi—which may be divided into three core areas: legitimacy through closer relations with the imperial court, stability through a series of laws that completely regulated all aspects of society, and the creation of an ideological framework justifying the need for a military government and obedience to it.

Regarding the Kyoto court, the Tokugawa needed to be able to have a connection with the nobility and the royal family, because although they were the ones who held real power, the court still had great symbolic importance. In fact, theoretically, the shōgun were nothing more than the emperor's vassals and were not considered part of the nobility, which meant that within the aristocratic hierarchy, any noble, even the lowest of them, outranked the Tokugawa. It was not enough to have Kyoto surrounded by the domains of trusted samurai lords, it was also necessary to control the court from within. For this reason, the Tokugawa began to employ the same strategy others had already used in the past: directly link oneself to the imperial family though marriage. So, Hidetada married one of his daughters to the emperor, and their daughter became the reigning empress in 1629, aged just five, to be known as Empress Meishō (AD 1624-1696)—the first case of a reigning empress since the end of the eighth century.

Back in 1615, with Ieyasu still alive, the bakufu had published an edict known as Buke Shohatto, which consisted of just thirteen very specific articles laying down various regulations to be applied to the way of life of the samurai class:

1. The samurai must devote themselves to those tasks which are inherent to the warrior aristocracy, such as archery, swordsmanship, equestrianism and classic literature.
2. Leisure and entertainment must be kept within reasonable limits and must not involve excessive expenditure.
3. Fiefdoms must not give refuge to fugitives and outlaws.

Portrait of an elderly samurai in formal
attire by Ogawa Kazumasa (1860–1929).

Bushi by Adolfo Farsari (1841–1898), an Italian photographer who
moved to Japan in 1873 and established his studio in Yokohama.

Kumamoto Castle in 1902.

Charles King Dillaway and his Japanese students Hanabusa
Kotaro, Hiraga Isasaburo, Tsuge Zengo, and Aoki Yoshihira,
ca.1890. Photograph by Antoine Sonrel (? -1879).

KIOGOKU NOTONO KAMI.

Envoy to England in 1862.

Envoy to England in 1862.

Archer, by Felice Beato (1833/4–1909),
British photographer who lived in
Japan between 1863–1884.

Japanese warrior with armor,
unknown date and author.

Verbeck's mysterious photograph

Guido Verbeck (1830–1898) was a Dutch Protestant missionary who arrived in Nagasaki in 1859 and for a few years taught Western languages, science and politics to young people from samurai families, among whom were some of the future leaders of the restoration and the Meiji government. Years later he became one of the most influential foreign advisors of the new government.

This photograph of a group of samurai surrounding Verbeck is a mystery about which Japanese historians have discussed at length. The only facts that we can give for certain are that Verbeck himself appears on it and that it was taken by the photographer Ueno Hikoma (1838–1904) in his own studio in Nagasaki. The date has not been determined exactly, although it is believed that it could be dated between 1865 and 1868. This is a crucial fact since, depending on the exact moment, some of the samurai believed to be accompanying Verbeck may or may not be in fact in the photo. There is even doubt about the identity of the child the missionary has on his knees. The most accepted theory is that it is his son William, but others defend that it is his daughter Emma. Verbeck himself sent this photograph to the United States –where he came from despite being Dutch– and in the accompanying letter he mentioned that some of the samurai were currently important politicians and that one of them was prime minister. We have seen in this book some of the famous names that are considered to appear in this photograph, such as Saigō Takamori, Sakamoto Ryōma or Katsu Kaishū, but there is still no consensus on this.

Harakiri by Kusakabe Kimbei (1841–1934).

Recreation of an execution
by Felice Beato (1833/4–1909).

Samurais with armor by Kusakabe Kimbei (1841–1934).

Members of the Ikeda Mission in 1864 in
Paris photographed by French photographer
Nadar (Gaspard-Félix Tournachon).

Satsuma daimyo vassals in 1863 by
Felice Beato (1833/4–1909).

Samurai with bow, 1863 by
Felice Beato.

Samurai with katana, 1863
by Felice Beato.

Portrait of Japanese officers
in Nagasaki, 1868.

Young noble of Satsuma portrayed
by Felice Beato (1833/4–1909).

Men dressed as ancient samurai, by Kusakabe Kimbei (1841–1934).

Shimazu Hisamitsu, of the Satsuma clan, surrounded by his vassals.

Ikeda Nagaoki (1837–1879).

Portrait of a samurai with armor in 1880, by Adolfo Farsari (1841–1898).

Sakamoto Ryoma (1836–1867).

The samurai escorts of the Dutch diplomatic mission in Nagasaki in 1863.

Samurai looking to the right (1875), photograph by
Baron Raimund Von Stillfried (1839–1911).

Samurai (ca. 1890), portrait by Ogawa Kazumasa (1860–1929).

Samurai of the Satsuma clan during the Boshin wars, by Felice Beato.

Shimazu Uzuhiko, 26 years old, 1869,
portrait by Uchida Kuichi (1844–1875).

Portrait of Hitotsubashi Yoshinobu during his brief period as the last shogun of the Tokugawa family (1866–1867).

Shimazu Uzuhiko with Satsuma clan soldiers during the Boshin wars.

Portrait of samurai Harada Kiichi in Nagasaki, by Ueno Hikoma (1838–1904).

Yakunin (ca.1860–1861), photograph attributed to August Sachtler.

4. The daimyō must eject rebels and criminals from their service and banish them from their lands.
5. The daimyō will not maintain relations with people from other fiefdoms, regardless of whether or not they are from the samurai class.
6. Castles must be repaired as and when necessary, but the bakufu must be informed whenever this occurs; enlarging castles or introducing structural innovations to them is forbidden.
7. The bakufu must be informed immediately of the development of revolts or conspiracies in neighboring fiefdoms. The same applies to improvements to fortifications or other defenses, or the build-up of military forces.
8. Marriages between daimyō and powerful or important people must not be organized in private.
9. The daimyō must report to Edo to serve the bakufu.
10. The rules relating to formal attire must be followed.
11. Commoners must not be carried in a palanquin.
12. Samurai must lead a frugal lifestyle.
13. The daimyō must choose their most skillful men to work as administrators and bureaucrats.

Among several theoretically fairly innocent articles and others aimed at improving the samurai's ethical behavior, a number stand out that were clearly intended to keep the daimyō under control (although it is not stated explicitly, they were mainly aimed at the tozama). For example, notice how any type of relationship between different fiefdoms is prohibited, and how marriages involving a daimyō must be authorized by the bakufu. Both these measures were designed to avoid the lords forming alliances. Notice also how Article 7 effectively makes all the daimyō their neighbors' keepers. Two things are now crystal clear: it is the shōgunate that has the final say when it comes to the allocation of territories, and any daimyō can lose his domains if he fails to rule them well or follow the central government's laws. This was no idle threat, as was borne out by the fact almost a hundred of these lords lost their lands, or at least part of them, (there were even some cases involving fudai) by 1650. In the same period, there were also more than twice that number of inter-territorial transfers.

Hidetada devoted himself to applying these policies, which his father had devised before him, to connecting the bakufu to the imperial family—as was already explained—and, after 1623, when he abdicated as shōgun to become ōgosho just as Ieyasu had done, he threw himself into the persecution of Christianity. Back in his father's time, the bakufu had shown themselves to be very interested in boosting trade with Europe, and especially with Castile, via its Mexican territories in New Spain. But, over and over again, Ieyasu's attempts to establish commercial agreements were met with an exasperatingly slow reply from the Castilians. When it came, this always included two prior conditions: that Japan should expel the Dutch and English, and they should accept the sending of more Catholic priests. In fact, the Castilian court was not particularly interested in promoting trade with the Japanese at that time and simply wanted to keep on good terms with them. The reason being that on their journey from Manila to Acapulco, the Castilian merchant ships had to pass very close to the Japanese coast, and were often shipwrecked on it by storms. The Tokugawa grew tired of this situation: on the one hand, the Dutch and English seemed to have no interest in converting Japan and only acted to further their commercial interests; on the other, Catholicism was under suspicion of being a Castilian tool of conquest. In 1614, they finally decided to ban this religion on Japanese soil. Logically, the prohibition did not come into effect from one day to the next, and the process of persecuting Japanese Christians and expelling foreigners would take several decades to be completed.

Shōgun Iemitsu may be considered the architect responsible for perfecting his predecessors' systems, and this is most clearly seen in the review he introduced of the Buke Shohatto in 1635, in which he explained the original thirteen articles in more detail, extended their remit and added seven more. Regarding the existing articles,

Fig. 9.5. Tokugawa Hidetada, anonymous portrait,
in Tokugawa Memorial Foundation, Tokyo.

he spelled out more clearly how they were to be implemented. In all cases, these changes were intended to exercise greater control over the daimyō, who had to obtain the bakufu's authorization for an increasing number of matters, and abide by ever more specific regulations. Out of all of them, the old Article 9 was one that was greatly modified and described in great detail, becoming one of the most important articles and among those that would have the greatest impact over the course of the following centuries, and not just when it came to the control of the daimyō. This article now institutionalized a system called *sankin kōtai*, which had already been used by Hideyoshi on a much smaller scale. At first, it was only applied to the tozama, and forced them to maintain a residence in Edo, where their wives and children, along with some of their trusted retainers, had to live permanently. The daimyō themselves had to spend alternate years living in their fiefdom and in this residence in the bakufu's capital. Some exemptions were made for lords from faraway fiefdoms, who only had to come to the capital every three years and, exceptionally, some lords whose fiefdoms were very close by had to come at six-month intervals.

This practice was very useful, firstly because the family that stayed behind in Edo would obviously be held hostage by the bakufu in the event of the feudal lord in question's involvement in a revolt or conspiracy against the shōgun; but also because keeping two homes and organizing the frequent trips between them, with the thousands of people and the resources that implied, meant the daimyō incurred enormous expenses—generally amounting to around a third of their annual income—which made them weaker and thus easier to control. Just seven years later, this was extended to include all the daimyō, including the fudai. With the passing of time, this system had other consequences, such as the fact that by the end of the seventeenth century almost all of Japan's daimyō had been born and raised in Edo; while their fathers travelled back and forth between the capital and their fiefdoms, they were kept hostage with their captive families. As a result, these new daimyō considered Edo their home and the year they had to spend in their territories as almost a temporary banishment. In this way, the bond with their region and to an extent with their ancestors, was lost, which was also to the bakufu's advantage since it made rebellion against the central government less likely as the latter was no longer seen as some far-off alien entity.

As far as this second version's new articles are concerned, what stands out is the strict country-wide prohibition of Christianity (the daimyō were pressured into persecuting and repressing it in their territories) along with the ban on building large ships—something that had already been banned in certain provinces in 1609 and was aimed at restricting foreign trade. Over the following years, Iemitsu implemented more policies along these lines, increasingly restricting merchants' comings and goings and at the same time cranking up the persecution of Christianity. As a result, the English left voluntarily in 1623 and a year later the Castilians were expelled. In 1637 there was a peasants' revolt in Shimabara, near Nagasaki. Despite the fact the almost forty thousand rebels were mainly motivated by the dire economic situation the peasantry found itself in, many of them were also Christians, and from the bakufu's point of view, this is what made them more united and their protest better organized. The revolt was harshly put down and almost all the peasants executed. The Shimabara Rebellion has gone down in history as the end of Christianity in Japan, and went hand in hand with the expulsion of the Portuguese the very next year. In the end, foreigners were banned from entering Japan (nor were the Japanese living abroad allowed to return), and the Japanese were banned from going to other countries—this situation would hold firm throughout the entire Edo period. The Tokugawa government's isolationist policy has been called *sakoku*, "closed

Fig. 9.6. Tokugawa Iemitsu, anonymous portrait, in Tokugawa Memorial Foundation, Tokyo.

country" or, literally, "chained up country," although the term did not emerge until the beginnings of the nineteenth century and the extent to which the policy was adhered to has been exaggerated. There were exceptions to this closure to the outside world, since they continued to trade with the Dutch the whole time—albeit with many restrictions—and a degree of commercial contact was maintained with China, Korea and the Ryūkyū Islands.

Dejima

After 1638, the Dutch were the only Europeans authorized to trade with Japan, and only within the narrow confines of the small man-made island of Dejima, in Nagasaki Bay. The trade carried out there was basically in Chinese silk and all kinds of objects from Europe and south-east Asia, in exchange for copper, porcelain, gold and silver. The island had been constructed in 1634 to be used by Portuguese traders, but after 1641, with the Portuguese no longer in the country, the Dutch were moved there. It was a fan-shaped island, just 120 meters in length, 75 wide and had two access points: a dock for small boats and a bridge connecting it to *terra firma*. Both were guarded by Japanese soldiers, since nobody could enter or leave without a special authorization, which was only granted on very rare occasions. The Dutch personnel, some twenty or so people, lived under close guard. Their houses or belongings could be searched at any time by the Japanese officials and numerous restrictions were imposed on them, one of the most important being that they were not allowed to have any religious books. Whenever a Dutch ship arrived, the captain was expected to tell the Nagasaki authorities what was happening in the rest of the world, and some historians believe this was actually Japan's main interest in keeping the island of Dejima open to Dutch trade. Likewise, during the annual visit all the island's occupants were required to make to Edo to pay homage to the shōgun, they were also asked about any news from abroad.

Over the more than two hundred years the Dejima trading post was in operation, some of its residents went down in history for the part they played both in spreading Japanese

Fig. 9.7. Model of Nagasaki Bay, with the island of Dejima
at the bottom, Nagasaki Municipal Museum.

knowledge in Europe and European knowledge in Japan, especially those who had the task of working on the island as the Dutch company's doctors. In the initial period, the laws governing the exchange of Western knowledge were very strict, as the Tokugawa government was still very worried about the possible introduction of Christianity to Japan. This explains why, in the first few decades, information flowed almost entirely in one direction, from Japan to Europe. For example, numerous aspects of Japanese culture, society and religion became public knowledge in Europe thanks to the Dutch on Dejima (knowledge largely gleaned from what they learned on their trips to Edo). But what was even more important, sometime later, was the introduction to Japan of European knowledge, particularly in the fields of medicine and science. Once the Dutch trading post on Dejima had been operating for a few decades, the laws concerning contact with foreigners and their books were gradually relaxed, and by 1720 the dissemination of Western knowledge had been given free rein and a certain degree of private trade was permitted. As a result, the Dutch began to buy and sell books as well as all kinds of objects: clocks, maps, medical instruments, etc. All this Western knowledge came to be known as *Rangaku* (what we could call "Dutch studies"), which basically included medicine, military technology, natural sciences and the Dutch language, and was taught in some public schools and Buddhist temple seminaries.

The forcible opening of Japan to the rest of the world in 1854, which put an end to the Dutch commercial monopoly, made the Dejima trading post unnecessary and it closed down just six years later. In the following decades, the man-made island fell into disuse and the city of Nagasaki grew around it, reclaiming territory from the bay, as a result of which Dejima was joined to the mainland and swallowed up by a swarm of buildings. The government purchased the land in 1951, and after that they began to think about restoring Dejima, although it was not until the 1980s, and particularly in the 1990s, that they started to do so. In 1996 a process of restoration and archeological excavation was initiated and by 2000, coinciding with the 400th anniversary of the start of relations between Holland and Japan, the first phase (consisting of just five buildings), had been opened to the public. Since then, new phases have been worked on, with more buildings inaugurated and a large number of objects and artefacts excavated on the island have been put on display. It now amounts to a kind of theme park or open-air museum, which receives around four hundred thousand (mainly Japanese) visitors a year. The most ambitious plan for the future is to restore Dejima's island status, eliminating the surrounding buildings, creating new canals and diverting the course of both the River Doza and a freeway. This project, though, appears rather complicated to carry out if one looks at the map of present-day Nagasaki.

The Samurai and the Organization of the New Country

The Tokugawa's political system, which differed from those of the two previous governments, is normally called *bakuhan*, a word that springs from the combination of bakufu and *han* (which is what each daimyō's fiefdom came to be known as), since the shōgunate operated as a kind of federation or coalition with the feudal lords—both the fudai and the tozama. This two-tier system, which was already employed to a greater or lesser extent in Nobunaga and Hideyoshi's time, was introduced gradually, and had the central government managing at a national level, while the daimyō ran things at a regional level, in their own territories. Here, these Edo period daimyō had considerably more autonomy and power than the shugo governors that had preceded them. We thus see how the bakufu was continually having to strike a dangerous balance: on the one hand, the daimyō were given greater regional autonomy so they could take responsibility for running their lands, but on the other hand, they wanted to keep them under strict supervision and tightly controlled through the raft of aforementioned policies.

To achieve this, the shōgunate needed the daimyō to be efficient administrators on the one hand and worthy of their trust on the other—albeit under the watchfulness of their neighbors and with the threat of reprisals against their families who resided in Edo. As long as they met these conditions, they could rule their lands with almost absolute power. The bakufu did not exact taxes or tributes from them and they were allowed to keep whatever taxes they collected in their domains. In addition, they could—and indeed were obliged to—maintain an army, whose size was stipulated by a central government law and based on how large their territory was. In exchange, they had to fulfill the terms of the Buke Sho-hatto articles and, from time to time, provide the necessary finance and labor either for the various public works the bakufu decided to carry out, or for the construction or maintenance of buildings belonging to the shōgunate or the court. Some areas fell under the central government's jurisdiction alone and no other body had the right to appeal against its rulings.

There were generally around two hundred fifty fiefdoms during the Edo period, although the fact that at any time some could disappear or new ones be created meant about 540 existed in total at one time or another. They came in all shapes and sizes and many belonged directly to the shōgunate, where the country's largest cities were found. Only one castle was permitted per fiefdom, around which the new cities inhabited by the samurai, merchants and craftsmen sprung up (a process already seen in the Sengoku period), which served as a base from which to control the peasants.

In the social sphere, movement between classes was prohibited as a continuation of Hideyoshi's policy. Moreover, the classes were defined and ordered hierarchically following the classic Chinese Confucianist method, which considered the literati as the highest class, followed by the peasants, then the craftsmen and, finally, the merchants; but in the Japanese case, the samurai took the place of the literati. Apart from these four main classes, there was the court nobility and the clergy, who were formally left out of this social order—but were at the top of it—and the so-called eta and hinin, those marginalized for having professions considered taboo or for being prostitutes or beggars. The eta and hinin did not even appear within the social hierarchy since they were regarded as subhuman. This social model was not the only thing to be taken from Confucianism—the ideology became the shōgunate's official philosophy, known as Neo-Confucianism, with thinkers like Hayashi Razan (AD 1583-1657), who was adviser to the first four Tokugawa shōgun. His ideology and that of his colleagues and followers was instrumental in justifying the Edo period's new social order; it fostered values such as loyalty to superiors, whether within the same social class or between them, and stated each person had to accept the position they found themselves in within society—a doctrine that was undoubtedly beneficial to those whose social status placed them at the top of the pyramid.

And at the top were the samurai, who in turn were divided into different ranks. They were a privileged elite that now you could only be born into and accounted for about 6% of the population. Since the country had largely been at peace since 1615, only a few of them had military or police tasks, the rest were entrusted with bureaucratic or administrative work and many had no job to do at all. All of them, though, received a public stipend, either from the bakufu or from a daimyō, depending on which fiefdom they lived in. As the Edo period went by, samurai numbers kept on growing and the upkeep of this structure in times of peace, when it had been designed for wartime, meant an enormous and growing cost. The shōgunate, therefore, soon became reluctant to grant stipends to new family branches. In times of peace these warriors devoted their ample leisure-time to studying the Confucianist classics, just as the bakufu encouraged them to do, and in the case of the highest-ranking ones, to all kind of genteel hobbies.

A kind of high bushi culture developed, with a boom in arts like painting or ceramics, fostered by the arrival of numerous Korean potters brought from their country—i.e., kidnapped—during the invasion by Hideyoshi's troops, whose techniques were adapted to suit Japanese tastes. These high-class samurai began to immerse themselves in a life of luxury, becoming ever more like courtiers and less like warriors, above all when they lived in Edo, where they had to appear to be richer and more refined than the rest, showing their expertise in poetry, calligraphy, painting or in celebrating the tea ceremony. Both those of high-rank and the rest also occupied themselves with intellectual matters in their free-time. They were able to do this thanks to the education they had received as children in schools exclusively reserved for their social class. As a result, in the seventeenth century practically all the country's intellectuals belonged to samurai families. Some of them chose to give up their station in order to join the liberal professions, for example as writers or artists, thus contributing to the flourishing culture associated with city inhabitants, the so-called *chōnin*. In this way, the typical samurai ideology began to influence the rest of the urban population. In reality, a good proportion of the warrior class spent their days resting or frequenting the city's red-light district, often getting into trouble and in some cases even having to leave their masters' service after having committed some crime or other, thus becoming *rōnin* (samurai with no lord to serve), and thereafter devoting themselves to roaming the country, often making a living as mercenaries or bandits.

The court was outside this social order. The bakufu simply asked the courtiers to recognize it was the legitimate government and in exchange allowed them to carry on dedicating themselves to ritual tasks and leading an easy idle lifestyle. The clergy, who were also outside this social order, had been dispossessed of a large part of their wealth and lands and of all the political power they had wielded in previous centuries, and restricted themselves to administering their temples and shrines following the laws dictated by the shōgunate. They were also entrusted with checking that the daimyō prohibited and persecuted Christianity as the official policies required them to do.

The peasants were the most numerous class and the economic base of the entire system. Although they were more highly regarded socially—in theory—than the craftsmen and merchants, they were generally very poor and barely had enough to survive. They did not own the lands they worked, which belonged to the daimyō or the shōgunate, and they had to pay one or the other a percentage of their harvest in the form of a tax, which was normally around 40% or 50%, but very often rather more. For their part, the craftsmen and merchants did not at first have to pay so many taxes as the peasants, since both the daimyō and the bakufu were interested in attracting them to their cities, but with the passing of time, many of their activities would incur levies, whether they dealt in production, commercialization or consumer goods.

Despite their lowly status within the social order, many of them became progressively wealthier, even becoming more powerful than many samurai. In general, both for the craftsmen and merchants and even more so for the peasants, the fiefdom they lived in was their entire world, which they normally never left, and the central government nothing more than an abstract concept; they knew no other authority than the daimyō—unless they resided in a fiefdom that was owned by the bakufu. Traveling around the country was, like most things in the society of that time, very tightly controlled. There were better paths, roads and bridges than there had been prior to the Edo period, but far fewer of them, and numerous checkpoints to verify if a traveler had the corresponding and obligatory letter of safe-passage or authorization. Along this transport network, country-wide commerce was fostered, which was also influenced by the large number of samurai constantly traveling between their domains and the capital because of the sankin kōtai. As a result, Edo grew enormously in a short space of time and its customs and culture quickly spread around the country, helping, for example, to create a standardized Japanese dialect.

We could say the Edo period molded a new Japan and had a greater impact on the country's idiosyncrasy than any other period, both at an institutional level and socioculturally. Curiously enough, the picture of the samurai today appeared at the same time their *raison d'être* disappeared, although that shall come later.

CHAPTER 10

The Keichō Diplomatic Mission

The Project

The so-called Keichō Mission, a Japanese diplomatic expedition that lasted seven years and brought a number of samurai to Europe, was a relatively minor event in Japanese history, particularly within the context of the samurai. While it was fairly irrelevant its odd nature makes it deserving of a place in our tale. Undoubtedly wherever they went it was a real social event, although this was more down to the fact it was such an anomaly rather than to it having any real importance. Although its importance has been greatly exaggerated in the last few years, it was in fact quite a minor project really, given both its initial objectives and (above all) its non-existent results. It was not even the first project of its kind, since another Japanese expedition to Europe had been organized as early as 1582. In 2013, on the occasion of the 400th anniversary of this Keichō Mission, even generalist Spanish media began to talk about it, spreading the idea the mission represented the start of four centuries of Japanese-Spanish relations. As shall be seen throughout this chapter, nothing could be further removed from the truth, since it is much more a case of the end of the relations (which were poor and few and far between) that the two countries had maintained up until then. Quite simply, a noteworthy date was made the most of for political, diplomatic and commercial ends. Nevertheless, the commemoration should be celebrated because it brought with it a whole series of interesting cultural initiatives related to Japan, which is not something that happens every day. But let us now explain the story of the mission.

The Tenshō Mission

In 1582, the Jesuit Alessandro Valignano organized a Japanese diplomatic mission which would travel to Catholic Europe to meet the leading authorities and see the great cities of Portugal, Spain and Italy. The twin aims of the project were: first, to spread word of Japan and of what the Jesuits were doing there, in a striking fashion and in keeping with his conviction that knowledge can only be gained through personal experience. This was to be done through showing off actual Japanese so the Europeans might see not only how civilized they were—just as his letters and reports argued – but also how different and strange a people they were. This was to demonstrate to his ecclesiastical superiors that different strategies also had to be employed with the Japanese. Secondly, it was meant to show the Japanese the grandeur and splendor of Europe and of the Catholic Church, so that on their return they could tell others about this, help to improve the image the Japanese had of the nanban and make it easier to convert them.

Fig. 10.1. Article about the mission in a German newspaper of 1586. Top: Nakaura, the Jesuit accompanying them, Ito; bottom: Hara, Chijiwa. University of Kyoto archive.

The chosen few were four upper class samurai adolescents, who were relatives of Christian daimyō from Kyūshū and students of Jesuit schools; their names were Mancio Itō, Miguel Chijiwa, Martinho Hara and Julião Nakaura. Valignano argued, it was preferable to send such young men because they would cope with the hardships of the long return journey better, but we might suspect the real reason was that their youthfulness would also make them more impressionable and easier to handle, especially seeing as they had received a Christian education from the Jesuits themselves.

The trip lasted eight years during which they visited the main Portuguese bases in Asia and Africa en route to Europe, followed by Lisbon, Toledo, Madrid and Rome, and were received by public figures such as Philip II and popes Gregory XIII (AD 1502-1585) and Sixtus V (AD 1521-1590). They made a good impression wherever they went and it was a real event in the Europe of that period—in stark contrast, as we shall see, to the Keichō Mission. A curious anecdote from a reception with Gregory XIII, is that the Japanese youths delivered the pope a personal gift from Oda Nobunaga: a painting showing the city of Azuchi, crowned by the magnificent castle Nobunaga had ordered built there. This would not be so extraordinary if it were not for the fact this castle was standing when the mission left Japan, but had already been destroyed by the time the gift was delivered. What is more, it is the only pictorial representation known to have existed of the building. Unfortunately, the painting's current whereabouts are unknown.

In the first years of the Edo period, Date Masamune, a powerful daimyō from the country's north-east region (who appeared briefly in Chapter 7) showed a keen interest in benefiting from the trade with the Castilians and Portuguese, which until then, essentially, just a few lords from Kyūshū had profited from. To that end, as others often did, he did not hesitate to grant the Church all kinds of favors. He authorized the priests to preach in his vast territory and even encouraged his subjects to convert, something which he himself never did. In 1612, Date met Luis Sotelo (AD 1574-1624), a peculiar Franciscan father, who had been trying for some time to organize an expedition to Europe with the aim of asking King Philip III (AD 1578-1621) and Pope Paul V (AD 1550-1621) to send more Franciscan priests to Japan. The fact was Father Sotelo had few friends even within his own order—there are many rather unkind Franciscan reports about his person—and his superiors suspected that the real aim of this whole expedition business was to ask the pope to create a diocese in the northern region of Japan (independent of the Nagasaki one, controlled by the Jesuits) and to name him bishop of it. Date saw this expedition as the perfect opportunity to contact the King of Castile and Portugal directly in order to establish trading relations with New Spain and Europe, which would then have to be conducted through his domains. So, he decided to finance the costly trip, provided this commercial request was included as one of its main objectives. The expedition had the (rather unenthusiastic) permission of Tokuwa Ieyasu, Date's son's father-in-law, despite the shōgun having banned Christianity in Edo that very year 1612 and all the signs pointing to the policy spreading to the rest of Japan before much longer. Although he was aware of this situation, the lord of Sendai decided to go ahead with the project.

Date Masamune

Date Masamune is unquestionably one of the most popular daimyō in Japan, and was one of the most powerful ones of his age, another of those individuals whose star shone more brightly in the firmament of the Sengoku period than his family name had done until that time. The Date are meant to have descended from a branch of the Fujiwara and to have been given their territory in the north of the country by Minamoto Yoritomo himself after the Genpei Wars, as a reward for fighting for him in this conflict as well as in the following one to get rid of his brother Yoshitsune. For many years they were entrusted with the task of putting down the "barbarian" peoples of the country's northern region.

Masamune was born in 1567 and apparently he was a melancholic lonely child. It is believed his personality was a consequence of him being blind in his right eye; although it has traditionally been believed he was one-eyed, (his nickname, Dokuganryū, "one-eyed dragon" stems from this), recent discoveries seem to indicate he did have both eyes, but could not see with the right one. Whether that was due to some kind of defect, or because a piece was missing for some reason, is not clear. In any case, this led to even his own mother rejecting him—she did not consider him fit to be clan chief and preferred his younger brother to be the successor. But his father, Date Terumune (AD 1543-1585), did not agree with her and, when Masamune was eighteen years old, the leadership was handed over to him. From then on, Masamune threw himself into a ceaseless ferocious conquest of neighboring territories (which, by the way, was nothing unusual in the Sengoku period), putting the region's daimyō on alert. One of these families decided to kidnap Terumune to pressure his son, but when Masamune turned up at the head of his troops to rescue his father, Terumune

Fig. 10.2. Statue of Date Masamune in Sendai, Miyagi prefecture.

himself ordered them to launch an all-out attack, even if that led to his death. Masamune did what his father wished, knowing that he would be executed the moment the attack began, and then took his revenge by killing all the members of the opposing family. But not only did he have enemies outside his domains, he also had to fight the ones he had within his own house: his very own mother continued to want her youngest son to lead the clan, and did not hesitate to hatch a plan to end Masamune's life by poisoning his food; but the plot failed and the one-eyed dragon decided to put an end to the matter once and for all by executing his brother.

In early 1590—as we saw earlier—Hideyoshi controlled all of Japan, except for the territories held by the Hōjō and the Date, who had refused to recognize the supremacy of Nobunaga's successor. When Hideyoshi and his armies headed for Odawara to finish off the Hōjō in May, Date Masamune saw that once they had fallen, he would not resist for long either, so there was no choice but to bow down before the peasants' son. He thus decided to go to Odawara as well and surrender to Hideyoshi, knowing he would most likely be executed for having taken so long to do so. But, as we have seen before, Hideyoshi was not much given to revenge and punishments, especially when it came to valuable men who could be of more use to him alive and as allies. So, when the two met, what he did was to ask Date for advice about the best way to conquer Odawara Castle. Henceforth, he would be just another of the daimyō forming part of the federation led by Hideyoshi, and even took part in the attempted invasion of Korea, leading his armies there. Although while the Taikō lived there were continual rumors of the Date leader's plans and strategies to take over the country, the truth is no attempt at anything like that ever happened; Date had a reputation for being an ambitious man, so it is highly likely the idea had occurred to him, but he was also known to be very intelligent. So, he was surely aware of the difficulty of the undertaking, and realized it was not worthwhile risking his—it must be said—rather well-off position.

It was this very intelligence that quickly led him to see that once Hideyoshi was dead, the one who had the best chance of taking over the country was Tokugawa Ieyasu, with whom he had had good relations for decades. For Ieyasu it was also a good idea to count on the friendship of the powerful northern lord, so the two decided to seal their alliance through the marriage of their children. From that point on, Date remained forever faithful to the Tokugawa, fighting alongside them both at Sekigahara and at the Siege of Osaka Castle. And not only at Ieyasu's side; he was also one of the main advisers to his son Hidetada, as he was to his grandson Iemitsu. In fact, it was while he was visiting the latter in Edo that he died, aged sixty-eight, after having spent the final years of his life at peace, a state of affairs brought about by the Tokugawa government. This life of peace was too dull for a seasoned warrior like Date, who told the shōgun on his deathbed that he lamented not leaving in the manner befitting a soldier—on the battlefield. Even with his dying breath, he gave him a good piece of advice—to keep his samurai ever ready for war, because so much peacefulness made men soft and left them unprepared to face danger when it finally arose. History would prove him right some two hundred years later.

The expedition included almost one hundred fifty Japanese and was led by one of Date's most trusted lieutenants, Hasekura Tsunenaga (AD 1571-1622) and coordinated by Father Sotelo, who also had an advisory capacity and was entrusted with interpreting tasks. They set sail from Sendai, to the north of Edo, aboard the ship San Juan Bautista, on October 28, 1613.

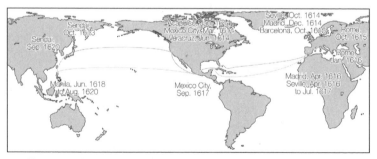

Fig. 10.3. Map of the Keichō Mission's route. Author's own drawing.

From Japan to Rome: Great Expectations

Carried on the Pacific Ocean currents, the ship reached Acapulco on January 25, 1614, after skirting the American coast down from California. The expedition members were met there by the Viceroy of Mexico, who equipped them with horses and all necessary supplies for the journey to Mexico City, which they reached on March 24. Once again they were received by the viceroy, in the Royal Palace, and after a solemn ceremony and all kind of celebrations, were granted permission to continue their journey to Europe. For his part, Hasekura handed the viceroy a letter written by his lord, Date Masamune, as well as various gifts.

This joyful warm atmosphere was disrupted when, shortly after the expedition's arrival in Mexico, numerous letters reached the viceroy bearing alarming news from Japan: the shōgun had just officially banned Christianity in the entire country, was expelling foreign priests, forcing Japanese Christians to abandon their faith, burning churches and executing everyone who refused to obey the new orders. In response to this situation, dozens of the Japanese who formed part of the expedition company decided to convert to Christianity and got baptized in Mexico, in an attempt to show their good intentions, notwithstanding the terrible news from Japan. But these tokens were not enough and the drastic change in the Japanese political situation had effectively doomed the expedition to failure. Quite obviously, they had lost all legitimacy to establish commercial relations with the Castilian leaders or those of other countries. Despite Father Sotelo's best efforts to keep the Mexican authorities' support, writing to the viceroy to defend Date and assure him the latter would not allow Christians to be persecuted in his lands, the expedition party ended up being completely marginalized and forgotten about.

Finally, they decided to leave Mexico behind and head for Europe, although the number of Japanese who remained in the expedition had fallen considerably: it is believed there were between twenty and thirty of them, since the rest had to return to Japan.

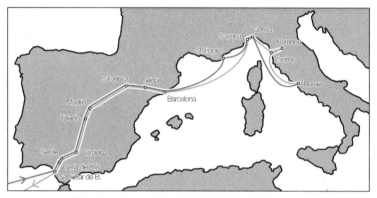

Fig. 10.4. Map of the Keichō Mission's European
route. Author's own drawing.

They set sail on May 29, 1614, calling at Veracruz and Havana, from where they left to cross the Atlantic.

On October 5, 1614, nearly a year after their departure from Japan, the expedition reached the Iberian Peninsula, making landfall in Sanlúcar de Barrameda, and from there they sailed up the Guadalquivir river as far as Coria del Río, the outer harbor of Seville and the place they would stay for several weeks. Later, great festivities were held in their honor in the city of Seville and they were welcomed by the mayor and church authorities, and given accommodation in the Alcázar Palace, a place normally reserved for high-ranking visitors, such as the royal family. The welcome they received here was far and away the best of the entire expedition, since Seville was Father Sotelo's hometown and he had close relatives in the local government promoting the visit. They gave greater prominence to Sotelo's name—who was heralded in pamphlets as virtually the most influential Christian figure in Japan—than to the Japanese envoys themselves.

In one of those gala dinners held in honor of the Japanese expedition, Hasekura handed the mayor a letter from Date Masamune, along with one from himself and two katana-*wakizashi* sets (the wakizashi is the other, slightly shorter sword, which usually goes with the katana). As for Father Sotelo, he lied when he described

Date as the most likely successor to Tokugawa Ieyasu, and himself as a personal envoy of the shōgun himself, while claiming Hasekura—rather than the two of them—represented Date. He also left out one or two minor details, such as the fact he had been condemned to death by Ieyasu not long before then and his life had only been spared thanks to the lord of Sendai's mediation. Nor did he mention anything about the expedition's commercial objectives. On November 25, 1614, the mayor of Seville presented the expeditionary group with several horse-drawn carriages so they could travel to Madrid, where they intended to have an audience with King Philip III, after visiting various religious authorities on their way through Córdoba and Toledo.

But by now the news of the prohibition of Christianity in Japan had also reached Madrid; ever since the start of the expedition, the court had been getting letters both from Japan and the Philippines, as well as from Mexico, about the Japanese political situation along with others concerning Father Sotelo's character. The Council of the Indies drew up a report for Philip III on October 30, 1614, informing him of these matters relating to Japanese current affairs and of Sotelo's lack of trustworthiness, and advising him to treat the Japanese well—among other things because they had a reputation for being warlike. However, they advised no reply be given to their demands, at least not until they had more information about what was happening in Japan. They also received reports about the Franciscan priest's real intentions, and others telling them Date was only interested in trade and that the Japanese government was systematically persecuting Christians. Armed with all this information, it was only to be expected that the Castilian court would distrust Sotelo in particular and the expedition in general.

As a result, when they arrived in Madrid, on December 20, 1614, there was no welcoming committee, nor did they get permission to have an audience with Philip III. They were lodged in an austere Franciscan monastery for the entire duration of their stay, a humble and undoubtedly rather inappropriate place for a foreign delegation. The court refused to treat the Japanese expedition as a diplomatic mission since they had only brought a letter from one of their nobles and not from their king or emperor. It was not until a month and a half later, on January 30, 1615—and after Father Sotelo's repeated insistence—that they were finally able to obtain an audience with the monarch. It was at this meeting that Hasekura handed Philip III the letter in which Date Masamune introduced himself and expounded how he wanted to maintain friendly relations with the Castilian monarch, who he considered one of the pillars of Christianity. In the letter Date also requested more priests and goods to be sent, and offered to pay for their transport, as well as granting Castilian traders privileges such as lands where they could settle, exemption from paying taxes and diplomatic immunity from possible legal actions. This warm letter, written before

Fig. 10.5. *Hasekura Tsunenaga in Rome,* oil painting by Claude Deruet, 1615, Borghese Gallery, Rome.

the expedition's departure, advocating terms which would benefit both parties, was in complete contrast to Japan's official position at that time regarding Christianity and foreign influence in general. It was hardly credible therefore that Date would be able to fulfill the conditions he promised in his letter to Philip III, and it was dismissed as not being worth the paper it was written on.

The Council of the Indies suggested it would be best if the monarch were to oppose any trade deal with Japan, not allow the trip to Rome and only accept the dispatch of a few missionaries—something the Castilians were usually more than happy to do. They also agreed to another of Hasekura's requests, namely for him to be baptized at the court in the king's presence. This duly took place on February 17, 1615, in the Descalzas Reales monastery, where he took the name Felipe Francisco Hasekura, thus honoring both Philip III and the Franciscan order. In any case, this goodwill gesture, which is believed to have been Father Sotelo's idea, had no effect on the king's attitude or that of the court or the Council of the Indies. Over the following weeks, despite the absence of any official reply, Sotelo kept on insisting tirelessly in an attempt to get the court to listen to his requests. Eventually, the king—maybe tired of the headaches the persistent Franciscan priest was causing him—authorized the group to visit Rome and acknowledged he would consider the trade deal, as long as Japan cut off all trade with Holland. So, on August 22, 1615, with a diffident verbal promise as their only guarantee, the expedition company left for the Vatican.

After visiting Zaragoza, Fraga, Lleida, Cervera, Igualada, the Abbey of Montserrat, Martorell and Esparraguera, the mission reached the city of Barcelona on October 3. From there, they set off on a sea journey, calling at Saint Tropez, Savona and Genoa, reaching Rome in late October 1615. But before their arrival in the Italian capital, Philip III's ambassador in the city had already received a letter which urged him to prevent any possible agreement between the expedition and the Holy See, and contained information the Council of the Indies had gathered about Sotelo, the situation in Japan, etc.

Fig. 10.6. Father Sotelo, Hasekura and the other Japanese delegates in Rome, fresco by the painter Giovanni Lanfranco in the Great Hall of the Cuirassiers in the Quirinal Palace, Rome.

The delegation was welcomed with great processions and celebrations in the city and was granted several audiences with the pope, both officially and unofficially. At one of these audiences, Hasekura gave a speech and handed the pontiff a letter written by Date Masamune in which he asked for his protection, the dispatch of Franciscan missionaries to Japan, his mediation in the negotiations with Philip III and assistance in establishing trade relations with Mexico—basically the same things he had requested of the Castilian monarch. The pope praised Date Masamune, but said nothing about his requests. Unlike Madrid, Rome decided to treat the visitors with great deference and courtesy, affording them the same treatment the ambassadors of any allied European country could expect. Ultimately, though, they behaved in the same way when it came to the important matters, which they ignored— clearly because of the warnings Philip III's ambassador had given the pontiff. On November 20, 1615, as a show of gratitude toward the mission, the city of Rome granted both Hasekura and the rest of the Japanese envoys citizenship, in yet another goodwill gesture of little consequence for the expedition's objectives. At one of the audiences with Paul V, Father Sotelo asked the pontiff to create a new diocese in Japan, putting himself forward as its bishop.

When this came to the attention of Philip III's court, their suspicions about Sotelo's real objective were confirmed. As a result, the king issued a command telling the expedition that on their return to the Iberian Peninsula, they had to head directly for Seville, without passing through Madrid, and once there immediately set sail on the return journey to Japan.

On January 4, 1616, more than two months after their arrival, Sotelo and Hasekura were received by the pope once again, who, seeing their insistence, assured them he would send more missionaries to Japan and gave them a letter for Philip III, which asked him to take charge of the matter. With this promise, the delegation set off on their return journey.

From Rome to Japan: Empty-handed

On January 25, 1616, the expeditionary group were traveling through Genoa when they received the order telling them to go directly to Seville without stopping off in Madrid, but Sotelo, who still had no concrete answer from the monarch, opted to disobey the orders, and reached Madrid in the month of April. Despite his insistence, the Madrid court (as a result of the ever-worsening news coming from Japan, added to the fact they had been disobeyed) refused to receive the delegation and again ordered them to head to Seville. What is more, when they reached the Andalusian capital, a new order from the Council of the Indies was waiting for them, which commanded them to return to Japan as soon as possible. To avoid this hasty departure, Sotelo and Hasekura pretended to be sick to gain time to allow them to contact Philip III and ask him for an official letter confirming the dispatch of more missionaries to Japan. In April 1617—worried about how badly his reputation had been damaged in his own city—Sotelo wrote to the Seville City Council, claiming that despite the worsening news from Japan,

Christians were not being persecuted in Date Masamune's fiefdom because they were under the protection of the powerful daimyō. Sotelo and his family had a good deal of influence in the city council, which wrote to the court defending the Franciscan and asking for his requests to be answered. The answer, when it came from Madrid, was once more that the mission had to leave as soon as possible to return to Japan. But Sotelo still refused to accept defeat and sent another letter to the court, which was answered with yet another order to leave immediately, but this time with the promise that the longed-for letter from Philip III would be given to him when he called at the Philippines.

So, on 4th July, the delegation finally left Seville. It was then that some of the Japanese delegates (it is believed, around six or seven of them), terrified by the situation back in Japan, not wanting to be forced to abandon the Christian doctrine or die, and having gotten used to life in Coria del Río, their home for the last year, decided to stay.

The Surname *Japón*

The main and most tangible legacy left behind by Hasekura Tsunenaga's expedition—if not the only one—was the surname *Japón*. It appears the samurai who decided to stay in Coria del Río ended up pairing off with local women and having children with them; for some reason—doubtless for the sake of convenience—it was decided to give these children the surname *Japón* instead of their fathers' surnames. The first known case of the use of this surname dates from the early seventeenth century and was found in the baptism register of the Santa María de la Estrella church, in Coria del Río, where the details of a child thus named appear. A few centuries on, there are more than six hundred fifty Coria residents with the surname in question, some of whom even have it as both their paternal and maternal surnames.

In Japan, on the other hand, the discovery of this surname is quite recent. In 1989, thanks to the commemoration of the foundation of the city of Sendai by Date Masamune, they started to investigate the city's history and found several documents written by the daimyō which talked about Hasekura's voyage. Hence began the first contact with Coria del Río, and other cities the expedition had visited, with a view to getting their version of events and additional details of the visit. Since then, an effort has been made to maintain respect and improve intercultural relations between the two countries through ambassadors both in Spain and Japan, and there have been many events involving the two countries. One such example was the 1992 Seville Expo, where a meeting was held between the Japanese ambassador and various supposed descendants of the historical expedition members. We should also mention that in a nice corner of Coria's Carlos de Mesa Park, by the River

Fig. 10.7. Statue of Hasekura Tsunenaga in Coria del Río. Photograph taken by the author, July 2014.

Guadalquivir, stands a statue of Hasekura Tsunenaga, donated by the government of Sendai in 1992. This, along with those delivered to other cities, such as Acapulco, Havana, Rome and Livorno, is a copy of the original one located in Sendai.

After passing through Mexico in mid-September 1617, the delegation reached the Philippines on June 20, 1618, and remained there in Manila for one and a half years. The long-awaited letter from Philip III arrived while they were there, but its contents were a great let-down, since it was merely a protocolary document that made no reference to the dispatch of missionaries or to any kind of trade agreement. Finally, on August 20, 1620 they set off for Japan. Not so Father Sotelo, who was ordered to remain in the Philippines, and shortly afterwards sent to New Spain by the Council of the Indies, who prohibited him from returning to Japan. Despite this ban, the irrepressible friar secretly stowed away on a Chinese ship two years later and managed to reach Japan, only to be discovered and imprisoned for two years. We know he then wrote to Date Masamune asking him for help, but this time got no reply from the daimyō and was executed in 1624, burned alive by orders of the shōgun. He was beatified two and a half centuries later.

As for Hasekura and the rest of the expedition, they arrived in the port city of Nagasaki in September 1620 and then crossed much of the country to get to their original starting point, Sendai, on 22nd September, practically seven years after having begun their voyage. One month later, the daimyō sent a letter to the Tokugawa court, informing them the delegation had returned home and reminding them it had been sent by Ieyasu himself, and that he, Date Masamune, had merely acted as an intermediary. At this time Christianity was under scrutiny throughout the country and Date was undoubtedly trying to protect his back, playing a double game: on the one hand, to King Philip III and the pope, he painted a picture of himself as a powerful lord and proposed trade agreements, whereas, on the other hand, to the shōgunate, he showed himself in favor of persecuting Christianity and washed his hands of the European expedition. There are no documents which explain what became of Hasekura Tsunenaga—we only know he died in 1622 and that his tomb is to be found in the Enfuku-ji Buddhist temple, in the modern-day Miyagi prefecture, although two other places claim the same thing.

This then has been the account of a failure, as we might rate any mission or project that fails to achieve a single one of its objectives. Date Masamune did not get to trade with Europe, or even with New Spain or Manila, and clearly was not Tokugawa Ieyasu's successor either, as Father Sotelo had proudly announced. The Franciscan priest did not get the Vatican to send more priests to Japan, nor did he come close to achieving his dream of becoming the bishop of a new Japanese diocese—perhaps his only triumph was to end up being beatified sometime after his martyrdom. Hasekura Tsunenaga, in so far as he had been charged with leading the expedition, failed along with it, returning home seven years later without having achieved anything he had set out to do. At the same time, this failure fits into a larger failure, that of the Catholic mission to preach the Gospel in Japan, which also represents the failure of a meeting of two civilizations.

On the other hand, perhaps it is this very failure that makes the mission so interesting, imbuing it with the appeal of lost causes, of pipe-dreams that are doomed even before they get underway. Perhaps that is what makes them so great.

CHAPTER 11

The End of the Samurai

Domestic Dynamite: The Waning of the *Bakuhan*

After the first fifty years of the Edo period, the Tokugawa government had achieved its longed-for stability, and from then on it could be said that things ran themselves for more than a century, almost through inertia, with no need for much effort on the part of the bakufu. The different systems for controlling the daimyō seen in Chapter 9 turned out to be effective and the warlords were involved in no significant revolts. The ones led by the peasants every so often, normally coinciding with periods of famine, were put down relatively easily. Japan continued its process of urban development, begun after the Sengoku period, and generally speaking the population's standard of living started to rise significantly; the growth of the cities stimulated commerce since the demand for all kind of products rose, and agricultural productivity—the foundation of the entire system—also grew, with the amount of arable land doubling and new farming techniques being applied. But this climate of economic prosperity mainly benefited the traders, who—let us not forget—theoretically occupied the lowest rung on the social ladder. This was due, among other things, to the fact they could regulate their prices more effectively, as they were not subject to the ups and downs that are part and parcel of agriculture, unlike the peasants, who were clearly affected by this, as were the samurai, who earned part of their stipends in rice. Some of these businessmen became increasingly wealthy over time and in times of economic difficulty for the bushi, became their moneylenders, even loaning money to the daimyō.

The Tokugawa system was not perfect and one of the places where the cracks began to appear was the economic sphere. Clearly it is not easy to explain a country's economy over the course of more than two centuries, nor does it concern us here, but we might say— greatly simplifying things—one of the main factors that caused economic problems was the samurai class's new lifestyle. Oddly enough, given it was a time of peace, military spending increased, since both the daimyō and the bakufu had to maintain standing armies. And unlike previous ages when the warriors would work on the land when they were not mobilized, now they had no other work to do and had to be paid a stipend even if they did not enter into combat. And although some of them carried out bureaucratic or administrative tasks, the majority led a very idle life. Added to this was the fact that in times of peace soldiers did not die on the battlefield, which meant they lived longer and their stipend became a long-term outlay for the state coffers. Those who accompanied their daimyō when he had to live in Edo incurred more expenses, immersing themselves in a new consumerist lifestyle which bore no relation to the frugality that samurai were supposed to prac- tice, because not only were they the elite of society, but they had to look like it too. It has already been mentioned that the journey to or from the capital was a massive undertaking and represented a great expense for the daimyō, but once in Edo the costs were also considerable because the lords competed among one another to have the most luxurious residence and the highest standard of living. As a result of having to cover all the costs incurred by the samurai class, the regional governments soon began to neglect the rest of the population (which represented 90% of the total) and adopt several economic measures, which tended to involve anything except cutting back on the elites' budgets.

The first step they took was to make the peasants pay more taxes. The ones who were supporting the system were forced to support it even more and went from handing over 40-50% of their harvests to 70% or more, and in some cases they were asked to pay the following year's taxes in advance. Logically, this stirred up discontent among the already suffering peasant class and made their revolts toward the end of the eighteenth century more and more frequent and on a larger scale, revolts which were normally cruelly put down, which in turn increased popular discontent. Cutting back on the samurai's stipend was another measure to be applied, at first only on certain occasions, but little by little this became common policy. By and large the warriors were understanding of these cutbacks, firstly because of their feeling of loyalty to their daimyō and secondly because a lower stipend in exchange for barely working was still better than having to earn a living with the sweat of one's brow. This measure obviously affected the lower-ranking samurai, and many of them had to turn to doing extra jobs as school teachers or, in the case of the women of the house, sewing tasks.

With the passing of time, acceptance and loyalty to the daimyō gave way to discontent among the samurai class too. The final measure to be taken to deal with the economic problems was to get into debt: most fiefdoms had to resort to loans, granted by the very people who were on the lowest rung of the social ladder—the traders—especially the rich and powerful merchants of Kyoto and Osaka. Both, the samurai and the daimyō got used to living in debt and on more than one occasion the government had to decree a general cancellation of the debts of this entire social class, as has happened on previous occasions. Clearly this was not at all to the liking of the traders who had loaned this money and discontent grew among them as well. This also made them loathe to lend more money when, despite the amnesty, the samurai required further loans; some of these businessmen then took advantage of the opportunity to gain access to privileges supposedly reserved for the warrior class, such as carrying two swords, or even to buy the title of samurai for a son, something which was theoretically prohibited. Thus, with the passing of time, the system employed in the Edo period—the bakuhan—created an economic situation that led to practically the entire population struggling and becoming dissatisfied with the system, and by association, with the government.

But with the passing of time, this system showed itself to not only be vulnerable economically speaking, but also politically. Another of the consequences of the sankin kōtai—which, as we are starting to see, were numerous—was that it made it impossible for the daimyō to govern their domains directly while they were living in Edo, not just because of the distance, but also because of the busy life of leisure they led there. So, the task of ruling the territory was left in the hands of some of the trusted vassals belonging to each fiefdom's highest samurai class, who virtually ended up governing even when the daimyō was back home.

The Tokugawa bakufu strongly endorsed the principle of hereditary succession for the feudal lords, which meant the title was not always inherited by the most suitable candidate, and the heir—in the absence of wars which had previously acted as a kind of natural selection mechanism—could be in charge of the fiefdom for many years. So, if we add the fact that the daimyō were not always the most suitable candidates for the job to the fact they lived half the time in Edo (where they led an agreeable carefree life, and on top of that had been born and raised there, regarding it as their home more than the faraway provincial territory they owned), it is clear they were not really fit to rule. What might at first glance appear to be a good solution to the problem—putting those trusted vassals in command—ended up being perverted for the same reasons: in each fiefdom the same three or four families always occupied the positions of greatest responsibility, since they also adhered to the principle of hereditary succession rather than merit-based criteria. The same delegated power system was found within the bakufu, where the shōgun gradually gave up ruling personally and increasingly delegated political decision-making to ministers, with the incumbent Tokugawa leader taking on a mere symbolic role (a phenomenon we have by now seen occur many times), far removed from that of Ieyasu, Hidetada and Iemitsu at the beginning of the period.

If added to all this erosion of the bakuhan system is the fact that—despite more than two centuries having gone by—the tozama never forgave the Tokugawa for their victory at Sekigahara and for having relegated them to the side-lines ever since (forever under watch and unable to apply for positions within the government), we have an explosive mixture ready to go off. Only the touch-paper was missing, and it would come from outside.

External Detonator: The New Western Threat

Japan had managed to emerge unscathed from the two previous occasions when other countries had fetched up on its shores: almost miraculously beating the Mongolian-Korean-Chinese coalition at the end of the thirteenth century and expelling the Portuguese and Castilians in the seventeenth century. After the latter, the country had decided to close itself off from the world almost completely and just like the rest of the measures adopted by the Tokugawa to maintain stability, for a time it had been successful. But this bakufu policy also began to founder from the final years of the eighteenth century.

As early as 1792, a Russian ship visited Hokkaidō, the most northerly of Japan's four main islands (which went by the name of Ezo until 1869), which had been taken from the Emishi one piece at a time on the battlefield and at that time was controlled by the Matsumae clan as a kind of protectorate; precisely because of the perceived Russian threat, the Japanese government put the island under direct rule and from then on it may be considered part of Japan—you will notice that until this point this has not been included in the maps. On this occasion, the Russians accepted the Japanese refusal to initiate any type of relations, just as they did when they visited Nagasaki in 1804. But from that moment on, the visits and sightings of both Russian and English ships were quite frequent, so much so that in 1825 the bakufu ordered the coastal defenses to be improved and all foreign ships to be expelled from Japanese waters, by force if necessary, as occurred twelve years later, when an American ship was met with cannon-fire. But Japan could not carry on fending off the arrival of foreigners forever, as their Dutch allies—let us recall, the only ones authorized to trade with Japan—warned them in a letter to the government in 1844. In it, they explained to them the world had changed and was becoming an ever more global market, and that Japanese isolationism would not manage to keep them divorced from that for long.

Moreover, the bakufu knew perfectly well what had been happening in East Asia for decades, where the Western Powers had humiliated and stepped all over no less a nation than the once all-powerful China. For part of the Japanese government, the Chinese case was precisely a reason for remaining closed off to the outside, not for opening up to it, but they also knew they could not go to war with the foreign Powers; ironically, keeping the army ever ready to face any potential threat had meant an enormous expense both for the shōgunate and for the daimyō, but when the threat finally arrived, the army was unable to stand up to it. They decided to further improve the coastal defenses but to rescind the 1825 order. This was because the government thought the best thing to do when faced with any proposals they might receive was not to respond aggressively but to give way initially until such time as they could attain the same technological and military level as the Western countries so as to then be able to face up to them. However, it was also feared that this concessionary policy might weaken the government at home.

Events would gather pace after 1853, when the roughly fifteen-year period referred to as *bakumatsu* (or end of the bakufu) began. This was a time of great confusion (at times it is difficult to follow the twists and turns of the various protagonists involved) and instability—just what the shōgunate had tried to avert ever since its foundation. In July of that year, a US Navy commodore, Matthew C. Perry (AD 1794-1858), arrived in Uraga harbor (modern-day Kanagawa prefecture), at the entrance to the Bay of Edo, in command of four gunboats, two of them steam-powered, all armed with the most modern heavy artillery. It is often said that

Perry's arrival was an enormous surprise for the Japanese. However, the fact is the government was warned in good time of the expedition's arrival, first by the Dutch in Dejima, who informed the Nagasaki authorities, and then by the authorities in Kagoshima, who had jurisdiction in the Ryūkyū archipelago, where Perry had docked before heading for Japan. For the common people though, the arrival of the so-called "Black Ships" was both astonishing and terrifying, and thousands of people gathered to see them in the port for the eight or nine days the visit lasted. The reason behind the visit was the delivery of a letter for the shōgun from the President of the United States. The bakufu hoped for a trouble-free delivery and that they would leave as soon as possible. There were certain rules of protocol to be followed and much negotiating to be done: through Japanese interpreters who spoke Dutch—considered the international *lingua franca* in Japan at that time—they insisted that Perry should relocate to Nagasaki along with his fleet, since

Fig. 11.1. Japanese view of one of the Black Ships,
in an engraving from the period.

this was where business was done with other countries, but faced with Perry's flat refusal, they ended up dealing with him in Uraga. He delivered his letter, which proposed a friendly collaborative relationship between the two countries. The Americans were particularly interested in being allowed to use one of the ports in the north of the country, for the purposes of their whaling activity in the North Pacific; Perry specified that this friendship proposal—for the time being they did not mention trade—should be replied to a year later, when he would return with a much larger fleet.

In between the American's two visits, a Russian admiral also arrived in Japan, first of all at the end of 1853 and again in early 1854, although Japanese diplomats managed to get rid of him without making any commitments for the time being. But just one week after the Russians had left, on February 13, Perry returned and this time he came with a fleet of ten ships, aboard which were around one thousand six hundred men—somewhat excessive for what was supposed to be a simple diplomatic negotiation, unless of course they wanted to make it clear what the consequences of a Japanese refusal would be. The bakufu's goal, once more, was for Perry to leave as soon as possible and the more empty-handed the better. To that end, they argued they had still not been able to deal with the matter because they had been very busy with the death of the previous shōgun—barely a week after the Americans' first visit—and the accession of the current one, so it would be better to pick up the conversations at a later date. But the commodore was not about to make it easy for them, and would not take no for an answer, making it clear at all times that he had not come to beg a favor, but to demand his rights.

He also made demands of his own, on top of those the American government had assigned him. This second visit by Perry ended up lasting four months, during which time countless meetings took place and there was a succession of paperwork, formalities, ambiguous replies, documentation and all kinds of protocol, bureaucracy and the going around in circles that tend to form part of any negotiation involving the Japanese. Finally, they signed what is known as the Kanagawa Treaty, by the terms of which Japan gave the United States permission to use the following ports: Shimoda, in today's Shizuoka prefecture; Hakodate, in Hokkaidō; and Naha, in the Ryūkyū Islands; they also promised to open up two more ports to them later—in Niigata and Hyōgo, rather than in Nagasaki. This was on Perry's personal insistence, apparently based simply on his wanting to antagonize the Japanese government, who insisted on sending them there. The amity and collaboration agreement between the two countries was accepted but, for the time being, trade was not; Japan inserted a clause by which no American would be able to live on Japanese soil, and the United States added one determining that any subsequent agreement the Japanese might sign with third parties would also have to be applied to them, the so-called "most favored nation clause" which is typical of this kind of treaties. All in all, Perry's expedition was a success and achieved more than it had been entrusted with; but it was merely the first step—neither the United States nor the other Powers (that same year identical treaties were signed with Russia and the England) were going to settle just for that.

In 1856 a new American appeared on the scene, Townsend Harris (AD 1804-1878), who was sent as consul general and who—as was to be expected—came ready to negotiate a trade treaty. This also included a clause which would allow Americans to live in the free port cities included in the Kanagawa Treaty, to enjoy diplomatic immunity and to be judged by courts of their own country in the event of committing any crimes. It should be said that in principle this clause was no big deal for the Japanese, who were used to running things this way between the different fiefdoms, but years later when they found out this was not how things were done between Western countries and was only applied to colonial relations, they regarded it as a humiliation. The negotiations with Harris were even slower and more exasperating than those held with Perry and it took nearly two years to seal a new deal, known unofficially as the Harris Treaty, in 1858. Once again, before very long, matching treaties were signed with other countries, with

Fig. 11.2. Commodore Perry, shown in a Japanese engraving of the period, and a photograph of him.

Russia, England, France and Holland to be exact. All these Powers would operate mainly from Yokohama, where the bakufu decided to relocate the foreigners, and this location would go from being a modest fishing village to the most modern and cosmopolitan city in the country, with the largest port in the whole Kantō region.

The years of conversations with Perry and Harris had been anything but an easy time for the bakufu, or for Japanese domestic policy in general. And if the negotiations with the Americans had been complicated and almost chaotic, domestic affairs had been a nightmare, and the worst was still to come.

Explosion: The Wrecking of the *Bakufu*

When Perry sailed away from Japan for the first time, the bakufu only had a few months to decide what to do on his return, and things became even more complicated with the aforementioned death of Shōgun Tokugawa Ieyoshi (AD 1793-1853). Although, at this point in history the shōgun no longer held real power within the government and his death had simply been used as an excuse to buy time—unsuccessfully in any case. At this point, in an unexpected and unprecedented turn of events, the bakufu decided to send each daimyō a copy of the letter brought by Perry and ask them for their opinion about what should be done—a decision they would come to regret. Although this consultation was in theory limited to this one matter, it was revolutionary since in practice it opened the way for the daimyō to henceforth believe they had the right to give their opinion about anything, including how the bakufu itself was run. And some fiefdoms had been wanting to have their say for some time, since Sekigahara to be exact. The dissatisfaction with the shōgunate's policies at the start of the chapter was much more intense in some tozama territories. This was perhaps less evident among their daimyō and ruling classes, (who at the end of the day were the ones who had been pardoned and were allowed to run their regions with a good deal of autonomy), but it was rife among the middle and low-ranking samurai classes, who made up the great majority.

Three of these fiefdoms would play a crucial role over the following years: Chōshu, Satsuma and Tosa. In addition, another dissenting voice would appear in the Mito fiefdom, despite it being, in principle, close to the central government—so close in fact it belonged to an offshoot of the Tokugawa family tree. As early as the mid-seventeenth century, a school had been founded there for the study of the history of Japan, which led in turn to the study of the indigenous religion—Shinto—and, as the years went by, to the defense of the idea that the country's uniqueness sprang from its imperial dynasty. This was supposedly uninterrupted and descended from the very gods of creation, thus lionizing the figure of the emperor—who had been ignored as never before during the Edo period. These ideas were compatible with those of other important schools of thought of the era, such as the National Studies movement. When the foreign threat appeared, the idea of recovering the respect for the emperor was joined by another notion: a concept called *sonnō jōi*, or "revere the emperor and expel the barbarians," which was taken from a fifth century bc Chinese saying, began to be promoted. In principle, this movement was not

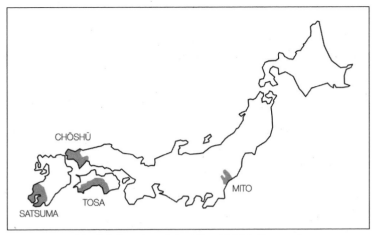

Fig. 11.3. Location of the Mito, Chōshū, Tosa, and Satsuma fiefdoms. Author's own drawing.

predicated on criticism of the bakufu—remember that the Mito fiefdom belonged to an offshoot of the Tokugawa family tree—but it would soon head in that direction, when the government's policies started to seem as though they were aimed at anything but expelling the barbarians. In Chōshū, Satsuma and Tosa this intellectual current of thought would be well received, and these were large fiefdoms with an enormous number of warriors, both in terms of the percentage of the population they accounted for and their absolute numbers; the clearest case was Satsuma, where 40% of the families belonged to the samurai class, a very different proportion from the national level of 6%. Moreover, these territories belonged to very long-standing clans, whose warriors regarded both the Tokugawa and the great majority of the fudai—generally speaking, clans that had been around for just three centuries or so—as nothing more than upstarts. As a result of all of these factors, they felt very little affection for Edo and when the sonnōjōi movement appeared, began to feel much more sympathy for Kyoto.

The bakufu got all kinds of replies from their poll of the daimyō, some in favor of opening up the country and others who completely opposed it, but in reality, even before posing the question, the government already knew it could ill afford to stand up to the Western threat: Japanese military resources were not equal to foreign technology, and the shōgunate's finances were too weak to invest in the said technology to bring their military up to speed. Clearly, this was not something that could be made public because it would leave the bakufu in a very fragile position when facing its opponents, but caving in to all the American demands would have the same effect, so there was really no easy way out. Coastal defenses were improved thanks to private financing—from well-off businessmen—and the old prohibition decreed by Shōgun Iemitsu regarding the construction of large ships was annulled. Other than that, the shōgunate had no choice but to sign the amity treaty dictated by Perry. Within the shōgunate, those in favor of maintaining the isolationist policy were logically very critical of the signing of such treaties and advocated the imperial court's involvement in these affairs.

Until then, the court's only involvement in the matter had been to ask the Ise Grand Shrine to have the gods expel the foreigners from Japan as they had in the thirteenth century. The bakufu, for its part, also knew that the Western countries wanted to broaden the scope of the treaties with new concessions and the opening up of trade, and that they would not be able to say no to this. They could only hope that at least they would be able to control this trade (just as they had done for centuries with the Dutch in Dejima) rather than it being private free trade. At the same time, they bought some modern warships from Holland and founded a shipyard and a sailing school in Nagasaki. What is known today as the Japanese flag (which is usually called Hinomaru) was ordered to be flown as the insignia in these new ships. It was already a very ancient and widely-used emblem, but until then its use had not become standardized as the national symbol.

During the negotiations with Harris, things became even tougher for the bakufu, because after only five years in the post, Shōgun Tokugawa Iesada (AD 1824-1858) died and he did so without leaving an heir. The daimyō who were critical of the bakufu took advantage of this to put the Mito daimyō's son forward as successor, rather than the government's preferred candidate, a twelve-year-old youth, who would clearly be easier to handle. Many daimyō then lobbied for the emperor's opinion to be sought about both the signing of the trade treaty and the appointment of the new shōgun before going ahead with either matter. In principle, the government had no problem with this—on the contrary, they believed the court would be in agreement and that it would help to silence the critics. But the court nobles, who yet again were the ones who really conditioned the emperor's opinion, believed the foreigners' ultimate objective was the invasion of Japan and moreover were convinced that if it came to a conflict with them, Japanese victory was assured. They even felt it offensive that the bakufu could see it any other way. As far as the shōgun was concerned, the court, which was heavily influenced by the daimyō of Satsuma and Chōshū, also preferred the Mito candidate. As a result, the imperial response was very negative for the government, and while it was only an opinion and not an order, not obeying it would constitute a betrayal for all the sonnō jōi followers. And this is how they took both the signing of the treaty with Harris and the appointment of the young Tokugawa Iemochi (AD 1846-1866). Both decisions had been taken by the new president of the council of elders —the ones who really ran the bakufu—Ii Naosuke (AD 1815-1860), who was in favor of a return to an authoritarian government that would not consult the rest of the daimyō or the imperial court over its decisions. This roused the passions of those who opposed the shōgunate and there was fierce criticism, but Ii responded by forcing many of the daimyō who questioned him to give up their positions and by imprisoning or executing tens of opponents, which only increased tensions. Just two years later, the president of the council was assassinated in full view of the entrance to Edo Castle by a group of young samurai from Mito.

From then on, such attacks became commonplace, and were always carried out by low-ranking young samurai (those who were the most dissatisfied with the system), who were normally from

Mito, Satsuma, Chōshū and Tosa. Due to their strong Confucianist education and the supposed samurai values which were ingrained in them, they regarded the emperor as the symbol of Japanese identity and unity and were prepared to use violence against those who, in their opinion, wanted to open Japan up to the barbarians. But these actions were not only committed against Japanese people—from the start, foreigners were also targeted by these sonnō jōi activists. In fact, one of the reasons why the main free port was moved to Yokohama was that it was further away from the main routes traveled by the samurai on their way to or from Edo on their sankin kōtai trips. Among this city's new residents were some Protestant missionaries, which did not please the Japanese, especially these young samurai activists, because Christianity was still banned and considered to be a threat.

Sakamoto Ryōma

Many of these young low-ranking samurai who rebelled violently against the bakufu, moderated their posture over time and some even devoted themselves to politics. The most famous case is probably that of Sakamoto Ryōma (AD 1836-1867), one of the most popular and best-loved historical characters in the collective Japanese imagination, seen over and again in countless novels, plays, television series and movies. Sakamoto was born in Tosa to one of the lowest-ranking samurai families, one of his ancestors, a wealthy sake merchant, having purchased samurai status for his descendants. He left school very young as he was not interested in studying and joined a fencing school, a pastime he was much more interested in and which it seems he excelled at. Like many other young samurai of his generation in his province, he identified with the Mito school of thought and the sonnō jōi precepts, so much so that he also leaned toward direct action. Consequently, in 1862 he decided to assassinate Katsu Kaishū (AD 1823-1899), a naval specialist and Rangaku scholar, who worked for the bakufu as an adviser and argued that opening Japan up to the world was the only way to survive in the international climate of the time.

When Sakamoto entered his home, sword in hand ready to kill him, Katsu only asked to be allowed to explain the reasons why he believed the opening up of the country was the best solution, and Sakamoto agreed to this. Apparently, after hearing the explanation, the young samurai sheathed his sword, apologized and asked Katsu to be his master. And so he was for some time. Sakamoto went on to devote himself to studying the political systems and constitutions of several Western countries and to designing a suitable government model for Japan, based on meritocracy. He also had a prominent role as an intermediary in the negotiations between Satsuma and Chōshū, thus playing a fundamental role in the course of the period's history, and later con vinced these same two provinces to negotiate a peaceful end to the bakufu. However, Sakamoto himself would just miss out on seeing that moment: in December 1867, while he was in hiding at a Kyoto inn, knowing the pro-bakufu militia were looking for him, the militia discovered he was there, attacked the site and killed him.

Fig. 11.4. Sakamoto Ryōma in 1866. Photograph by Inoue Shunzō.

Particularly noteworthy was an incident that occurred in 1862 when four Englishmen who were enjoying a pleasant day out horse-riding suddenly came across the retinue of none other than the daimyō of Satsuma; there are different accounts of what happened next, but it seems one of them decided not to dismount despite having been warned that would be seen as a lack of respect—sure enough, in response to the Englishman's insolence, one of the samurai officers stepped out of the entourage and killed him right there and then. When events like this happened, the bakufu was forced to pay compensation to the victim's country of origin and sometimes even had to hand over the killer. This in turn caused more discontent among the Japanese because, in contrast, when a foreigner committed a crime, he was brought before a judge from his own country, and normally judged in a scandalously benevolent fashion. But violent action was not the preserve of those opposed to the bakufu. Militia made up of lordless samurai who were loyal to the government were also created, and devoted themselves to searching for and killing opponents.

In addition, the anti-government daimyō applied as much pressure politically speaking as the young samurai did on the streets. And this happened despite the new government adopting a much more conciliatory tone after Ii's assassination and trying to introduce economic reforms at the same time as political and military ones. In general terms, they looked for closer ties with the court, to at least please the supporters of the sonnō ideas ("revering the emperor"), since for the time being they could not sort out the jōi part ("expelling the barbarians"), and to that end they married the young Shōgun Iemochi to one of the emperor's sisters. Another important reform adopted in 1862 was nothing less than the repeal of the sankin kōtai system, eliminating the daimyō's obligation to keep their families in Edo. The bakufu thereby lost these valuable hostages and the samurai leaders' finances also benefited from an important saving, which had the effect of allowing the fiefdoms to spend more on improving their armies; it was crystal clear that both factors represented an enormous risk of uprising, since this system had been created precisely to avoid this happening.

Straight away, Edo found itself emptied of all the daimyō, their vassals and families, but instead of returning to their respective domains, those opposed to the bakufu moved to Kyoto, from where they declared the shōgunate was incapable of handling the situation and therefore should hand power over to the imperial court. Strengthened by the new situation, the emperor asked for foreigners to be expelled—remember that when we talk of the emperor we are really talking about the court since he personally had little say in things. The bakufu then decided to send the shōgun to the capital in person to discuss the matter—another almost unprecedented gesture. The previous visit by a shōgun to the emperor had happened in 1634, although the two occasions had absolutely nothing in common; when Iemitsu had arrived in Kyoto he had done so accompanied by an enormous army of over three hundred thousand soldiers as a demonstration of the shōgunate's power over the court, and on this occasion, in 1863, Iemochi took with him a retinue of just three thousand men in a gesture of near submission to the court. While there, he was informed that 25th June had been chosen as the day the expulsion of the barbarians would begin, something the imperial court nobles thought would be resolved in less than ten years.

In point of fact, when the great day came, the bakufu did nothing, because they were aware it was an impossible undertaking. From Chōshū though, they did start to fire their artillery shore defenses at the foreign ships passing by their coasts. This was met both by official protests to the government and by the attacked ships also firing broadsides (with far greater accuracy), to Chōshū's misfortune. For their part, in Satsuma they were starting to realize Chōshū was coming out on top, placing itself at the head of this anti-government revolution, while Tosa was expressing more moderation and Mito, despite having laid the movement's ideological foundations, had lost the leadership some time ago. The daimyō of Satsuma therefore decided, in a strange turn of events, to side with the bakufu and attacked the Chōshū, managing to force them to leave Kyoto.

The Shinsengumi

Just as many young masterless samurai were opposed to the bakufu, some defended it—what they had in common was a liking for direct action. The most famous group of the second faction was the so-called Shinsengumi, which the government entrusted with the defense and pacification of Kyoto. At one point it had as many as three hundred members—mostly of non-samurai origin—and had a hierarchy composed of a commander, two deputy commanders, a military adviser and ten captains. Dressed in a striking uniform of a light blue kimono jacket with white triangles on the sleeve ends and at the hem, they were behind several successful operations: for example, avoiding the burning down of Kyoto in 1864; they are also credited with the assassination of, along with many others, Sakamoto Ryōma, although it has never been proved it was them and not another pro-bakufu militia. With the advent of the new age, its leaders quickly began to fall, because of desertions as well as arrests and executions carried out by the Meiji government. Despite having only really played a very limited role over a very short period of time—which should relegate them to the footnotes of history—they are hugely popular in Japan even today and have been the subject of numerous novels, comics, television series and movies.

This led to Chōshū becoming the place to be for all the (increasing number of) dissatisfied low-ranking samurai. Many of them abandoned their clans and fiefdoms to move to this kind of true sonnō jōi sanctuary. From this base, shortly afterwards, they attacked Kyoto to secure the emperor, but once again the bakufu's forces and their allies, including Satsuma, managed to defeat them, and those responsible for the attack were arrested and executed. The bakufu could then breathe more easily as it seemed they were back in control of the situation, and they continued to carry out a number of reforms: there was an attempt to have positions both in the central government and in the fiefdoms filled by those who were most capable (even if they came from the lower ranks of the samurai class) and promises were made to take measures such as closing the port of Yokohama to foreigners after a short interval of time. Thanks to all these policies, there was relative calm in the country for a couple of years.

But in mid-1866, aged just twenty, Shōgun Iemochi died of vitamin deficiency, and the bakufu decided his successor would this time indeed be Tokugawa Yoshinobu (AD 1837-1913), the daimyō of Mito's son. This was evidently a clear concession to the opposition sector. But Mito had long ceased to lead the way among the opposition and Yoshinobu's appointment did not help to resolve things. The new shōgun wanted to institute a completely new system of government, based on those in place in Western countries—and very similar to the system Japan would end up having a few decades later—but with the proviso that this new government would continue to be run by the Tokugawa. Understandably, the idea was not particularly appealing to all the samurai who were still gathered in Chōshū. The dissidents who had flocked there from different parts of the country had been organizing themselves militarily for a couple of years, and curiously they had done so using Western techniques and technology, and even incorporated some peasants into their ranks. In Satsuma, something very similar was happening, although in this case focused more on the navy than on land forces, with the help of British advisers. The two fiefdoms combined had a powerful army at that time, but the bakufu only distrusted the Chōshū maneuvers, since Satsuma had been an ally of theirs for some time. What they did not know in Edo was that the two fiefdoms had been engaged in secret conversations for months, using Tosa as an intermediary, and had already forged an alliance. So, when the bakufu opted to attack Chōshū out of fear of its growing military power and asked Satusma for help, the latter did not budge, and the government forces were defeated. Not only was it an enormously humiliating defeat, but it also left the shōgunate in a clear position of weakness; other discontented sectors of society took advantage of this to foster all kind of revolts and protests, both in the countryside and in the cities.

The aftermath of this defeat was the perfect time for Satsuma and Chōshū to deal the death blow to the bakufu. Their leaders then planned a military attack on Edo, which ultimately was not carried out because they were convinced by Tosa to first try to talk the shōgun into stepping down. In effect, Yoshinobu, agreed to abdicate and leave power in the emperor's hands, but only if he were guaranteed the Tokugawa would keep their lands and riches, and that he would have a special place within the chamber which would run the new government. But, once again, this was not enough for Satsuma and Chōshū, who occupied Kyoto and took advantage of the emperor's death (officially caused by smallpox, although there are rumors blaming the anti-bakufu forces) to make his successor, the fifteen-year-old Emperor Meiji (AD 1852-1912), officially declare the bakufu abolished and imperial power restored in the first days of 1868. In this new model—things could hardly be otherwise—the emperor would have symbolic power, while a new government made up of nobles and daimyō would run the country on his behalf. It may seem as though, essentially, nothing had really changed, and it hadn't, except for the fact the Tokugawa no longer formed part of the system.

Yoshinobu obviously tried to resist, and there were a few battles between those forces who still supported the bakufu and those of the dissident fiefdoms, in what is known as the Boshin War. The already extinct shōgunate, though, suffered important defeats. This was due in part to the modern Western weapons used by their enemy—let us not forget, the very people who did not want to open the country up to foreign influence—and partly to the fact numerous daimyō who had until then been on the bakufu's side, decided now was an opportune moment to switch sides. France, which until then had supported the bakufu, did likewise. England had favored the rebels, but the Western powers suddenly agreed to remain neutral. Osaka then fell that very January and Edo surrendered in May, while a group of daimyō who sided with the Tokugawa continued fighting in the northern region of the country, but were defeated in early November; a few of them took refuge in Hokkaidō, where they went so far as to set up an independent republic—with the unofficial help of the French—but this only lasted until May 1869.

A little earlier, at the end of October 1868, Edo was renamed Tokyo, literally "the capital of the east," the emperor moved there to take up residence at what had until then been Edo Castle and from then on was known as the Imperial Palace, and the city became the capital of Japan. The Meiji era had begun.

Meiji: The Construction of a New Japan

This new age began with a clear objective in mind—placing the country on the same level as the Western Powers; it was no longer a question of adapting foreign technology and techniques so as to manage to stand up to them, and thus be able to cut themselves off from the world again—now it was a matter of "if you can't beat them, join them." So, in this brief period, Japan launched itself on a dizzying race toward modernization, making it clear the country was not like its Asian neighbors, which were now living under Western colonial governments, and therefore did not deserve to be treated like them; they also made it clear the unfair treaties signed during the years of the bakumatsu had to be annulled. Although there was an attempt to instill the people with due reverence toward the emperor, few commoners even remembered his existence by that stage, and the sonnō jōi slogan was abandoned in favor of the official adoption of the *fukoku kyōhei* motto: "rich country, powerful army," the two goals Japan had to reach if it was to be a world power.

Sovereignty, as we said earlier, was theoretically in the hands of the emperor, but he was expected not to meddle in political affairs. The task of government fell to a council of nobles and daimyō (mainly from Chōshū and Satsuma),which went to great lengths to make it clear, as we just said, that sovereignty was in the emperor's hands. One of the Meiji government's first edicts explained that the imperial dynasty was descended from the gods themselves and therefore posited the following: everything in the world legitimately belonged to the emperor; his government was the fairest; proof of that was the chaos that had reigned for the preceding three hundred years because of the Tokugawa having usurped his power; all Japanese should respond to his beneficence by being forever loyal and obedient toward him. Soon afterwards, this self-same text was included in schools, where students recited it on a daily basis until the end of the Second World War. So, it was a matter of drumming into people the idea that what had taken place was a restoration of the emperor's power, a task they succeeded at, since these days we still talk about the Meiji Restoration, when in fact nothing whatsoever was restored. The emperor neither ruled before the Tokugawa came on the scene, nor did he rule now; in fact, rarely throughout Japan's history has an emperor held real power, perhaps ten or so of them, and the young Meiji was—officially—the 122nd.

The forces who had been opposed to the Tokugawa since as far back as Sekigahara were the ones who ruled now. To achieve that, they had used the emperor as a figurehead and played the anti-foreigner card, but now they were in power, they did not reject foreigners at all. In fact, the ones who had previously opposed opening up the country to the outside world, opened it up more than ever before—not only when it came to technological or technical fields, but they also adopted the French judicial system, a British-style navy, and a constitution almost identical to the Prussian one. The Chōshū, Satsuma, Tosa and Hizen daimyō renounced their fiefdoms in favor of the emperor, knowing full well the rest of the lords would then do likewise of their own free will—or perhaps out of fear. And once all the land officially belonged to the emperor, in 1871, the fiefdoms were abolished and the prefectures were born. At first there were around two hundred seventy of them, but a couple of decades later only 46 would remain.

The daimyō were compensated for the loss of their territories, but the thousands and thousands of samurai, including those who had fought for the supposed restoration of the emperor, suddenly found themselves without a lord to serve and with no stipend to

Fig. 11.5. Emperor Meiji, photographed by Uchida Kuichi in 1872, with the requisite court outfit, and in 1873, with a Western-style military uniform.

draw. They were granted a salary, but it was much lower than the stipend. Moreover, with the abolition of the division into social classes, they ceased to be a defined and differentiated stratum, as a result of which they lost their privileges, such as the right to wear two swords or sport their characteristic hairstyle and the rest of the classes no longer had to bow to them respectfully. The final measure was the creation of the new imperial army, which initially was made up of ex-samurai from Chōshū, Satsuma and Tosa, but would soon be opened up to the rest of the former classes, through recruitment among the entire population, although the ex-samurai tended to take all the officers' positions. Many other former samurai joined the new national police force—at first they even used to wear their two swords while on patrol—or switched to being teachers or working in any other trade in which their superior academic training gave them an edge, such as law or journalism. But they also worked in jobs previously considered to be beneath them, for example as farmers, craftsmen or traders.

Fukuzawa Yukichi

The samurai class had the best intellectual training, not only because they had a school education as children, but also because they could devote their entire lifetime to study since they had ample free time. The greatest intellectuals born in the Edo period are to be found among the bushi families. So, when the samurai ceased to exist officially as a class with the arrival of the Meiji period, many of them devoted themselves to these kinds of tasks. The most influential and popular of them all was undoubtedly Fukuzawa Yukichi (AD 1835-1901), writer, journalist, and, above all, political philosopher; his image currently appears on the 10,000-yen bills (the highest denomination), which shows his historical importance to Japanese society. He was born in the bosom of a low-ranking samurai family—like almost all the important figures of his generation—and sent at the tender age of nineteen to study Rangaku in Nagasaki, where he coincided with Commodore Perry's visits. A little later, in 1858, he visited Yokohama and discovered to his surprise that none of the foreigners there spoke Dutch, a language he had studied and wished to practice, but which apparently was not really as im

Fig. 11.6. A young Fukuzawa Yukichi during a trip to Paris in 1862.

portant internationally as the Japanese had been led to believe. As his political theory would later show, Fukuzawa was a resolute proponent of pragmatism and adapting to changing circumstances, so that very day he began to devote himself to studying English—or at least this is what he explains in his autobiography.

Just two years later, he formed part of a shōgunate mission to the United States and various European countries. Upon returning from this trip, he published his famous book *Things Western*, a literary work that would make him one of the foremost experts on Western culture for the Japanese. He was even more successful with *An Encouragement of Learning*, of which no fewer than three and a half million copies were sold—a real best-seller. In this book he spoke out in favor of the overriding need for a new more pragmatic type of education, removed from Confucianist morality. Precisely for this reason, he founded his own school, called Keiō Gijuku, which over time would become Keiō Daigaku, still today the country's most important private university. He also set up a popular debating society as well as his own newspaper, which would henceforth serve as a platform for his numerous writings on a wide range of issues, including national and international politics, economics, education, language, women's rights, etc.

Fukuzawa was very critical of the way the other countries in East Asia had dealt with the European Powers' arrival, and it is within this context one of his most controversial articles, from 1885, should be placed: "Datsuaron," roughly "Leaving Asia" (although some scholars claim it went relatively unnoticed at the time, and only much later did the controversy appear). In any case, in this article, Fukuzawa expressed disappointment with the way China and Korea had failed to react to the unstoppable influx of Western civilization, which he compared to a measles epidemic or a powerful wave, in the face of which you had to decide whether to float above it or perish below it. He believed Japan had to take advantage of the opportunity to raise itself to the same level as these Powers, distancing itself from Asia if necessary, being independent from the rest of the countries on the continent so as not to come to depend on the Western countries either. He openly recognized the West's manifest superiority, as a result of which he saw no other way than to adapt pragmatically to the new circumstances in order to maintain national independence, severing the bonds with any kind of cultural or historic dependency.

Some of them still resisted things ending this way, although they only managed to put it off for a very short time. Leading them was precisely the man who had been one of the architects of the fall of the Tokugawa government and the success of the Meiji Restoration, Saigō Takamori (AD 1828-1877), from Satsuma, popularly known as "the last samurai," although others prefer to use this term with general Nogi Maresuke (AD 1849-1912). Saigō was one of the many low-ranking bushi who managed to stand out during the bakumatsu years, leading the Satsuma troops after 1864 and negotiating the secret alliance with Chōshū—with Sakamoto Ryōma acting as an intermediary between the two provinces. An ardent critic of the bakufu, he was one of those most strongly opposed to allowing the Tokugawa to form part of the new government. During the Boshin War, he led the pro-emperor army in several successful campaigns, including the taking of Edo after its surrender—which, oddly, he negotiated with Katsu Kaishū, Sakamoto Ryōma's "accidental master." With the arrival of the Meiji period, he became a member of the new government and his main contribution was to take charge of creating the new imperial army. As he was more unswerving in his approach than many of his colleagues, he continued to oppose what, according to him, was the excessive opening up of Japan to the rest of the world, especially when it came to trade or technological breakthroughs he considered unnecessary, such as the railway, and was very critical of the reforms regarding the disappearance of the samurai class.

Disenchanted with these policies, he resigned from his positions and returned to Kagoshima, the new prefecture which included what had previously been the provinces of Satsuma and Osumi. But in 1873 he went back to Tokyo to propose the invasion of Korea, with the argument that country did not recognize Emperor Meiji as the sovereign of Japan, although it is more likely his real objective was to increase the samurai's stock by giving them the one thing they existed for: a war. He put forward this idea taking advantage of the fact much of the government was travelling, on what is known as the Iwakura mission. This was an almost two-year-long expedition that took around fifty politicians, diplomats and intellectuals to the United States, a dozen European and half a dozen Asian countries with the aim of renegotiating the unequal treaties and collecting all kinds of information that might be useful for the modernization of Japan. Saigō's proposal to invade Korea was rejected and he felt completely let down by the country's new government. Back in Kagoshima, along with many other samurai who had also given up their political, army or police posts, he created a school that defended the old order's values and customs, and for a few years the state laws ceased to be applied in this region and it operated as a kind of autonomous state where samurai and their privileges still existed. Logically, this situation was frowned upon in the capital, and the government sent spies to Kagoshima to find out what was going on; these spies were captured but the incident made it clear Tokyo would not allow them to carry on living in this kind of samurai haven for much longer. This led to thousands of dissatisfied bushi advocating a rebellion against the government and they pressured Saigō—who was initially reluctant—to lead it. Thus began what is known as the Satsuma Rebellion in the West and the Southwestern War in Japan.

Nogi Maresuke

Although Nogi Maresuke did not lead a samurai's life, we could say his life both started and ended as such. Born in 1849 to a bushi family from Chōshū, he initially received French-style military training, first served in his daimyō's army and then at the age of twenty-one, within the new imperial army, where he quickly rose through the ranks. In 1877, while a lieutenant colonel, he fought Saigō Takamori's rebel forces and during the battle lost his regiment's standard. He tried to get it back by throwing himself into a near suicide mission, but his superiors prevented him from doing so—he would carry the shame around for the rest of his days. In 1894, he took part in the First Sino-Japanese war as a divisional general; from 1896 to 1898 he was governor of Taiwan, which was occupied at the time by the Japanese; and in 1904-1905, at this stage as a general, he directed the attack on the fortress of Port Arthur in the Russo-Japanese War. The siege lasted five months and was an absolute massacre for both sides, but especially so for the Japanese, who suffered nearly fifty-six thousand casualties, including one of the general's own sons—his other son died in another battle of the same war.

They finally managed to take the fortress and Nogi became a great national hero, but the victory came at the expense of

Fig. 11.7. General Nogi Maresuke.

another intolerable disgrace for him. He then asked the emperor for permission to commit suicide and thus unburden himself of his feeling of guilt, but the request was rejected. After the war, he mainly devoted his time to teaching, having Emperor Meiji's grandson—little Hirohito, who would some time later be known as Emperor Shōwa (AD 1901-1989)—as one of his pupils. In addition, he donated a large part of his fortune to hospitals that treated wounded soldiers and to raising monuments in honor of those killed on both sides in the Russo-Japanese War. In 1912, when Emperor Meiji died, Nogi decided to behave like a samurai and accompany his lord into death, an act known by the name *junshi* (a practice already considered outdated and unnecessary back in the Edo period), and was accompanied by his wife, who committed suicide just before him. In his suicide note, he referred to the loss of the standard in 1877 and to the fallen at the taking of Port Arthur as disgraces that he wanted to atone for with his death, included a poem about Mount Fuji, asked the Japanese to remain united and also stated he wished his body to be donated to science. The event caused a great impact in the Japan of the time and meant the end of an era, at the same time as reminding the Japanese where they came from, now they had almost transformed into a Western-style power. Nogi's name was much vindicated by the Japanese ultra-nationalists in the following decades, somewhat abandoned after the Second World War, and his reputation restored some time later.

In February 1877, Saigō set off at the head of his army, intending to reach Tokyo to meet with the government and negotiate a peaceful solution, but the letters he wrote on the way proposing a negotiation were rejected. He also had to combat both the armies of the various lords whose territories he passed through and the new imperial army—which he had helped to create—which was sent to the area. During his journey, he was joined by other samurai who were equally discontented with the new Japan, and ended up leading more than forty thousand men, who used modern Western armament as well as the typical samurai weapons—Saigō himself wore his French-style Imperial army uniform. Facing them was a much larger force of some three hundred thousand men, even better armed and organized, thanks to which Saigō's journey would come to a swift end.

After several unsuccessful battles over the course of six months, the rebel army had just five hundred or so troops left when it faced up to thirty thousand imperial soldiers in what could be considered the last samurai battle in history, at Shiroyama. There, on September 24, 1877, Saigō rejected the enemy general's petition of surrender and was readying himself for certain defeat when his forces were attacked by a head-on assault. For years it was believed he had committed suicide when he realized he was beaten, but forensic investigations have revealed he was killed by a shot and his head was cut off afterwards by one of his trusted vassals, undoubtedly to preserve his honor. Despite having rebelled against the imperial government, Saigō always considered he was fighting for the emperor, trying to free him from the corrupting influence of the politicians around him, and this is how it was seen

Fig. 11.8. Statue of Saigō Takamori in Ueno Park, Tokyo.
Photograph taken by the author in February 2015.

by the people, who had felt great affection for this character from the start. So much so that popular pressure led to Emperor Meiji himself decreeing an official pardon and a statue of him was built in Ueno Park, in Tokyo.

On that day, September 24, 1877, the modern Gatling machine-guns recently purchased by the brand-new Imperial Army finished off the rest of Saigō's army, and brought an end to the rebellion, snuffing out the last breath of what by then was already an anachronistic figure: the samurai. They had ruled Japan for seven centuries, but, like everything in this world, were destined to disappear sooner or later; at this final point in our story, we may remember the first lines of the *Heike Monogatari*, (which was in Chapter 2), which belong to the very beginnings of the history of the samurai:

The sound of the Gion Shōja bells echoes the impermanence of all things; the color of the sāla flowers reveals the truth that the prosperous must decline. The proud do not endure, they are like a dream on a spring night; the mighty fall at last, they are as dust before the wind.

Epilogue:
The Samurai Myth

And that is the history of the samurai. Throughout a conscious effort has been made to try to keep as far as possible to the historic facts, at least to the extent that the passing of time and the possible none existence of documentation allowed. So, although some obviously mythological and legendary information has been mentioned here and there (such as the tengu who trained the young Minamoto Yoshitsune, for example), I have tried not to overuse those types of anecdotes which are either unlikely to be true or downright impossible, and have always pointed out any lack of veracity. For example, when talking about the Shinsengumi, their insignificant historical role was made clear. This is why the reader has yet to see some words he or she was perhaps expecting to find, the ones which are usually found in books dealing with the samurai, like *ninja* or *bushidō*, while others like honor and harakiri have only briefly raised their heads.

Undoubtedly, this attempt to keep to the facts will not have been entirely successful because the passing of time and the none existence of certain documents have an important part to play here. In addition, the samurai myth is so attractive and suggestive that it is very hard not to let yourself be carried away by it at times, or indeed to realize you are perpetuating the myth without meaning to. In fact, it is so attractive there are an infinite number of essay books about the samurai myth, especially in the didactic sector, some of which are really interesting and well worth reading. The problem with these books is that many of them—intentionally or inadvertently—pass themselves off as History books, when in fact they are story books. These stories are even more prevalent in novels and movies, but the public approach these products assuming that what they are going to see or read is a work of fiction based loosely on historical facts, rather than reality. Therefore, they do not contribute much to fostering the samurai myth as something real. Unfortunately, this does happen with much of the didactic writing on the subject, but not with academic literature.

In the West, anything originating in Japan, or East Asia in general, is almost automatically regarded as old and traditional, and we quickly label it millenary when talking about it. And apart from being very old, everything is also very profound, philosophical and mystical, imbued with a spirit that mixes strange religions and mythologies—millenary, of course—with values such as honor, duty and loyalty, which perhaps should be universal, but sound exotic since they are so rare. The samurai myth thus finds itself perfectly at home within this collective imagination of what "Japanese" or "Oriental" means, because it has all those aforementioned characteristics: the samurai are imagined to be millenary warriors—we can indeed grant them that, since they were around for more than a thousand years—who behave according to a strict code of honor and follow the Zen precepts, which makes them loyal to the very end, preferring to die rather than suffer the shame of defeat—this stereotype is so widespread and ingrained there is no need to describe it any further here. Yet, in our account we have seen ceasefires used to finish off enemy defenses before attacks are resumed, sons executing their own fathers, brothers ordering the deaths of their own siblings, massacres of civilians, whose corpses have their noses cut off, entire families executed to put an end to a family line, schemes for controlling the four-year-old occupant of a throne, important battles—Dan no Ura and Sekigahara no less—being decided by people switching allegiance at the last minute, etc. All of this does not make the samurai some kind of heartless treacherous warriors with no sense of ethics—at least no more so than the warriors of any other time and place, but nor does it make them any better.

If we are to talk about the samurai myth, it befits us to differentiate between the bushi who lived before the Edo period and the ones who lived during it: in other words, between the bushi who waged war and those who did not. The former had but one simple ideology that governed their acts on the battlefield: surviving. That does not seem like a bad ideology for a warrior to have. The first thing we must remember is that in the early centuries of the samurai's existence, they were not a closed well-defined social class, and with the exception of a few small elites, anybody could be a samurai when they were needed on the battlefield, spending the rest of their time as a farmer. All of this made it very difficult for these part-time warriors to share a code of honor or an elaborate set of rituals. What we know of those early times has come to us primarily from the gunki monogatari, but we have to take into account they give us rather biased information, and have also been subject to numerous re-editions and revisions over the centuries. Yet even in these half-reality half-fiction chronicles, what we can find there is quite a long way from the romantic image of the honorable samurai warrior. Both in these texts and in any other document from the period, for every "honorable" deed that turns up, there are five or ten switches of allegiance, betrayals, executions of four-year-old children, etc. So, does that mean the samurai were without honor? Well, quite simply they did not know what it meant. In point of fact, the type of honor the samurai myth credits them with having is a very modern concept, which would not even have registered in the world view of a twelfth century warrior. For them, everything came down to their standing as bushi, but this reputation depended on their victories on the battlefield and not on the manner in which they had been achieved. If we had to choose a virtue that stands out in these first warriors, it would not be honor, but pragmatism.

From our twenty-first century Western outlook based on Christian traditions, it may be difficult for us to understand, but we should forget about concepts such as "fair" and "unfair," "good" and "evil," "honorable" and "dishonorable," when judging these warriors' actions. Minamoto Yoritomo probably had no internal moral debate when he ordered the death of his brother Yoshitsune after he had almost single-handedly won the Genpei wars—quite simply he thought it was what had to be done for the stability of his government. When the first firearms appeared in Japan, the samurai saw no ethical problem in starting to make use of them as soon as possible; they did not scorn them as dishonorable or contrary to the tradition of fighting with the katana (or "the samurai's soul" as fans of the myth insist on calling it). Firstly, because the samurai's main weapon was always the bow, which shared its *raison d'être* with the harquebus: killing at a distance. And secondly because, in the context of an all-out civil war, the bushi had no time for metaphysical questions and were more interested in pragmatic evidence. And if the samurai on the battlefield simply wanted to survive, then the elites that sent them there were purely motivated by such practical matters as possessing more land and collecting more taxes; this (and not some slight toward a rival or slur on their honor) was what lay behind practically all the wars and conflicts. So, throughout these centuries, truces were broken, promises forgotten and blood ties were unimportant—but all of this only held true if victory required it. Likewise, it could be necessary to maintain an alliance for life, fight to the death to avenge a father, or commit suicide rather than fall into the enemy's hands; all these actions, both those which seem vile to us and the ones that appear heroic, were equally justified for a samurai if they were needed to win—in the widest sense of the word.

So, where does the widespread image of the samurai as incorrupt honorable knights fighting for justice come from? It is down to the second group of bushi we differentiated beforehand, those of the Edo period. And not because this was how they behaved (we have to take into account the fact they could not show themselves to be honorable on the battlefield for the very good reason they never set foot on one), but because they said the samurai had always behaved that way... and everybody, including them, believed it.

When describing this period, we already saw how the samurai

made up a social class devoted almost entirely to a life of leisure,— to painting, practicing calligraphy, writing poems, holding tea ceremonies, etc.—and how within this easy laid-back life, they began to feel a kind of nostalgia for what they themselves as a group had been in the past, when they were real warriors. The Edo period samurai themselves were very critical of the bureaucratic role they had then and there was a kind of adulation of the supposed deeds of their ancestors: old war chronicles were dusted off and rewritten, performed on the stage and in song, and new novels were also written starring valiant noble warriors. In all of these works, the samurai were motivated by a strict code of honor and decency, always showing an unshakeable loyalty toward their superiors, and prominence was given to combat, bravery, the glory of the fight and victory, all of which were values and concepts that had ceased to exist in the samurai's day-to-day life. When they were revising historical episodes, they made sure they chose the ones that best fit their idea of what the past had been like, not just out of self-indulgence, but also to legitimize their privileged position as hereditary landlords to the rest of Japanese society. This legitimization was built on two connected foundations: the Neo-Confucianist doctrine that we commented on in a previous chapter, and the samurai myth. So, based on what these bureaucrat-samurai believed their ancestors (the warrior-samurai) had been like, an ideology began to emerge that created a code of how a samurai should behave; a false past, created in the present, determined how their class's present and future should be, in order to carry on imposing themselves on the other classes. One of the most prominent followers of this new ideology was a disciple of Hayashi Razan called Yamaga Sokō (AD 1622-1685), who along with almost all these armchair warriors had been born in a time of peace and had only had to unsheathe his sword to clean it. When he was already forty years old, Yamaga repudiated the Neo-Confucianist doctrine he had studied all his life in favor of advocating the original Confucianist texts, as a result of which he was banished from Edo for going against the bakufu's official ideology.

The 47 *Rōnin*

The Akō incident, the story of the 47 rōnin, is unquestionably one of the most popular historical episodes in Japan. It is almost a national legend and has been recreated in a huge number of plays, novels, series and movies; in fact, just a few weeks after the event, it was already been performed in a puppet theater in Edo. Although it is a true story, it has often been portrayed by a fictionalized version of events, adding an increasing number of subplots and extra characters. In the West, it also became quite a popular story in the late nineteenth century, after appearing in 1871 in the book *Tales of old Japan*, written by an English diplomat stationed in Japan called A. B. Mitford (AD 1837-1916).

The story—which we recount here only in a brief summary—begins in 1701, when the daimyō Asano Naganori (AD 1667-1701), from the Harima province, attacked a bakufu official called Kira Yoshinaka (AD 1641-1703), who as master of ceremonies was instructing him about the protocol required for a task he had just been assigned within the government. Asano felt deeply offended and insulted by the way Kira treated him and decided to kill him, but his attack failed and he only managed to leave him with a wound to the forehead. Since at that moment they were both in the shōgun's residence, the aggression was considered a grave affront to the government itself, and consequently Asano was condemned to death by seppuku and his family to losing their domains—a territory called Akō—and all their property, thus automatically making all their vassals rōnin. Some of them decided to avenge their lord's death by killing Kira, who they considered responsible for what had happened, but they believed that first they would have to wait for a while and only attack when their target no longer feared revenge and was over-confident. They therefore spent months pretending to do all kinds of jobs or serve other lords. They were led by the man who had been the daimyō's chief adviser, Ōishi Yoshio (AD 1659-1703)— although he has gone down in history as Ōishi Kuranosuke, the latter word really being the term for his position. He moved to Kyoto and devoted himself to drinking and hanging out in brothels there, which came to Kira's attention and made him believe Asano's leading vassal was none too interested in avenging his lord. Meanwhile, some of the other rōnin had returned to Edo and managed to infiltrate Kira's residence to gather all kind of information about the dwelling itself and about its soldiers and other servants. With more than one and a half years having gone by since Asano's death, Ōishi also returned to Edo in secret to meet with his men—with his own son numbering among them—and begin his mission. On December 14, 1702, in the early hours of a morning battered by a great snowstorm, they attacked Kira's residence and, after finishing off his guards, found him cowering in a hut. Once they had taken him prisoner, Ōishi told him who they were and what they had come for, then asked him to que carry out seppuku to atone for his insult; as Kira refused to do so, Ōishi himself killed him, cutting his head off. Then with Kira's head in a bucket,

Fig. 12.1. Statue of Oishi Kuranosuke, Tokyo. Photograph taken by the author, February 2015.

they went without a care in the world to Sengaku-ji Temple, where Asano was buried, to place it on his grave as an offering and wait there for whatever punishment the bakufu wished to deal out to them. Finally, almost two months later, they were condemned to death by seppuku and buried at the same temple, next to their lord.

The government had found itself facing a dilemma, given that on the one hand the rōnin's behavior deserved the worst possible punishment, since they had attacked a shōgunate official, but on the other hand, they had also acted in accordance with the idea of being loyal to one's master that the Neo-Confucianist doctrine promoted by the Tokugawa bakufu itself so ardently defended. So, they opted for a Solomonic solution: the rōnin deserved to die for their crime, but they had earned the right to an honorable death, by seppuku instead of simply having their heads cut off like common criminals. Also, from a practical point of view, the revenge achieved an additional objective, since the shōgunate decided to restore the Asano house, allowing Asano Naganori's younger brother to inherit the title and possessions, although they decreased to just a tenth of what they had been.

The 47 rōnin's graves can still be visited today in Sengaku-ji, as can a small museum within the temple grounds, where some tattered items of clothing are on display, along with what is left of a few homemade weapons and coats of chainmail and some documents the rōnin carried with them, such as the following: the plan of Kira's house; a piece of paper they all had a copy of, explaining the rōnin's plan and their reasons for it, signed by Ōishi; another letter that was placed on Asano's grave along with Kira's head, which explains what happened and dedicates the exploit to their lord's memory. Undoubtedly the strangest document is the receipt the temple keeps which certifies the return of Kira's head to his family, as if it were just any other object or merchandise.

He spent the rest of his life in different places in Japan, devoting himself to writing about the way of the samurai—one of these places was the Akō fiefdom, which linked him to the famous story of the 47 rōnin—and influenced the following generations of intellectuals who wrote about the same subject. For example, Yamamoto Tsunetomo (AD 1659-1719), author of the famous *Hagakure*, finished in 1716, but not published until the early twentieth century. This is one of the genre's classics, a literary work which sets out all the aspects of the life a samurai should lead. But with Yamamoto we have yet another case of a samurai who had spent his life devoted to administrative tasks; he had not even received military training due to the poor health he had suffered since he was a child, so he and the ideal samurai he describes to us in his book could not be more different. In fact, the Edo period samurai were also in reality something very far removed from the picture painted in this kind of texts; they not only devoted themselves to bureaucratic tasks, but also to a life of luxury, consumerism, and had an affinity for the theatre, alcohol and brothels. Other influential literary works of this style were *Budō Shoshin-shū*, which was widely read throughout Japan in its time, written by Daidōji Yūzan (AD1639-1730), who had been a disciple of Yamaga; and the famous *Go Rin no Sho (The Book of Five Rings)*, by the even more famous Miyamoto Musashi (c. AD 1584-1645).

Miyamoto Musashi

Miyamoto Musashi is probably the most popular samurai of all time, but had not turned up in our account until now because, despite his reputation, Musashi is in fact historically irrelevant; he is believed to have taken part in three events that we have already referred to: the Battle of Sekigahara, the Siege of Osaka Castle, and the Shimabara Rebellion, but as a mere soldier. What is more, in the first two he fought on the losing side. But what he is famous for is being a great dueller, rather than a great soldier.

They have been talking about Musashi's life for so long and he has appeared in so many fictional accounts—even in his own lifetime—that it is difficult to differentiate between facts and fantasy. We know hardly anything about his childhood since he did not belong to an important family and there are no chronicles describing his early years. Furthermore, the texts he wrote himself were mainly devoted to matters related to military strategy or combat and focused very little on autobiographical data. We know he was born in the province of Harima around 1584 and it is normally said he was the son of Shinmen Munisai (n.d.), a renowned martial arts master, although this is also unconfirmed and he may just have been his master. Musashi himself tells us that he had his first duel at the age of thirteen, the second aged sixteen and won both of them. At around that age he fought for the western armies at Sekigahara, although some historians question this. Some years later, at the age of twenty-one, he traveled to Kyoto for a series of duels with disciples of one of the capital's prestigious sword-fighting schools. While he tells us he beat sixty of them without suffering a single defeat, the records of the family running the school only talk of one duel with Musashi, although they do recognize his victory.

Apparently from then on, he devoted his time to traveling around the country with the sole purpose of challenging famous

Fig. 12.2. Self-portrait of Miyamoto Musashi, Shimada Museum of Arts, Kumamoto.

swordsmen; this has created all kinds of stories, legends and myths, which form part of the romanticized image of the wandering rōnin who finds himself caught up in a thousand adventures. This stage of his life is when the most famous of his duels happened, with Sasaki Kojirō (AD ?-1612), a popular sword-fighting master who used a *nodachi* (a much longer sword than the katana). This duel took place on a small island between Honshū and Kyūshū, known at the time as Funajima, but shortly afterwards renamed Ganryūjima in honor of Sasaki, who is also known by the nickname Ganryū. This encounter has been described thousands of times and in many different ways, but what they normally agree on is that Musashi arrived very late for the meeting, used a long piece of wood he had fashioned from an old oar with his wakizashi on his journey by boat as a weapon, and that he killed his opponent. The next we hear of him is when he fights in the two Osaka siege campaigns on Hideyori's side. Soon after this, he entered the service of a daimyō from the Harima province and over the following years devoted himself to teaching his combat style, which was mainly distinguished by its simultaneous use of the two samurai swords (katana and wakizashi), one in each hand. In 1633, when he was nearly fifty, he moved into the service of the Hosokawa clan, in Kumamoto, and four years later formed part of the forces sent by the bakufu to put down the Shimabara Rebellion. He spent his last two years living as a hermit in the mountains while writing *The Book of Five Rings*, a treatise on military strategy, combat technique and samurai philosophy, which he finished barely two weeks before he died.

Miyamoto Musashi had already become quite famous during his lifetime, supposedly embodying the perfect romantic samurai figure that was so appreciated in the novels of the Edo period. He would not become hugely popular though until the mid-1930s, when the writer Yoshikawa Eiji (AD 1892-1962) began to publish his book *Miyamoto Musashi* in instalments in *Asahi Shinbun*, a newspaper specialized in historic novels. Yoshikawa based his tale both on the existing documents and on the legends and fantasies going around about Musashi, and also added his own fictional events. Despite it being a novel—and an excellent one—the combination of its great success and the decades that have gone by since its publication has led to much of what it describes ending up seeming like something that actually happened and these days it is taken to be a factual account. Musashi's own artwork has led to his recognition as a skilled painter and calligrapher, but above all it is his book that has been very successful, albeit in a rather strange fashion; it is often cited as bedside reading by leading company directors and businessmen, in much the same way as happens with *The Art of War* by Sun Tzu or *The Prince* by Niccolò Machiavelli (AD 1469-1527).

When Japan found itself forced to open up to the rest of the world and began the breakneck race to reach the same level as the Western Powers in the Meiji period, the samurai became an uncomfortable remnant of the past that had no place in a forward-looking country. They represented an enormous unnecessary expense that might otherwise be saved and invested in Western technology instead, and they were also a permanent potential threat. Moreover, the common people, despite adoring the bushi of the distant past—the ones starring in novels and plays—were quite unsympathetic toward the samurai class of their own time, and were more than happy to see them disappear and quickly pass into obscurity. On the other hand, the new Meiji government—let us not forget, made up of ex-samurai from Satsuma and Chōshū—despite having put an end to its own and the rest of the different social classes, retrieved, renewed and promoted this ideal samurai philosophy, which had first been created during the Edo period. At first this was done to promote loyalty to the emperor, which was the pillar the entire new system was built on, a loyalty easily comparable to that of the samurai vassal towards his lord and master. One of Fukuzawa Yukichi's disciples by the name of Ozaki Yukio (AD 1858-1954), who would for decades be an important progressive-thinking politician, would be key to this process of renovating and adapting the samurai myth.

At the end of the 1880s, Ozaki went on a trip that took him to the United States, and to some European countries, and the English society of the time made such an impression on him that he decided to study it in depth. He then came to the conclusion one of the reasons why it was the most advanced country in the world was a quality its inhabitants had—gentlemanship: a refined and polite upbringing that at the same time gave a lot of importance to honor, reputation, the value of giving one's word, etc. When studying this characteristic, he saw its connection to the European tradition of the medieval knights errant and thought that a similar behavior could be promoted in Japan based on their own medieval knights, the samurai. To that end he coined the term *shinshi* as a synonym of "gentleman" and wrote prolifically about the subject, playing a very active role in a magazine founded in the year 1898 called *Bushidō Zasshi*. In this, many intellectuals of differing origins and tendencies theorized about the Japanese people's identity, the samurai myth and the Edo period texts that talked about it, and above all about how Japan should face up to the future. Obviously, any reference to the relationship with gentlemanship and the European medieval knights was eliminated from the discourse, and the idea that there was a unique and ancient system of genuinely Japanese values was promoted.

It is in no way coincidental that at this point, in 1898, the word bushidō has finally put in an appearance. We could have used it in preceding paragraphs when describing the ideology that was attributed to the samurai of past epochs in the Edo period; or we could have used it even before, when explaining that those bushi from ancient times lacked a code of conduct; likewise, we could even have used it in many earlier chapters of this book, instead of using it for the first time right at the end, in the Epilogue. But as part of the conscious effort to stick to the historical facts and keep away from the myth, the most apposite thing to do was not to use it until this point. Because it is at this moment, in the final years of the nineteenth century, that it first appears (although it is unclear whether it was with the name of the magazine or a little earlier), notwithstanding the common preconception of bushidō as something—of course!—ancient. This idea was fueled by a good deal of the popular literature on the subject of the samurai, which would have us believe that, as early as the Kamakura period, the warriors followed a perfectly structured and organized strict code of honor known as bushidō.

In those years, some of the texts written about the subject in the Edo period were dusted off but only a carefully selected few—it was at this time that the *Hagakure* was published, for example—and some long forgotten historical characters were revived, many of whom we have come across during our account. The culmination of this bushidō construct also came at this time, with the publication of the book that even today is still taken to be gospel when it comes to the genre: *Bushidō, the Soul of Japan*, by Nitobe Inazō (AD 1862-1933). Its English name has been used here—and not the Japanese original as elsewhere—because in this case, the English name IS the original. It turns out that the classic and best-known work about the supposedly ancient samurai code of honor was written in English by a Christian Japanese economist while he was living in the United States, in the year 1899. What is more, he barely knew the history of Japan and used hardly any Japanese sources. Nitobe's education was entirely in English, first at a Christian school in Hokkaidō and later in the United States, and his Christian faith led to him wanting to find an equivalent to Christianity's values system and ethics in his own culture; he would find it in bushidō, an ideology he wanted to make the rest of the world aware of and which he attributed to the whole of Japanese society, not just to the samurai.

Thus, we see how the whole narrative and theory of bushidō is in reality something very recent: an ideology little more than a century old that was created from a romantic biased vision of the past and not based on historical facts, despite claiming to be so, since its theorists' ideas were sourced exclusively from a small number of texts written in the Edo period, but only rarely from before then. It combines elements cherry-picked from Confucianist ethics, from the European knights, from Christianity and from

Shintō. It is worth pointing out that the Shintō cited here was also redefining and reinventing itself at that time from the perspective of the new modern Japanese state; it was also being mixed with elements pertaining to Confucianism and Christianity, and being distanced from the essence of ancient Shintō. In the latter, for example, there was nothing worth dying for since nothing existed after death and there was neither reward nor punishment for the life one had led—it did not even have a defined doctrine. This is completely at odds both with bushidō and with the interests of the government of the time and even more so with those of later governments. Because the role of successive governments is crucial in this whole matter. On the one hand, contact with the rest of the world after more than two centuries of isolation meant that in the Japan of the period a patriotic nationalist feeling emerged, which had been unnecessary until then, and on the other, this very same feeling was taken advantage of, channeled and nurtured by the State to unify in a single national identity what until then had been a considerable regional diversity.

Up until 1945, the Meiji, Taishō (AD 1912-1926), and Shōwa (AD 1926-1989) governments benefited from this bushidō ideology, which had indoctrinated the entire population, and was one of the foundations on which Japanese militarism was based, especially during the First Sino-Japanese War, in 1894-1895, the Russo-Japanese War, in 1904-1905, and the Second World War. It was even used by Japan's enemies in the latter conflict to depict the Japanese as unemotional unfeeling creatures, motivated solely by strict codes of conduct. We can see its influence in one of the portraits of Japanese society that for decades had the most impact in the West: *The Chrysanthemum and the Sword*, by the anthropologist Ruth Benedict (AD 1887-1948), which the American government commissioned her to write and which she wrote without setting foot in Japan, basing it on nothing more than Japanese literature and interviews with Japanese residents in the United States.

After World War II, bushidō was both marginalized by the Japanese population and banned by the American forces of occupation, as it was part of all that was connected to the radical nationalism that had led the country to imperialism and war; but a few decades later it reappeared, above all in the 1980s, although on this occasion stripped of its nationalist spirit (only the meager Japanese extreme right-wing have kept it as part of their spiel). Today it continues to be used when talking of Japan, and we associate it with virtually all aspects of Japanese society—many other parts of the world also created romantic visions of their past in the nineteenth century to define their identity but we do not make the same association with them. Perhaps this is because, as we said at the start, when it comes to Japanese matters, everything seems ancient, set in stone, mystical and spiritual to us.

This realist vision of the samurai myth as an artificial modern construct is standard knowledge within the academic world, both in Japan and in the West; it is perfectly well-known both that it was created in the Edo and Meiji ages and that it was promoted out of self-interest later. Even more importantly, the historians specialized in twelfth to sixteenth century Japan state that they have found no bushi ethical code that may be considered the precursor to what is now known as bushidō. So, does that mean everything we thought we knew about the samurai is a lie and their history in reality is not worth knowing? No. In fact, there is no need to resort to myths and legends, since historically and objectively speaking, the history of the samurai is fascinating in itself and needs no window dressing—its study can be highly satisfying. In any case, I hope you have found the whole tale to be similarly interesting. This epilogue should not be taken as an attack on the samurai myth, because in no way is it intended to be one (there are few myths as attractive as that of these Japanese warriors). Its purpose is simply to advocate a distinction between two fields: history and mythology. It is always advisable to know to which we are referring.

Bibliography

Alvar, Manuel. "La embajada japonesa de 1614 al rey de España." *Thesaurus,* Tomo L 1-2-3, 1995, 518–525.

Andressen, Curtis. *A Short History of Japan, from Samurai to Sony.* Canberra: Silkworm Books, 2002.

Asao Naohiro. "The Sixteenth-century Unification." In John W. Hall, ed., *The Cambridge History of Japan, vol. 4, Early Modern Japan.* Cambridge, UK: Cambridge University Press, 1991, 40–95.

Bayle, Constantino. *Un siglo de Cristiandad en el Japón.* Barcelona: Editorial Labor, 1935.

Beasley, William G. "The Foreign Threat and the Opening of the Ports." In Marius B. Jansen, ed., *The Cambridge History of Japan, vol. 5, The Nineteenth Century.* Cambridge, UK: Cambridge University Press, 1989, 259–307.

_____. *La restauración Meiji.* Gijón: Satori Ediciones, 2007.

Bellah, Robert N. *Imagining Japan. The Japanese Tradition and its Modern Interpretation.* Berkeley: University of California Press, 2003.

Benedict, Ruth. *El Crisantemo y la Espada.* Madrid: Alianza Editorial, 1974.

Benesch, Oleg. *Inventing the Way of the Samurai: Nationalism, Internationalism, and Bushido in Modern Japan.* Oxford, UK: Oxford University Press, 2014.

Berry, Mary Elizabeth. *Hideyoshi.* Cambridge, MA: Harvard University Press, 1982.

Boletín de la Real Academia de la Historia. Tomo CCV, No. 1, Madrid: Royal Academy of History, 2008.

Bolitho, Harold. "The Myth of the Samurai." In Alan Rix and Ross Mouer, eds., *Japan's Impact on the World.* Melbourne: Japanese Studies Association of Australia, 1984, 2–8.

_____. "The Han." In John Whitney Hall, ed., *The Cambridge History of Japan, vol. 4, Early Modern Japan.* Cambridge, UK: Cambridge University Press, 1991, 183–234.

Boxer, Charles R. *The Christian Century in Japan, 1549–1650.* Manchester, UK: Carcanet Press, 1993.

Brading, D.A. "Europe and a World Expanded." In Euan Cameron, ed., *The Sixteenth Century.* Oxford, UK: Oxford University Press, 2006, 174–199.

Brower, Robert H., and Earl Roy Miner. *Japanese Court Poetry.* Palo Alto, CA: Stanford University Press, 1988.

Brown, Delmer M. "The Impact of Firearms on Japanese Warfare, 1543–98." *The Far Eastern Quarterly, 7* (3), 1948, 236–253.

_____ and Torao Toshiya, eds. *Chronology of Japan.* Tokyo: Business Inter-communications, Inc., 1991.

Brown, Philip C. "Unification, Consolidation, and Tokugawa Rules." In William M. Tsutsui, ed., *A Companion to Japanese History.* Malden, MA: Blackwell Publishing, 2007, 69–85.

Buruma, Ian. *Inventing Japan, 1853–1964.* New York: Modern Library, 2004.

De Bary, William Theodore, Donald Keene, George Tanabe and Paul Varley, eds. *Sources of Japanese Tradition: From Earliest Times to 1600.* New York: Columbia University Press, 2001.

_____, Carol Gluck and Arthur E. Tiedemann, eds. *Sources of Japanese Tradition: 1600 to 2000.* New York: Columbia University Press, 2005.

Cabezas, Antonio. *El siglo ibérico de Japón. La presencia hispano-portuguesa en Japón (1543–1643).* Valladolid, Spain: University of Valladolid, 1995.

Cameron, Euan. "The Turmoil of Faith." In Euan Cameron, ed., *The Sixteenth Century.* Oxford, UK: Oxford University Press, 2006, 145–173.

Chamberlain, Basil Hall. *The Invention of a New Religion.* London: Rationalist Press, 1912.

Cooper, Michael. *They Came to Japan: An Anthology of European Reports on Japan, 1543–1640.* Berkeley: University of California Press, 1982.

_____. *The Japanese Mission to Europe, 1582–1590.* Folkestone, UK: Global Oriental, 2005.

Cullen, L.M. *A History of Japan, 1582–1941. Internal and External Worlds.* Cambridge, UK: Cambridge University Press, 2003.

Deal, William E. *Handbook to Life in Medieval and Early Modern Japan.* New York: Facts on File, 2006.

Delgado, James. *Kamikaze. History's Greatest Naval Disaster.* London: Vintage, 2010.

Elison, George. "The Priest Keinen and His Account of the Campaign in Korea, 1597-1598: An Introduction." In Motoyama Yukihiko, ed., *Nihon kyōikushi ronsō.* Kyoto: Kyoto Shibunkaku, 1988, 25–41.

Elisonas, Jurgis. "The Inseparable Trinity: Japan's Relations with China and Korea." In John Whitney Hall, ed., *The Cambridge History of Japan, vol. 4, Early Modern Japan.* Cambridge, UK: Cambridge University Press, 1991, 235–300.

_____. "Christianity and the Daimyo." In John Whitney Hall, ed., *The Cambridge History of Japan, vol. 4, Early Modern Japan.* Cambridge, UK: Cambridge University Press, 1991, 301–372.

Farris, William Wayne. *Japan to 1600. A Social and Economic History*. Honolulu: University of Hawaii Press, 2009.

Fernández-Armesto, Felipe. *1492. El nacimiento de la modernidad*. Barcelona: Random House Mondadori, 2010.

Friday, Karl F. *Samurai, Warfare and the State in Early Medieval Japan*. New York: Routledge, 2004.

Fukuzawa Yukichi. *The Autobiography of Yukichi Fukuzawa*. New York: Columbia University Press, 2007.

Genjō Masayoshi, ed. *Sengokushi*. Tokyo: Natsumesha, 2005.

Gil, Juan. *Hidalgos y samuráis. España y Japón en los siglos XVI y XVII*. Madrid: Alianza Editorial, 1991.

Gilbert, Marc Jason. "Deshima Island: A Stepping Stone between Civilizations." *World History Connected* 3 (3), Chicago: University of Illinois Press, 2006.

Goble, Andrew Edmund. "Medieval Japan." In William M. Tsutsui, ed. *A Companion to Japanese History*. Malden, MA: Blackwell Publishing, 2007, 47–66.

Goodman, Grant K. *Japan and the Dutch, 1600–1853*. Richmond, UK: Curzon Press, 2000.

Gordon, Andrew. *A Modern History of Japan: From Tokugawa Times to the Present*. New York: Oxford University Press, 2003.

Griffis, William Elliot. *The Mikado's Empire*. New York: Harper & Brothers, 1890.

Hall, John Whitney. *Japan. From Prehistory to Modern Times*. New York: Dell, 1970.

_____. *El imperio japonés*. Madrid: Siglo XXI Editores, 1973.

_____. "The Muromachi Bakufu." In Kozo Yamamura, ed., *The Cambridge History of Japan, vol. 3, Medieval Japan*. Cambridge, UK: Cambridge University Press, 1990, 175–230.

_____. "The Bakuhan System." In John Whitney Hall, ed. *The Cambridge History of Japan, vol.4, Early Modern Japan*. Cambridge, UK: Cambridge University Press, 1991, 128–182.

Hane, Mikiso. *Breve historia de Japón*. Madrid: Alianza Editorial, 2000.

Hanley, Susan B. "Tokugawa Society: Material Culture, Standard of Living, and Life-styles." In John Whitney Hall, ed. *The Cambridge History of Japan, vol.4, Early Modern Japan*. Cambridge, UK: Cambridge University Press, 1991, 660–705.

Henshall, Kenneth G. *A History of Japan: From Stone Age to Superpower*. New York: Palgrave Macmillan, 1999.

Hillsborough, Romulus. *Shinsengumi: The Shogun's Last Samurai Corps.* North Clarendon, VT: Tuttle Publishing, 2011.

Huffman, James L. "Restoration and Revolution." In William M. Tsutsui, ed. *A Companion to Japanese History.* Malden, MA: Blackwell Publishing, 2007, 139–155.

Hurst, III, G. Cameron. "Insei." In Donald H. Shively and William H. McCullough, eds. *The Cambridge History of Japan, vol.2, Heian Japan.* Cambridge, UK: Cambridge University Press, 1999, 576–643.

_____. "The Heian Period." In William M. Tsutsui, ed. *A Companion to Japanese History.* Malden, MA: Blackwell Publishing, 2007, 30–46.

Imatani Akira. "Muromachi Local Government: Shugo and Kokujin." In Kozo Yamamura, ed., *The Cambridge History of Japan, vol. 3, Medieval Japan.* Cambridge, UK: Cambridge University Press, 1990, 231–259.

Ishii Susumu. "The Decline of the Kamakurabakufu." In Kozo Yamamura, ed., *The Cambridge History of Japan, vol. 3, Medieval Japan.* Cambridge, UK: Cambridge University Press, 1990, 128–174.

Jansen, Marius B. "The Meiji Restoration." Marius B. Jansen, ed. *The Cambridge History of Japan, vol. 5, The Nineteenth Century.* Cambridge, UK: Cambridge University Press, 1989, 308–366.

_____. *The Making of Modern Japan.* Cambridge, MA: Harvard University Press, 2000.

Javier, Francisco. *Cartas de Japón escritas por Francisco de Xabier.* Pamplona, Spain: Government of Navarre, 2005.

Junqueras, Oriol, Dani Madrid, Guillermo Martínez and Pau Pitarch. *Historia de Japón. Economía, política y sociedad.* Barcelona: Editorial UOC, 2012.

Keay, John. *China: a History.* London: Harper Collins Publishers, 2009.

Kondo, Agustín Y. *Japón. Evolución histórica de un pueblo (hasta 1650).* Hondarribia, Spain: Editorial Nerea, 1999.

Lee, Christina H. "The Perception of the Japanese in Early Modern Spain: Not Quite 'The Best People Yet Discovered.'" *eHumanista* 11, 2008, 345–380.

Lisón Tolosana, Carmelo. *La fascinación de la diferencia. La adaptación de los jesuitas al Japón de los samuráis, 1549–1592.* Tres Cantos, Spain: Ediciones Akal, 2005.

López-Vera, Jonathan. "La misión jesuita en Japón y China durante los siglos XVI y XVII, un planificado proceso de adaptación." *Asiadémica* no. 1, 2012, 44–56.

_____. "La Embajada Keichō (1613-1620)," *Asiadémica* no. 2, 2013, 85–103.

_____. "Descripciones de Japón para Felipe II: El Imperio del sol naciente visto por el Imperio donde nunca se pone el sol." Osami Takizawa and Antonio Míguez, coords. *Visiones de un Mundo Diferente. Política, literatura de avisos y arte namban.* Madrid: Centro Europeo para la Difusión de las Ciencias Sociales y Archivo de la Frontera, 2015, 59–86.

Manegazzo, Rossella. *Japón.* Barcelona: Random House Mondadori, 2008.

Mass, Jeffrey P. "The Kamakura Bakufu. In Kozo Yamamura, ed. *The Cambridge History of Japan, vol. 3, Medieval Japan.* Cambridge, UK: Cambridge University Press, 1990, 46–88.

Massarella, Derek. *A World Elsewhere: Europe's Encounter with Japan in the 16th and 17th Centuries.* New Haven, CT: Yale University Press, 1990.

McCullough, Helen C. *The Tale of Heike.* Stanford: Stanford University Press, 1988.

Meriwether, Colyer. "A Sketch of the Life of Date Masamune and an Account of His Embassy to Rome." *Transactions of the Asiatic Society of Japan,* vol. 21. Yokohama: R. Meiklejohn & Co., 1893, 3–105.

Milton, Giles. *Samurai William: The Adventurer Who Unlocked Japan.* London: Hodder & Stoughton, 2003.

Mitford, A.B. *Tales of Old Japan.* London: Macmillan, 1871.

Miyamoto Musashi. *El libro de los cinco anillos.* Barcelona: Ediciones Obelisco, 2005.

Morillo, Stephen. "Guns and Government: A Comparative Study of Europe and Japan." *Journal of World History,* 6 (1), 1995, 75–106.

Morton, W. Scott and J. Kenneth Olenik. *Japan. Its History and Culture.* New York: McGraw-Hill, 2005.

Mungello, D.E. *The Great Encounter of China and the West, 1500–1800.* Oxford, UK: Lowman & Littlefield Publishers, 1999.

Murdoch, James. *A History of Japan, vol 2.* London: Kegan Paul, Trench, Trubner & Co., 1903.

_____. *A History of Japan, vol 1.* London: Kegan Paul, Trench, Trubner & Co. Ltd., 1925.

_____. *A History of Japan, vol 3.* London: Kegan Paul, Trench, Trubner & Co., 1926.

Mutel, Jacques. *El fin del shogunato y el Japón Meiji, 1853/1912.* Barcelona: Editorial Vicens-Vives, 1972.

Nakai Nobuhiko. "Commercial Change and Urban Growth in Early Modern Japan." In John Whitney Hall, ed. *The Cambridge History of Japan, vol.4, Early Modern Japan.* Cambridge, UK: Cambridge University Press, 1991, 519–595.

Nauert, Charles G. "The Mind." In Euan Cameron, ed. *The Sixteenth Century*. Oxford, UK: Oxford University Press, 2006, 116–144.

Nitobe Inazō. *Bushido: The Soul of Japan*. New York: Kodansha America, 2012.

Pastells, Pablo. *Catálogo de los documentos relativos a las Islas Filipinas existentes en el Archivo de Indias de Sevilla*. Barcelona: Compañía General de Tabacos de Filipinas, 1925.

Pratt, Edward E. "Social and Economic Change in Tokugawa Japan." In Tsutsui, William M., ed., *A Companion to Japanese History*. Malden, MA: Blackwell Publishing, 2007, 86–100.

Ravina, Mark. *The Last Samurai: The Life and Battles of Saigō Takamori*. Hoboken, NJ: John Wiley & Sons, 2004.

Reis Correia, Pedro L. "Alessandro Valignano, Attitude towards Jesuit and Franciscan Concepts of Evangelization in Japan (1587–1597)." *Bulletin of Portuguese/Japanese Studies*, vol. 2. Lisbon: New University of Lisbon, 2001, 79–108.

Reyes, Ainhoa. "La introducción de las armas de fuego en Japón." *Brocar, Cuadernos de investigación histórica*, 33, 2009.

Robertson, Lisa J. "Warriors and Warfare." In William E. Deal, ed. *Handbook to Life in Medieval and Early Modern Japan*. New York: Facts on File, 2006.

Rubio, Carlos (introduction, notes and translation) and Rumi Tani Moratalla (translation). *Heike Monogatari*. Madrid: Editorial Gredos, 2009.

Sadler, Arthur L. *The Maker of Modern Japan: The Life of Shogun Tokugawa Ieyasu*. Rutland, VT: Charles E. Tuttle Company, 1980.

Sansom, George. *A History of Japan, 1334–1615*. Palo Alto, CA: Stanford University Press, 1961.

Schirokauer, Conrad, and Miranda Brown. *Breve historia de la civilización china*. Barcelona: Edicions Bellaterra, 2006.

Shigeno Saburō. *Han Bushidōron*. Tokyo: Bungeisha, 2014.

Sola, Emilio. *Libro de las maravillas del Oriente Lejano*. Madrid: Editora Nacional, 1980.

_____. *Historia de un desencuentro. España y Japón, 1580–1614*. Alcalá de Henares: Fugaz Ediciones,1999.

Takeuchi Rizō. "The Rise of Warriors." In Donald H. Shively and William H. McCullough, eds. *The Cambridge History of Japan, vol.2, Heian Japan*. Cambridge, UK: Cambridge University Press, 1999, 644–709.

Takizawa, Osami. "La delegación diplomática enviada a Roma por el señor feudal japonés Date Masamune (1613-1620)." *Archivo de la Frontera,*

Centro Europeo para la Difusión de las Ciencias Sociales (CEDCS), 2009, 3–29.

_____. *La historia de los jesuitas en Japón (siglos XVI-XVII)*. Alcalá de Henares: Universidad de Alcalá, 2010.

Torres de Mendoza, Luis. *Colección de documentos inéditos, relativos al descubrimiento, conquista y organización de las antiguas posesiones españolas de América y Oceanía, sacados de los Archivos del Reino y muy especialmente del de Indias*, tomo VIII. Madrid: Imprenta de Frías y compañía, 1867.

Totman, Conrad D. *Japan before Perry*. Berkeley: University of California Press, 1981.

_____. *Tokugawa Ieyasu: Shogun*. San Francisco: Heian International, 1983.

_____. *Politics in the Tokugawa Bakufu, 1600–1843*. Berkeley: University of California Press, 1988.

Turnbull, Stephen. *Samurai Warfare*. London: Arms and Armours Press, 1996.

_____. *The Samurai Sourcebook*. London: Cassell & Co., 1998.

_____. *Samurai Invasion. Japan's Korean War 1592–1598*. London: Cassell & Co., 2002.

_____. *The Mongol Invasions of Japan, 1274 and 1281*. Oxford, UK: Osprey Publishing, 2010.

_____. *Toyotomi Hideyoshi*. Oxford, UK: Osprey Publishing, 2010.

Varley, H. Paul. *Japanese Culture*. Honolulu: University of Hawaii Press, 2000.

Wakita Osamu. "The Social and Economic Consequences of Unification." Hall, John W., ed. *The Cambridge History of Japan, vol. 4, Early Modern Japan*. Cambridge, UK: Cambridge University Press, 1991, 96–127.

Yamamoto Tsunetomo. *Hagakure. El camino del samurái*. Madrid: Dojo Ediciones, 2014.

Yamamura Kozo. "Returns on Unification: Economic Growth in Japan, 1550–1650." In John W. Hall, Nagahara Keiji, Yamamura Kozo, eds. *Japan Before Tokugawa: Political Consolidation and Economic Growth, 1500–1650*. Princeton, NJ: Princeton University Press, 1981, 327–372.

Chronology

Periods in Japanese history (those in which the government was in the hands of the samurai) are highlighted.

PALEOLITHIC	200,000–13,000 BC.	Paleolithic	
	13,000–300 BC	Jōmon Period	
ANCIENT	300 BC–AD300	Yayoi Period	
	300–552	Kofun Period	
	552–710	Asuka Period	
CLASSIC	710–794	Nara Period	
	794–1185	Heian Period	
	1185–1333	Kamakura Period	
	1333–1336	Kenmu Restoration	
FEUDAL	1336–1573	Muromachi Period	Nanbokuchō Period (1336–92)
			Sengoku Period (1477–1573)
	1573–1603	Azuchi-Momoyama Period	
EARLY MODERN	1603–1868	Edo Period	
	1868–1912	Meiji Period	
MODERN	1912–1926	Taishō Period	
			Pre-war and War (1926–45)
	1926–1989	Shōwa Period	USA Occupation (1945–52)
CONTEMPORARY			Post-occupation (1952–89)
	1989–2019	Heisei Period	
	2019–present	Reiwa Period	

Emperors of Japan

Although this is the official list of emperors, we should be cautious with the earliest dates. Most historians agree that the first nine or ten emperors on the list did not exist and the following twenty or so were in reality kings who controlled part of Japan. The dates of birth and death, the length of time they reigned, and many of the events of their lives are also more than debatable and full of contradictions. It is difficult to establish a precise moment after which time the data may be considered historically reliable.

1st	660 BC–585 BC	Jinmu	16th	313–399	Nintoku
2nd	581 BC–549 BC	Suizei	17th	400–405	Richū
3rd	549 BC–511 BC	Annei	18th	406–410	Hanzei
4th	510 BC–476 BC	Itoku	19th	411–453	Ingyō
5th	475 BC–393 BC	Kōshō	20th	453–456	Ankō
6th	392 BC–291BC	Kōan	21st	456–479	Yūryaku
7th	290 BC–215 BC	Kōrei	22nd	480–484	Seinei
8th	214 BC–158 BC	Kōgen	23rd	485–487	Kenzō
9th	157 BC–98 BC	Kaika	24th	488–498	Ninken
10th	97 BC–30 BC	Sujin	25th	498–506	Buretsu
11th	20 BC–AD70	Suinin	26th	507–531	Keitai (2)
12th	71–130	Keikō	27th	531–535	Ankan
13th	131–191	Seimu	28th	535–539	Senka
14th	192–200	Chūai	29th	539–571	Kinmei
	201–269	Empress Jingu (1)	30th	572–585	Bidatsu
15th	270–310	Ōjin	31st	585–587	Yōmei

32nd	587–592	Sushun	55th	850–858	Montoku
33rd	592–628	Empress Suiko	56th	858–876	Seiwa
34th	629–641	Jomei	57th	876–884	Yōzei
35th	642–645	Empress Kōgyoku	58th	884–887	Kōkō
36th	645–654	Kōtoku	59th	887–897	Uda
37th	655–661	Empress Saimei	60th	897–930	Daigo
38th	661–672	Tenji	61st	930–946	Suzaku
39th	672	Kōbun	62nd	946–967	Murakami
40th	672–686	Tenmu	63rd	967–969	Reizei
41st	686–697	Empress Jitō	64th	969–984	En'yū
42nd	697–707	Monmu	65th	984–986	Kazan
43rd	707–715	Empress Genmei	66th	986–1011	Ichijō
44th	715–724	Empress Genshō	67th	1011–1016	Sanjō
45th	724–749	Shōmu	68th	1016–1036	Go-Ichijō
46th	749–758	Empress Kōken	69th	1036–1045	Go-Suzaku
47th	758–764	Junnin	70th	1045–1068	Go-Reizei
48th	764–770	Empress Shōtoku	71st	1068–1073	Go-Sanjō
49th	770–781	Kōnin	72nd	1073–1087	Shirakawa
50th	781–806	Kanmu	73rd	1087–1107	Horikawa
51st	806–809	Heizei	74th	1107–1123	Toba
52nd	809–823	Saga	75th	1123–1142	Sutoku
53rd	823–833	Junna	76th	1142–1155	Konoe
54th	833–850	Ninmyō	77th	1155–1158	Go-Shirakawa

78th	1158–1165	Nijō		1371–1382	Go-En'yū (4)
79th	1165v1168	Rokujō		1382–1392	Go-Komatsu (4)
80th	1168–1180	Takakura	97th	1339–1368	Go-Murakami
81st	1180–1185	Antoku (3)	98th	1368–1383	Chōkei
82nd	1183–1198	Go-Toba (3)	99th	1383–1392	Go-Kameyama
83rd	1198–1210	Tsuchimikado	100th	1392–1412	Go-Komatsu
84th	1210–1221	Juntoku	101st	1412–1428	Shōkō
85th	1221	Chūkyō	102nd	1428–1464	Go-Hanazono
86th	1221–1232	Go-Horikawa	103rd	1464–1500	Go-Tsuchimikado
87th	1232–1242	Shijō	104th	1500–1526	Go-Kashiwabara
88th	1242–1246	Go-Saga	105th	1526–1557	Go-Nara
89th	1246–1260	Go-Fukakusa	106th	1557–1586	Ōgimachi
90th	1260–1274	Kameyama	107th	1586–1611	Go-Yōzei
91st	1274–1287	Go-Uda	108th	1611–1629	Go-Mizunoo
92nd	1287–1298	Fushimi	109th	1629–1643	Empress Meishō
93rd	1298–1301	Go-Fushimi	110th	1643–1654	Go-Kōmyō
94th	1301–1308	Go-Nijō	111th	1655–1663	Go-Sai
95th	1308–1318	Hanazono	112th	1663–1687	Reigen
96th	1318–1339	Go-Daigo	113th	1687–1709	Higashiyama
	1331–1333	Kōgon (4)	114th	1709–1735	Nakamikado
	1336–1348	Kōmyō (4)	115th	1735–1747	Sakuramachi
	1348–1351	Sukō (4)	116th	1747–1762	Momozono
	1352–1371	Go-Kōgon (4)	117th	1762–1771	Empress Go-Sakuramachi

118th	1771–1779	Go-Momozono	123rd	1912–1926	Taishō
119th	1780–1817	Kōkaku	124th	1926–1989	Shōwa
120th	1817–1846	Ninkō	125th	1989–2019	Heisei
121st	1846–1867	Kōmei	126th	2019–present	Current emperor (5)
122nd	1868–1912	Meiji			

1. Jingu was Emperor Chūai's consort and Emperor Ōjin's mother, acting as regent between the death of the former and the appointment of the latter—supposedly for no less than 68 years, which is rather difficult to believe. For along time, she was included on the list of empresses, but later eliminated from it, although still referred to as an empress.

2. Today it is believed that in reality a new dynasty began with Keitai that continues into the present-day, despite the fact that traditionally Japan has been considered to have had only one imperial dynasty.

3. When the Taira fled the capital with the little Emperor Antoku, they took the Imperial Treasures with them. This is why, despite Emperor Go-Toba ascending the throne in 1183, Antoku is still considered emperor until his death in 1185,and why for two years there were two emperors.

4. Emperors of the northern imperial court, during the Nanbokuchō period.

5. In Japan, the current emperor is called just that—Kinjō Tennō "reigning emperor"—and his emperor's name is not used until his death. Outside Japan, the custom is to use his first name—as in the case of the current emperor, Naruhito.

Shōgunate of Japan

Kamakura Shōgunate

1st	1192-1199	Minamoto Yoritomo (1147-1199)
2nd	1202-1203	Minamoto Yoriie (1182-1204)
3rd	1203-1219	Minamoto Sanetomo (1192-1219)
4th	1226-1244	Kujō Yoritsune (1218-1256)
5th	1244-1252	Kujō Yoritsugu (1239-1256)
6th	1252-1266	Prince Munetaka (1242-1274)
7th	1266-1289	Prince Koreyasu (1264-1326)
8th	1289-1308	Prince Hisaaki (1276-1328)
9th	1308-1333	Prince Morikuni (1301-1333)

Ashikaga Shōgunate

1st	1338-1357	Ashikaga Takauji (1305-1358)
2nd	1359-1368	Ashikaga Yoshiakira (1330-1367)
3rd	1368-1394	Ashikaga Yoshimitsu (1358-1408)
4th	1395-1423	Ashikaga Yoshimochi (1386-1428)
5th	1423-1425	Ashikaga Yoshikazu (1407-1425)
6th	1429-1441	Ashikaga Yoshinori (1394-1441)
7th	1442-1443	Ashikaga Yoshikatsu (1434-1443)
8th	1449-1473	Ashikaga Yoshimasa (1436-1490)
9th	1474-1489	Ashikaga Yoshihisa (1465-1489)
10th	1490-1493	Ashikaga Yoshitane (1466-1523)
11th	1494-1508	Ashikaga Yoshizumi (1481-1511)

10th	1508-1521	Ashikaga Yoshitane (1466-1523)
12th	1521-1546	Ashikaga Yoshiharu (1511-1550)
13th	1546-1565	Ashikaga Yoshiteru (1536-1565)
14th	1568	Ashikaga Yoshihide (1538-1568)
15th	1568-1573	Ashikaga Yoshiaki (1537-1597)
		(Oda Nobunaga (1534-1582))
		(Toyotomi Hideyoshi (1537-1598))

Tokugawa Shōgunate

1st	1603-1605	Tokugawa Ieyasu (1543-1616)
2nd	1605-1623	Tokugawa Hidetada (1579-1632)
3rd	1623-1651	Tokugawa Iemitsu (1604-1651)
4th	1651-1680	Tokugawa Ietsuna (1641-1680)
5th	1680-1709	Tokugawa Tsunayoshi (1646-1709)
6th	1709-1712	Tokugawa Ienobu (1662-1712)
7th	1713-1716	Tokugawa Ietsugu (1709-1716)
8th	1716-1745	Tokugawa Yoshimune (1684-1751)
9th	1745-1760	Tokugawa Ieshige (1712-1761)
10th	1760-1786	Tokugawa Ieharu (1737-1786)
11th	1787-1837	Tokugawa Ienari (1773-1841)
12th	1837-1853	Tokugawa Ieyoshi (1793-1853)
13th	1853-1858	Tokugawa Iesada (1824-1858)
14th	1858-1866	Tokugawa Iemochi (1846-1866)
15th	1866-1867	Tokugawa Yoshinobu (1837-1913)

Maps of Japan

Current prefectures of Japan

Hokkaidō Region
1 Hokkaidō

Tōhoku Region
2 Aomori
3 Iwate
4 Miyagi
5 Akita
6 Yamagata
7 Fukushima

Kantō Region
8 Ibaraki
9 Tochigi
10 Gunma
11 Saitama
12 Chiba
13 Tōkyō
14 Kanagawa

Chūbu Region
15 Niigata
16 Toyama
17 Ishikawa
18 Fukui
19 Yamanashi
20 Nagano
21 Gifu
22 Shizuoka
23 Aichi

Kinki Region
24 Mie
25 Shiga
26 Kyōto
27 Ōsaka
28 Hyōgo
29 Nara
30 Wakayama

Chūgoku Region
31 Tottori
32 Shimane
33 Okayama
34 Hiroshima
35 Yamaguchi

Shikoku Region
36 Kagawa
37 Tokushima
38 Ehime
39 Kōchi

Kyūshū Region
40 Fukuoka
41 Saga
42 Nagasaki
43 Kumamoto
44 Ōita
45 Yamazaki
46 Kagoshima
47 Okinawa

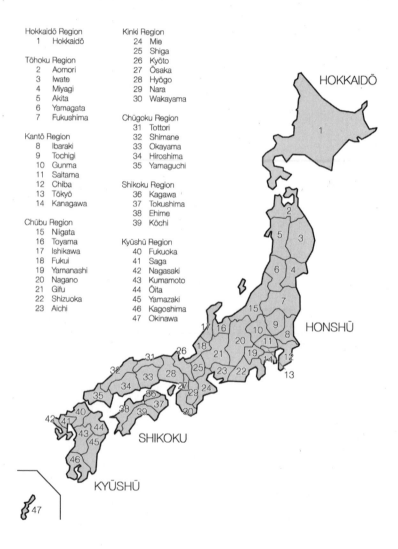

Former provinces of Japan

1	Mutsu
2	Dewa
3	Sado
4	Echigo
5	Kōzuke
6	Shimotsuke
7	Hitachi
8	Shimōsa
9	Kazusa
10	Awa
11	Musashi
12	Shinano
13	Kai
14	Sagami
15	Izu
16	Suruga
17	Tōtōmi
18	Mikawa
19	Hida
20	Etchu
21	Noto
22	Kaga
23	Echizen
24	Mino
25	Owari
26	Shima
27	Ise
28	Iga
29	Ōmi
30	Wakasa
31	Yamashiro
32	Yamato
33	Kii
34	Kawachi
35	Izumi
36	Settsu
37	Tanba
38	Tango
39	Oki
40	Inaba
41	Tajima
42	Harima
43	Awaji
44	Hōki
45	Mimasaka
46	Bizen
47	Bitchu
48	Izumo
49	Bingo
50	Iwami

51	Aki
52	Nagato
53	Suō
54	Sanuki
55	Awa
56	Tosa
57	Iyo
58	Tsushima
59	Iki
60	Higo
61	Hizen
62	Chikugo
63	Chikuzen
64	Bungo
65	Buzen
66	Hyūga
67	Satsuma
68	Ōsumi

Significant battles in samurai history

1	Uji (1180)	13	Fourth of Kawanakajima (1561)
2	Kurikara (1183)	14	Attack on Mount Hiei (1571)
3	Awazu (1184)	15	Mikatagahara (1572)
4	Ichi no Tani (1184)	16	Nagashino (1575)
5	Yashima (1184)	17	Siege of Takamatsu castle (1582)
6	Dan no Ura (1185)	18	Yamazaki (1582)
7	Koromogawa (1189)	19	Siege of Odawara castle (1590)
8	First Mongol attack (1274)	20	Sekigahara (1600)
9	Second Mongol attack (1281)	21	Siege of Osaka castle (1614-1615)
10	Siege of Kamakura (1333)	22	Tennō-ji (1615)
11	Minatogawa (1336)	23	Shiroyama (1877)
12	Okehazama (1560)